Communications
in Computer and Information Science   1495

Editorial Board Members

Joaquim Filipe ⓘ
  Polytechnic Institute of Setúbal, Setúbal, Portugal
Ashish Ghosh
  Indian Statistical Institute, Kolkata, India
Raquel Oliveira Prates ⓘ
  Federal University of Minas Gerais (UFMG), Belo Horizonte, Brazil
Lizhu Zhou
  Tsinghua University, Beijing, China

More information about this series at http://www.springer.com/series/7899

Limei Lin · Yuhong Liu ·
Chia-Wei Lee (Eds.)

Security and Privacy in Social Networks and Big Data

7th International Symposium, SocialSec 2021
Fuzhou, China, November 19–21, 2021
Proceedings

Editors
Limei Lin (iD)
Fujian Normal University
Fuzhou, China

Yuhong Liu
Santa Clara University
Santa Clara, CA, USA

Chia-Wei Lee (iD)
National Taitung University
Taitung, Taiwan

ISSN 1865-0929   ISSN 1865-0937 (electronic)
Communications in Computer and Information Science
ISBN 978-981-16-7912-4   ISBN 978-981-16-7913-1 (eBook)
https://doi.org/10.1007/978-981-16-7913-1

This Springer imprint is published by the registered company Springer Nature Singapore Pte Ltd.
The registered company address is: 152 Beach Road, #21-01/04 Gateway East, Singapore 189721, Singapore

Preface

Social networks and big data have pervaded all aspects of our daily lives. With their unparalleled popularity, social networks have evolved from platforms for social communication and news dissemination to indispensable tools for professional networking, social recommendations, marketing, and online content distribution. Social networks, together with other activities, produce big data that is beyond the ability of commonly used computer software and hardware tools to capture, manage, and process within a tolerable elapsed time. It has been widely recognized that security and privacy are the critical challenges for Social networks and big data applications due to their scale, complexity and heterogeneity.

The 7th International Symposium on Security and Privacy in Social Networks and Big Data (SocialSec 2021) was held at Fujian Normal University in Fuzhou, China during November 19–21, 2021. It follows the success of SocialSec 2015 in Hangzhou, China, SocialSec 2016 in Fiji, SocialSec 2017 in Melbourne, Australia, SocialSec 2018 in Santa Clara, CA, USA, SocialSec 2019 in Copenhagen, Denmark, and SocialSec 2020 in Tianjin, China. The aim of the symposium is to provide a leading edge forum to foster interactions between researchers and developers within the security and privacy communities in social networks and big data, and to give attendees an opportunity to interact with experts in academia, industry, and government. The technical program of the conference included 16 regular papers selected by the Program Committee from 41 full submissions received in response to the call for papers. All the papers were peer reviewed by at least three (3.32 on average) Program Committee members or external reviewers.

We thank everyone who made this meeting possible: the authors for submitting papers, the Program Committee members, and external reviewers for volunteering their time to review conference papers. We thank Springer for publishing the proceedings in the Lecture Notes in Computer Science series. We would also like to extend special thanks to the chairs and conference Organizing Committee for their work in making SocialSec 2021 a successful event.

September 2021

Limei Lin
Yuhong Liu
Chia-Wei Lee

Organization

General Co-chairs

Jie Wu — Temple University, USA
Yang Xiang — Swinburne University of Technology, Australia
Li Xu — Fujian Normal University, China

Program Co-chairs

Limei Lin — Fujian Normal University, China
Yuhong Liu — Santa Clara University, USA
Chia-Wei Lee — National Taitung University, Taiwan

Publicity Co-chairs

Xiangjian He — University of Technology Sydney, Australia
Zhiwei Lin — Queen's University Belfast, UK
Hui Tian — Huaqiao University, China

Publication Co-chairs

Dajin Wang — Montclair State University, USA
Jianxi Fan — Soochow University, China
Zhiyong Yu — Fuzhou University, China

Local Co-chairs

Ayong Ye — Fujian Normal University, China
Hui Lin — Fujian Normal University, China
Xiaoding Wang — Fujian Normal University, China

Web Chair

Manli Yuan — Fujian Normal University, China

Program Committee

Shaoying Cai — Hunan University, China
Yang Chen — Fudan University, China
Baolei Cheng — Soochow University, China
Jintai Ding — University of Cincinnati, USA

Weibei Fan	Nanjng University of Posts and Telecommunications, China
He Fang	Fujian Normal University, China
Steve Furnell	University of Plymouth, UK
Sun-Yuan Hsieh	National Cheng Kung University, Taiwan
Yanze Huang	Fujian University of Technology, China
Yikun Huang	Fujian Normal University, China
Sokratis Katsikas	Norwegian University of Science and Technology, Norway
Kwok Yan Lam	Nanyang Technological University, Singapore
Chia-Wei Lee	National Taitung University, Taiwan
Aihua Li	Montclair State University, USA
Wenjuan Li	City University of Hong Kong, Hong Kong
Xiaoyan Li	Fuzhou University, China
Chao Lin	Fujian Normal University, China
Limei Lin	Fujian Normal University, China
Liwei Lin	Fujian University of Technology, China
Zhiwei Lin	Queen's University Belfast, UK
Xiaolong Liu	Fujian Agriculture and Forestry University, China
Ximeng Liu	Fuzhou University, China
Yuhong Liu	Santa Clara University, USA
Bo Luo	University of Kansas, USA
Xiapu Luo	Hong Kong Polytechnic University, Hong Kong
Chiara Pero	University of Salerno, Italy
Rishikesh Sahay	MAN Energy Solutions, Germany
Seonghan Shin	National Institute of Advanced Industrial Science and Technology, Japan
Hung-Min Sun	National Tsing Hua University, Taiwan
Dajin Wang	Montclair State University, USA
Feng Wang	Fujian University of Technology, China
Jianfeng Wang	Xidian University, China
Xiaoding Wang	Fujian Normal University, China
Jie Wu	Temple University, USA
Jinbo Xiong	Fujian Normal University, China
Li Xu	Fujian Normal University, China
Lei Xue	Hong Kong Polytechnic University, Hong Kong
Shaojun Yang	Fujian Normal University, China
Wun-She Yap	Universiti Tunku Abdul Rahman, Malaysia
Ayong Ye	Fujian Normal University, China
Xiucai Ye	University of Tsukuba, Japan
Zhiyong Yu	Fuzhou University, China
Manli Yuan	Fujian Normal University, China
Haibo Zhang	University of Otago, New Zealand
Jing Zhang	Fujian University of Technology, China
Lei Zhang	East China Normal University, China

Additional Reviewers

Chen, Yawen
Qin, Yue
Zhang, Yingjie

Contents

Applied Cryptography for Big Data

Distribution Key Scheme for Secure Group Management in VANET Using Polynomial Interpolation

Ankit Kumar[1], Kamred Udham Singh[2], Sun-Yuan Hsieh[3(✉)],
V. D. Ambeth Kumar[4], and Abhishek Kumar[5]

[1] Department of Computer Science and Engineering, Swami Keshvanand
Institute of Technology, Management, and Gramothan, Jaipur, India
[2] Department of Computer Science and Information
Engineering, National Cheng Kung University, Tainan 701, Taiwan
[3] Department of Computer Science and Information
Engineering, Institute of Medical Information,
Institute of Manufacturing Information and Systems,
Center for Innovative FinTech Business Models, and International
Center for the Scientific Development of Shrimp Aquaculture, National
Cheng Kung University, No. 1, University Road, Tainan 70101, Taiwan
hsiehsy@mail.ncku.edu.tw
[4] Department of Computer Science and Engineering, Pani-
malar Engineering College, Anna University, Chennai, India
[5] School of Computer Science and IT, JAIN
(Deemed to be University), Bengaluru, India

Abstract. Security is a major concern for vehicular ad hoc networks
(VANETs). Group-based communications in VANETs is a commonly
investigated topic. Creating a group and distributing a key to numerous fast-moving vehicles for secure communication is a major security
challenge for VANETS. Distributed keys in VANETs allow for the secure
participation of vehicles that may not have been present when the group
was formed. This paper presents a new distributed key scheme for secure
group management in VANET by using polynomial interpolation. The
proposed scheme not only provides a distributed key for vehicles to be
created, to join, and to communicate in the group but also provides and
manages the distribution of keys to maintain the security of VANETs.
The experimental results reveal that the proposed scheme is a secure
solution for group communication in VANETs.

Keywords: Key distribution · Privacy · Authentication · Polynomial · Interpolation · Vehicles

Department of Computer Science and Information Engineering, National Cheng Kung
University, 701, Tainan, Taiwan.

1   Introduction

Mobile ad hoc networks (MANETs) are a promising and emerging technology that enables the development of new decentralized applications. A MANET is a self-organized network formed by mobile nodes that connect to each without predefined infrastructure. If these mobile nodes are vehicles, the MANET is considered a vehicular ad hoc network (VANET). In a VANET, nodes move at high speed and the number of participating nodes is typically unpredictable. Consequently, VANETs must support numerous nodes entering and leaving the network. VANETs have many applications; for example, they can be used to disseminate warnings of road accidents or hazards (e.g., from fog or obstacles). Other applications include obtaining useful service information, such as that regarding nearby restaurants, hotels, or service stations.

The activities performed within a VANET must be protected against malicious attack. Attacks may occur against VANETs the numerous features of a VANET may cause vulnerabilities on connecting to a network. In terms of connectivity, VANETs and MANETs differ in that MANETs typically have no additional infrastructure. For VANETs, access points can be strategically transferred to road side units (RSUs). The difference constituting the greatest challenge for these networks is the movement of participants in a VANET. Vehicles in a VANET typically move at faster speeds than devices in a MANET do, frequently causing disconnections in the network. Security and privacy are key concerns for VANETs. In particular, gray hole attacks are a major security concern. In a gray hole attack, traffic is directed towards nodes that are not actually participating in the network [1]. In a black hole attack, a malicious node reveals its rationing protocol to express itself in order to prevent it from hiding the small path or packet of the destination node. The attacker node advertises the availability of new routes without checking its routing table.

The scope of this paper has expanded from what was originally intended in response to the technological developments and the growth of smart cities worldwide. The methods described herein increase the safety and convenience of driving techniques and enable vehicles to exchange information regarding safety and traffic. The proposed model improves the connectivity and protection of VANETs to achieve enhanced security and privacy in scenarios with various road conditions. Furthermore, a novel scheme was formulated to protect the privacy of VANET users while signaling with the distributed key during group communication.

2   Literature Review

Yang et al. [2] described the threats, vulnerabilities, and identification methodologies of ad hoc networks. They employed the OLSR (Optimized Link State Routing Protocol) routing protocol. OLSR is a proactive routing technology that establishes a network path prior to sending network packets. They simulated a network and describe threats to the OLSR routing protocol. Iwendi et al.

(2018) [3] noted that security packets are exchanged on a regular basis in VANET applications. They published information about a long-term attack, which they believe is feasible, for VANET packets. Each node in the VANET was responsible for determining where messages are to be sent. An attacker could use VANET vulnerabilities to launch an attack. The VANET defensive mechanism was used to prevent the attacker from receiving vital security signals from nearby nodes. Replay attacks could be performed with prior event information. Zhang and Chen (2019) [4] analyzed various attacks that can be performed in VANETs. They compared attacks and attack approaches. They discuss the importance of network security in ensuring the safety of ad hoc networks and proposed a tried-and-true method for handling VANET attacks. Attacks were classified into several categories, and a quantitative analysis was performed. They concluded that VANET attacks affecting the network and its features are a major problem. The advantages and strengths of VANETs cannot be realized until these security violations are resolved. Tan and Chung (2020) [5] presented a method for defining the true network position in a trust-based routing analysis using AODV, which was based on a thorough literature review. VANET was considered a tool for communicating with multiple nodes in a network at the same time. Unfortunately, the simulation results and default parameters were separated. The various models and methods used were discussed. Other scholars also have addressed these concerns, stating that trust is required to ensure secure and effective data transmission. They discuss multiple threats and means to defend against attacks with a confidence model. Zhang and Zhu (2018) [6] reconsidered the efficiency of enhanced protocol schemes, claiming that any attacker can enter a network and affect the VANET functions. For example, an infected node could be deployed in a VANET after an authentication procedure. They described a popular m-ary encoding algorithm for reducing the VANET overhead sequence. The algorithm reduces packet supply and the reduces of network invasions. Attackers are less inclined to attack VANETs because of this system.

3   Problem Definition

In this section, the research problem is detailed, including the network model and adversary model.

3.1   Network Model and Adversary Model

Network Model. A VANET is a wireless network that communicates with sensors or other computing devices embedded in vehicles. These networks can enable continuous monitoring and communication [7] with regard to road safety and road conditions. In a VANET, all nodes have a wireless communication interface that is IEEE 802.11p compatible. However, these nodes have limited energy, computational, and storage capabilities.

Adversary Model. A VANET faces greater vulnerability from the connected vehicles because the RSUs, which are equipped with better security features, are less vulnerable. A VANET could be attacked at any time through breaches in vehicle security [8].

A hacker can be anyone who has access to the vehicles' wireless network. They could also hack any of the vehicles and then pose as a genuine member of the network. Once inside the network, the hacker can perform a variety of actions such as jamming, modifying, forging, or eavesdropping on any device in their range. The hacker's main goal may be to intercept normal communication or to modify it to disrupt traffic and cause damage or loss of life. This is accomplished by altering the information being sent between nodes [9].

3.2   Interpolation

Polynomial equations are sums of monomials of the form $y_n(x^n)$, where

- x is the variable
- y is the coefficient of the variable
- n is the degree of the variable.

For any y and n, a polynomial function of degree n is represented as follows:

$$f(x) = y_n(x^n) = y_n x^n + \cdots + y_0 = 0.$$

Polynomials represent sets of ordered pairs $(x_0, y_0), (x_1, y_1), ..., (x_n, y_n)$. To represent data for an unknown pair at $n + 1$, a continuous function $f(x)$ is used. With this equation, we can find the value of y for any value of x. This process is known as interpolation if x is between the minimum and maximum x value in the provided data, and it is extrapolation otherwise. Polynomials are commonly used interpolating functions because they are simple to differentiate, integrate, and evaluate.

The Lagrangian interpolating polynomial displayed in (1).

$$f_n(x) = \sum_{i=0}^{n} L_i(x) f(x_i) \tag{1}$$

In (2), $f(x)$ indicates an nth order polynomial approximating the function $y = f(x)$ with $n + 1$ data points $(x_0, y_0), (x_1, y_1), ..., (x_{n-1}, y_{n-1})$ and (x_n, y_n).

$$L_i(x) = \prod_{j=0, j\neq i}^{n} \frac{x - x_i}{x_i - x_j} \tag{2}$$

$L_i(x)$ is a weighting function that includes the product of $n - 1$ terms with terms where $j = i$ omitted.

Experiments that reveal discoveries concerning interpolation or amalgamation with respect to the injection transfer property have been completed and are known as "interpolation experiments." Thus, we are able to recognize numerous concepts on their own terms.

4   Proposed Framework

A novel key distribution scheme for broadcast encryption based on polynomial interpolation is proposed. The proposed scheme is not a one-time scheme; that is, that the key does not need to be updated after each use. The method relies on Lagrange polynomial interpolation. In this section, we first introduce Lagrange polynomial interpolation, and we then discuss key distribution in the context of broadcast encryption by using Lagrange polynomial interpolation. The Lagrange interpolating polynomial is the polynomial $p(x)$ of degree $\leq (n-1)$ that passes through the following n points: $(x_1, y_1 = f(x_1)), (x_2, y_2 = f(x_2)), \cdots , (x_n, y_n = f(x_n))$. This polynomial is given by (3) as follows:

$$p(x) = \sum_{j=1}^{n} p_j(x), \tag{3}$$

where $p_j(x)$ represents

$$p_j(x) = y_j \prod_{k=1}^{n} \frac{x - x_k}{x_j - x_k} \text{ where, } k \neq j. \tag{4}$$

Written explicitly,

$$p_x = \frac{(x-x_2)(x-x_3)\cdots(x-x_n)}{(x_1-x_2)(x-x_3)(x-x_n)} y_1 + \frac{(x-x_1)(x-x_3)\cdots(x-x_n)}{(x_2-x_1)(x_2-x_3)(x_2-x_n)} y_2$$
$$+ \cdots + \frac{(x-x_1)(x-x_2)\cdots(x-x_n)}{(x_n-x_1)(x_n-x_2)(x_n-x_{n-1})} y_n.$$

For an example of an interpolating polynomial equation, consider $f(x) = x^3$ in the range $1 \leq x \leq 3$.

The points identified on the polynomial equation are $(x_0, y_0) = (1, 1)$, $(x_1, y_1) = (2, 8), (x_2, y_2) = (3, 27)$.

Equation 5 describes the interpolation.

$$p(x) = 1 * \frac{x-2}{1-2} * \frac{x-3}{1-3} + 8 * \frac{x-1}{2-1} * \frac{x-3}{2-3} + 27 * \frac{x-2}{3-1} * \frac{x-2}{3-2} \tag{5}$$

$$P(x) = 6x^2 - 11x + 6 \tag{6}$$

4.1   Use of Lagrange Interpolation to Share a Secret and to Reconstruct It from a Set of Point Pairs (x, y)

Let the secret be $D = 10$. We consider a three-share scheme in which all three shares are required to reconstruct the secret. We choose two numbers at random as the coefficients. The polynomial is constructed using the coefficients and the secrets as follows: $5x^2 + 2x + 10$. Here, 5 and 2 are the selected coefficients and

10 is the secret. By using the constructed polynomial, three points are generated $(1, 17), (2, 34), (3, 61)$.

To reconstruct the secret key D, we must use the constant part of Lagrange's polynomial.

$$l_0 = \frac{(x-2)}{(1-2)} * \frac{(x-3)}{(1-3)} = \frac{(x-2)(x-3)}{2},$$

$$l_1 = \frac{(x-1)}{(2-1)} * \frac{(x-3)}{(2-3)} = \frac{(x-1)(x-3)}{-1},$$

$$l_2 = \frac{(x-1)}{(3-1)} * \frac{(x-2)}{(3-2)} = \frac{(x-2)(x-3)}{2}$$

Again, we reconstruct the secret key pair D by ignoring the x axes, and we only consider constant parts as follows:

$$D = 17 * \frac{(-2)(-3)}{2} + 34 * \frac{(-1)(-3)}{-1} + 61 * \frac{(-1)(-2)}{2} = 10.$$

The same method is expected to work for a finite field $GF(2^8)$ as long as the arithmetic is replaced with finite field arithmetic.

4.2   Key Distribution in Broadcast Encryption Using Polynomial Interpolation

Now, we consider a VANET with a road side unit (RSU) and a set of vehicles with on board units (OBUs). The RSU provides the vehicle with prearranged keys when it joins the network. Figure 1 illustrates the scenario; C is the set of all users connected to the broadcast center $C = (C_1, C_2, C_3, \ldots, C_n)$. Suppose some messages are intended for a group of users T in C and that those messages ought not to be visible to other vehicles in C. Figure 2 illustrates this scenario. A possible solution is encrypting the messages prior to broadcasting. The proposed method is useful for key distribution in this scenario.

Suppose that M is the message that is intended for the group of users T. The broadcast center is expected to encrypt the message using a key K and send it to the users.

We can represent this scenario as follows:

$$C = E(M, K),$$

where M is the message, K is the key, E is the encryption scheme, and C is the encrypted message. The user must be able to decrypt the message; thus, the key K should be available to the user [10]. In our proposed method, instead of the original key K being shared with the users of group, a shared key based on the original key K is generated and distributed to the users.

Using the shared key, the users can now decrypt the message [11].

Algorithm 1: (a): Generation of Distributed Key for Group Communication

Input : K is the distributed key for group communication.

Output: $k_1, k_2, \cdots, k_n$ are distributed shares for key each group.

1 Choose a random number used as coefficients $C_1, C_2, \cdots, C_{z-1}, C_z$ of the polynomial equation.
2 Construct a polynomial $P(x) = C_1 x_z + C_2 x_{z-1} + \cdots + C_{z-1} x_2 + C_z x_1 + M$.
3 Select a separate token for each node such as $T_1, T_2, \cdots, T_n$.
4 Compute $f(T_1), \quad f(T_2), \cdots, f(T_n)$ values as the shares of the key $k_1, k_2, \cdots, k_n$.
5 For each node, select a random number R_i.
6 For each user, find two more quantities.
7 $k_i R = f(T_i + R_i), k_i 2R = f(T_i + 2R_i)$.
8 For each node, compute two more variables $k_i R = f(T_i + R_i), k_i 2R = f(T_i + 2R_i)$.
9 Combine the key factors for each node n as $K_i = (k_i, k_i R, k_i 2R)$.
10 For each node u_i, distribute the shared key K_i.

Algorithm 1: Describes the distribution of key shares among the users in a particular group. It describes the encryption using the key. Algorithm 2 describes the decryption for a user using the key shares. The number of users in the group T is

n. Initially, the broadcast center must select a key K and a constant z.

Algorithm 1: (b): Encryption process

Input : M is the message, and K is the key.

Output: C is the encrypted message for the users of group T.

1 Encrypt the message M by using the key K.
2 $C = E(M, K)$.
3 Broadcast the encrypted message C to the group T.

Assume that user i from group T decrypts the message using his/her own key share.

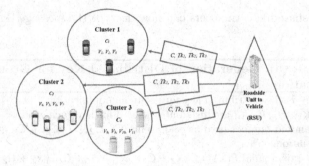

Fig. 1. Encryption used for RSU communication with vehicles.

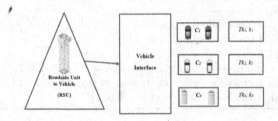

Fig. 2. Decryption used for RSU communication with vehicles

Algorithm 2: For Decryption

---

1 The vehicle provides a token number, random number, and the corresponding key pair value. The token value is verified by the vehicle OBU, for example, with the token value $TK_1 = 15$, random number $R_1 = 2$, and key pair values $K = 68550, 104770,$ and 136846.

2 Represent K_1 in pairs. $X_1 = 15, K_1 = 68850$, $X_2 = 15 + 1 * 2 = 17, K_2 = 104770, X_3 = 15 + 2 * 2 = 19, K_3 = 136846$

3 Compute as follows:

$$k = 68550 * \frac{-104770}{(15-17)} \frac{-136840}{(15-19)} + 104770 * \frac{(-68550)}{(17-15)} \frac{(-136840)}{(17-19)}$$
$$+ 136846 * \frac{(-68550)}{(19-15)} \frac{(-104770)}{(19-17)}$$

---

5   Implementation

In this section, the implementation is presented with simulation parameters and code to calculate the throughput and number of dropped packets.

5.1   Simulation Parameters

Tables 1 and 2 describe the simulation network, simulator parameters, interface type, queue type, radio propagation, length, routing protocol, MAC protocol, size of the broadcast, and the resulting time for implementing the VANET in the NS2 simulator.

Table 1. Network simulation parameters for VANET

S. No.	Parameter	Value
1.	Network simulator	NS-2.34
2.	Network interface type	Physical/Wireless/OFDM
3.	Queue type	Queue/PriQueue/DropTail
4.	Radio propagation	Propagation/Two ray ground
5.	Queue length	50
6.	Routing protocol	AODV
7.	MAC protocol	IEEE 802.16e
8.	Size of broadcast packet	1500 bytes
9.	Total simulation time (ms)	410–710 ms

Table 2. Vehicular mobility model parameters for VANET

S. No.	Parameter	Value
1.	Traffic simulator	SUMO 0.9.10
2.	Map Area	1212*4756 m
3.	Max. speed (road segment)	16.16 m/s
4.	No. of lanes (per road segment)	4
5.	Route length	3697 m
6.	Total no. of vehicles for simulation	25–85
7.	No. of Base station	4
8.	No. of road segment	5

5.2   Code for Throughput Calculation

To calculate throughput, the degree of the received packet and the package type are considered. An awk script was written to provide details of the number bundles of each package type received by any node in the network [12].

The formula to calculate the throughput is as follows:

$$Throughput = \frac{No.\ of\ bits\ received\ by\ the\ Node}{Simulation\ Time\ *\ 106\ Mpbs}.$$

5.3   Code for Calculating the Number of Dropped Packets

The network can also be investigated in terms of the number of bits or packets lost during transmission. To increase the network's effectiveness, data loss should be minimized [13].

6   Results and Discussion

The observed values of node bandwidth versus throughput are presented in Table 3.

Table 3. Bandwidth Versus Throughput (Proposed Algorithm)

Bandwidth utilization (Mbps)	25	30	35	40	45
Throughput per node (Mbps)	25	29.0014	32.1468	35.95	39.3627

The observed values of number of nodes versus throughput are presented in Table 4.

Table 4. Number of nodes vs. Throughput (Proposed Algorithm)

Number of nodes	20	40	60	80
Throughput per node (Mbps)	35.95	31.0485	28.1534	26.7302

Table 5. Number of nodes versus packet loss ratio (normal)

Number of Nodes	20	40	60	80
Packet Loss Ratio	44.778	60.712	136.654	180.361

We observed that as the number of nodes in the simulation increased, the throughput per node decreased even if the bandwidth was held constant at 40 Mbps [14]. To improve network efficiency, packet loss in the system must be reduced. We performed the experiment with a bandwidth of 40 Mbps to calculate the ratios; the results are presented in Table 5.

Table 6 detail the number of nodes and percentage packet loss.

Table 6. Number of nodes versus packet loss percentage (proposed algorithm)

Number of nodes	20	40	60	80
Percentage packet loss	46.642	46.815	46.818	46.945

The number of packets lost due to collision was observed to increase with the number of nodes. The ratio of packets lost due to collision and the total amount of packets sent can be used to calculate the packet loss ratio [15], as indicated in.

7   Conclusion

Encryption is vital for an ad hoc network, especially for one-to-group communications. We propose a scheme in which the RSU does not share the key with the vehicle. The key share is instead distributed for group communication. In the experiments, we observed that use of this encryption scheme increases VANET group communication security in terms of availability, authenticity, accountability, and data integrity. The proposed methodology has a better packet delivery ratio and a lower packet drop rate relative to its counterparts. The main advantage of this proposed algorithm is that the revocation of vehicles does not require the generation of a new shared key for encrypting and broadcasting the secret key.

References

1. Xie, L., Ding, Y., Yang, H., Wang, X.: Blockchain-based secure and trustworthy internet of things in SDN-enabled 5G-VANETs. IEEE Access **7**, 56656–56666 (2019)
2. Yang, J., Weng, N., Cheng, J., Ni, X., Lin, X., Shen, X.: DeQoS attack: degrading quality of service in VANETs and its mitigation. IEEE Trans. Veh. Technol. **68**, 4834–4845 (2019)
3. Iwendi, C., Uddin, M., Ansere, J.A., Nkurunziza, P., Anajemba, J.H., Bashir, A.K.: On detection of sybil attack in large-scale VANETs using spider-monkey technique. IEEE Access **6**, 47258–47267 (2018)
4. Zhang, X., Chen, X.: Data security sharing and storage based on a consortium blockchain in a vehicular Ad-hoc network. IEEE Access **7**, 58241–58254 (2019)
5. Tan, H., Chung, I.: Secure authentication and key management with blockchain in VANETs. IEEE Access **8**, 2482–2498 (2020)
6. Zhang, T., Zhu, Q.: Distributed privacy-preserving collaborative intrusion detection systems for VANETs. IEEE Trans. Signal Inf. Process. Netw. **4**, 148–161 (2018)
7. Guo, J.: TROVE: a context-awareness trust model for VANETs using reinforcement learning. IEEE Internet Things J. **7**(7), 6647–6662 (2020)
8. Wei, Z., Li, J., Wang, X., Gao, C.: A lightweight privacy-preserving protocol for VANETs based on secure outsourcing computing. IEEE Access **7**, 62785–62793 (2019)
9. Ma, Z., Zhang, J., Guo, Y., Liu, Y., Liu, X., He, W.: An efficient decentralized key management mechanism for VANET with blockchain. IEEE Trans. Veh. Technol. **69**, 5836–5849 (2020)
10. Lu, Z., Qu, G., Liu, Z.: A survey on recent advances in vehicular network security, trust, and privacy. IEEE Trans. Intell. Transp. Syst. **20**, 760–776 (2019)

11. Tangade, S., Manvi, S.S., Lorenz, P.: Trust management scheme based on hybrid cryptography for secure communications in VANETs. IEEE Trans. Veh. Technol. **69**(5), 5232–5243 (2020)
12. Tan, H., Gui, Z., Chung, I.: A secure and efficient certificateless authentication scheme with unsupervised anomaly detection in VANETs. IEEE Access **6**, 74260–74276 (2018)
13. Cui, J., Wei, L., Zhong, H., Zhang, J., Xu, Y., Liu, L.: Edge computing in VANETs-An efficient and privacy-preserving cooperative downloading scheme. IEEE J. Sel. Areas Commun. **38**(6), 1191–1204 (2020)
14. Javed, M.A., Hamida, E.B.: On the interrelation of security, QoS, and safety in cooperative ITS. IEEE Trans. Intell. Transp. Syst. **18**(7), 1943–1957 (2017)
15. Zhang, L., Wu, Q., Domingo-Ferrer, J., Qin, B., Hu, C.: Distributed aggregate privacy-preserving authentication in VANETs. IEEE Trans. Intell. Transp. Syst. **18**(3), 516–526 (2017)

Big Data System Security

Performance Evaluation of Fault Tolerant Routing Algorithm in Data Center Networks

Ningning Liu[1] , Weibei Fan[2(✉)] , and Jianxi Fan[3]

[1] Suzhou Vocational University, Suzhou 215104, China
[2] Nanjing University of Posts and Telecommunications, Nanjing 210003, China
wbfan@njupt.edu.cn
[3] Soochow University, Suzhou 215031, China

Abstract. Nowdays, the vigorous development of cloud computing technology has brought great changes to the development of the whole information industry. The traditional data center network topology construction method and the operation mechanism of the network layer control plane are solidified, which have been difficult to meet the increasing demand for high performance and high cost performance under the new situation. Researchers map the topology of the data center network to an undirected graph, and use graph algorithms to implement fault-tolerant routing in complex networks. However, the shortest path algorithm of some early graphs cannot be applied to all topological graphs. In this paper, we analyze the advantages and disadvantages of related algorithms, and propose a fault-tolerant routing algorithm for all networks, which can dynamically call different algorithms according to the current number of nodes and links. The experimental results show that it can effectively improve the accuracy and fault tolerance of the algorithm and reduce the consumption of time and memory.

Keywords: Data center network · Graph algorithm · Fault tolerant routing · Performance evaluation

1 Introduction

Cloud computing and its related technologies have made great development and progress, which have also brought great changes to the computer industry. Data center network refers to an infrastructure of data center network, which is connected with switches and servers by using high-speed links. The traditional data center network topology construction method and the operating mechanism of the network layer control plane are solidified. It has been difficult to meet the increasing demand for high performance and high cost performance under. Fault tolerant secure routing means that when there are a certain number of failed nodes in the network system, an efficient transmission route can still be found by using the concept of node security level. Therefore, it is more and more important to design a better fault-tolerant routing strategy to record the information of the optimal path in the system as much as possible, and realize more effective fault-tolerant routing in the case of failure in the system, so as to improve the

© Springer Nature Singapore Pte Ltd. 2021
L. Lin et al. (Eds.): SocialSec 2021, CCIS 1495, pp. 17–33, 2021.
https://doi.org/10.1007/978-981-16-7913-1_2

performance of the whole system. The optimization of fault-tolerant routing algorithm can effectively improve the security performance of data center network and ensure the reliable communication of data.

1.1 Related Work

Fault-tolerant routing algorithm is a significant and popular research direction in the field of computer networks. Many scholars have proposed an algorithm design or optimization for a specific network. At first, the routing algorithm mostly adopts the Equivalent Cost Multipath Routing (ECMP) [1], but with the emergence of Software Defined Network (SDN), the control surface and data surface of network equipment are separated, so as to realize the flexible statistical control of network traffic, which also provides a good platform for the proposal of some subsequent routing algorithms. Cai et al. proposed Software defined Hybrid Routing (SHR) [2], determined the threshold according to the statistical results, divided the data flow into large flow and small flow, adopted adaptive routing algorithm for large flow, and adopted traffic independent routing algorithm for small flow, meeting the transmission requirements of different large and small flows. Subsequently, Peng et al. proposed multi-path routing on link real-time status and flow characteristics (MLF) [3]. The algorithm proposed the idea of transforming topology into weighted directed graph, and adopted Dijkstra algorithm for the mapped graph of topology graph. The algorithm has higher link utilization and network throughput in Fat-tree environment. Then, Lei et al. proposed a multi path routing algorithm based on branch and bound in software defined data center networks (mpb-aa) [4], which gives priority to link delay and residual bandwidth according to the characteristics of large and small streams, and uses branch and bound method to find paths, compared with MLF, it has shorter end-to-end delay and higher throughput. Finally, Nan et al. proposed fault tolerance effect and cost function based multipath routing mechanism (feac) [5], designed a feasible path set generation algorithm using heuristic idea, and then used efficiency function and cost function to find the optimal solution. After that, some routing algorithms not only consider the failure of the node itself, but also consider the failure of the link or link connection error. Chang et al. proposed the miswiring tolerant routing protocol (MTR) in the cloud environment data center [6], which uses the openflow controller to complete the physical information collection, map the servers and devices in the physical network to the blueprint, detect wiring errors and facilitate the calculation of solutions, and then modify the configuration routing table through the controller to complete the routing correction.

1.2 Our Contributions

The main results of this paper are as follows:

1. According to the implementation of algorithms in the current data center network (DCN) and software defined network (SDN) environment, this paper analyzes various previous fault-tolerant routing algorithms, and implements Floyd algorithm and double algorithm based on double_stack. Based on this strategy, this paper

writes a program to encapsulate the two, and uses the ratio of edge ratio to node to automatically select an algorithm.
2. This paper reads TXT through the object-oriented high-level programming language Python to complete the construction of network topology and the display of topology shape.
3. We built several models such as bus network, Fat-tree, DCell and Bcube, and tested their algorithm speed, memory occupation, path finding accuracy and other performance indicators under different network topologies.
4. The results of the algorithm are analyzed and studied to find the appropriate threshold so that the algorithm can automatically adapt to different network conditions. The advantages and disadvantages of the algorithm are described, and the next work direction and goal are pointed out.

1.3 Organization of the Paper

The rest of this paper is organized as follows:

The second section mainly introduces the basic knowledge of fault-tolerant routing algorithm of data center network in cloud environment; the third section introduces the design of fault-tolerant routing algorithm in the ideal environment, including how to globally map the network topology to the undirected graph and a variety of graph routing algorithms, and how to dynamically call each routing algorithm according to the existing situation of the graph to obtain the highest efficiency; in the fourth section, the algorithm is tested experimentally; the last section mainly contains the summary of the full text and the outlook for the future.

2 Preliminaries

Cloud environment [7] refers to the Internet or big data environment that can provide computing power, storage capacity or virtual machine services to users or various application systems on demand from the dynamically virtualized resource pool.

DCN [8–10] refers to an infrastructure of data center network, which uses high-speed links to connect with switches and servers. Through unified planning and arrangement of resources, it can make full use of centralized large-scale resources to provide reliable and safe services for decentralized users.

2.1 Software Defined Network Mapping to Undirected Graph

With the development of software defined network SDN, we can map the data center network topology to undirected graph. The previously introduced algorithms such as MLF, mpb-aa and MTR have been mapped to graph, and some graph algorithms are used to complete fault-tolerant routing algorithms. This paper only discusses the situation in the ideal network, considers the shortest path finding algorithm based on the number of routing hops without bandwidth delay requirements, and realizes the efficient fault-tolerant path of dynamically calling Freud algorithm and double stack method in the case of node or link failure.

2.2 Data Center Network Definition Storage Mode

The data center topology is constructed here, and each link and node in the topology are recorded in text form. The format of each line can be defined as a ternary formula $L_i = \{node_s, node_d, value_{sd}\}$, where L_i represents a line in the plain text file of the stored data center network topology, $node_s$, $node_d$ here only represents the serial numbers of the two nodes connected by the link. Here, because they are mapped into an undirected graph, the sequence of the two nodes can be reversed. $value_{sd}$ represents the weight of the path between nodes s and d. Because this paper only discusses the ideal case, it defaults to 1, which can be extended according to the actual situation.

2.3 Undirected Graph Storage Mode

In all kinds of graph algorithms, undirected graphs usually have two storage methods: adjacency matrix and adjacency table. In this paper, the functions read_mtx() and get_map() are read from the data center network definition file and transformed into two storage forms respectively, so as to facilitate the call and search of fault-tolerant routing algorithm. The adjacency matrix stores the edge relationship between nodes in the form of matrix, and its corresponding relationship is shown in Fig. 1. Because of the characteristics of the relationship between nodes, the adjacency matrix is more suitable for storing dense graphs. This paper only considers the ideal data center network routing, and takes the number of routing hops as the optimization goal. Therefore, in Python code, the adjacency matrix is dynamically created by using a two-dimensional array. If there is a link between i and j, remember mtx[i][j] = 1 (i < j), otherwise set inf. The specific implementation steps of read_mtx() are as follows:

(1) Read the first line of the topology definition file to obtain the maximum node sequence number.
(2) Dynamically initialize a two-dimensional array mtx, all positions inf.
(3) Traverse the triplet $\{node_s, node_d, value_{sd}\}$ of each line in the text file and set mtx[s][d] = 1.
(4) Set mtx[s][d] = 1 on the other half of the matrix.

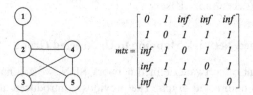

$$mtx = \begin{bmatrix} 0 & 1 & inf & inf & inf \\ 1 & 0 & 1 & 1 & 1 \\ inf & 1 & 0 & 1 & 1 \\ inf & 1 & 1 & 0 & 1 \\ inf & 1 & 1 & 1 & 0 \end{bmatrix}$$

Fig. 1. Temporary matrix storage.

The adjacency table can also store undirected graphs. Unlike the adjacency matrix, the adjacency table records the adjacent nodes of each node in the form of linked list array, and its corresponding relationship is shown in Fig. 2. The adjacency table does not have zero or positive infinite space occupation and will not consume too much space resources. The adjacency table is especially suitable for storing sparse graphs. In this paper, the dictionary (dict) in Python is used to realize the linked list array. The key of the dictionary represents the corresponding node in the diagram, and the value of the dictionary is a (list), which is used to store the serial numbers of other adjacent nodes. The specific implementation form of get_map() is as follows:

(1) Read the first line of the topology definition file to obtain the maximum node sequence number.
(2) Create a dictionary with the maximum node sequence number_map, all index values are set to an empty list.
(3) Traverse each triplet {$node_s$, $node_d$, $value_{sd}$} in the text file, add d to the value of key s, and add s to the value of key d.

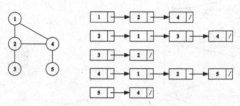

Fig. 2. Temporary connection table storage.

Finally, this paper realizes the visualization of data center topology definition, and realizes the topology diagram display through Networkx, a third-party library of Python.

2.4 Floyd Algorithm

Floyd algorithm [11] was proposed in 1962 and can be used without negative weight edge loop, which is consistent with the data center network in this paper. The algorithm can not only calculate the shortest path between any two nodes through a weighted matrix, but also record the shortest path between two nodes by introducing a successor node matrix. The algorithm flow chart is shown in Fig. 3, and its specific implementation ideas are as follows:

1. Read in the adjacency matrix. If there is a connection between two nodes, set it to 1, and if there is no connection, set it to infinity inf.
2. For every two nodes u and v, check whether there is a third node w, so that the path value passing through w is shorter. The specific method is as follows:

    (1) Define the adjacency matrix distance according to the above design scheme. If there is a reachable path from node u to v, set distance[u][v] = 1; otherwise, set distance[u][v] = inf.
    (2) Define another matrix route with the same size, record the information of the inserted point, and initialize route[u][v] = v.

(3) Insert each node into the diagram in turn, and compare the path value after inserting the new node with the original path value, that is, distance [u][v] = min(distance[u][v], distance[u][k] + distance[k][v]). If distance[u][v] becomes smaller, let route[u][v] = k.

(4) After traversing all nodes, the shortest path from any source node i to destination node j is generated through route matrix and output.

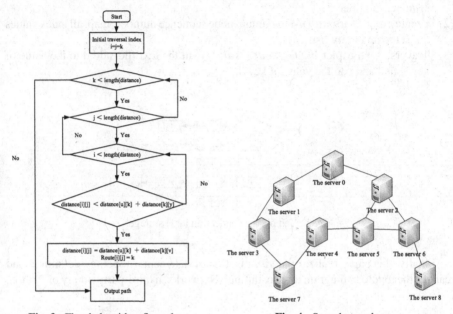

Fig. 3. Floyd algorithm flow chart.   **Fig. 4.** Sample topology.

The idea of Floyd algorithm belongs to dynamic programming, with time complexity of $O(n^3)$ and space complexity of $O(n^2)$. Floyd algorithm performs best in dense graphs. The efficiency of the algorithm is higher than that of Dijkstra algorithm or SPFA algorithm. When the topology has not changed, the shortest path between any two nodes can be obtained only by calculation once. The code implementation is very simple, compact and robust. However, its performance on sparse graph is not very ideal, and the algorithm itself has no memory function except the optimal path. When there is an error in the optimal path, the adjacency matrix needs to be modified and calculated again.

In order to supplement the performance of Floyd's fault-tolerant routing algorithm on sparse graph, this paper introduces the second algorithm, the depth first algorithm based on double stack, which dynamically calls the two algorithms by comparing the ratio of edge to node in the existing topology.

2.5 Depth First Algorithm Based on Double Stack

In order to avoid using recursion to realize depth first search, this paper uses two stacks to realize node expansion and path recording, in which main_stack stores a single node, which is used to record the path and side_stack is used to store a list of adjacent nodes of the current element. Take topology Fig. 4 as an example to calculate the optimal path from node 3 to node 6. The specific idea is as follows:

(1) Set two stacks, main_stack and side_stack. Always keep the stack height consistent.
(2) Put the source node into the main_stack and the list of adjacent nodes of the top element of the main_stack into the side_stack. As shown in Fig. 5.

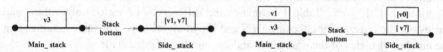

Fig. 5. Double stack based depth first algorithm step 1.

Fig. 6. Double stack based depth first algorithm step 2.

(3) Select a node in the top element of the side_stack and move it into the main_stack, and add the list of adjacent nodes of the top element of the new main_stack at the corresponding height of the side_stack, as shown in Fig. 6.
(4) When the top of the side_stack is empty, check whether the top element of the main_stack of the main_stack is the destination node. If not, an element will pop up both the main stack and the side_stack, as shown in Fig. 7.

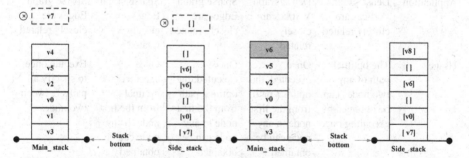

Fig. 7. Double stack based depth first algorithm step 3.

Fig. 8. Double stack based depth first algorithm step 4.

(5) Repeat steps (3) and (4) until the top of the main_stack is the target node. Record the main_stack sequence to get an available path, as shown in Fig. 8.
(6) All paths are sorted by path length to obtain the optimal path.

The depth first algorithm based on double stack needs the topology to adopt the form of adjacency table to facilitate the query of adjacent nodes. In this case, the time complexity $O(N + E)$ and space complexity $O(N)$ of the algorithm. The algorithm is very suitable for sparse graph. Its advantage is that it has memory ability for all paths, can quickly find a standby scheme in the case of a node or link error, and can make a rough judgment on the fault tolerance of a topology. Its disadvantage is that the worst time complexity of depth first is $O(n!)$. When there is no macro understanding of the whole topology, the blind use of the algorithm may not meet the time limit and be inefficient.

3   Design of Dynamic Fault Tolerant Routing Algorithm

3.1   Graph Algorithm Selection and Comparison

In addition to the above two graph path algorithms, the graph shortest path algorithm also includes Bellman-Ford algorithm [12, 13] and its improved algorithm (SPFA), Dijkstra algorithm [14, 15], etc. Table 1 compares the differences of various algorithms and writes out the reasons for choosing DFS and Floyd algorithms. The table assumes that the number of nodes of the graph is N and the number of edges is E.

Table 1. Comparison of shortest path algorithms.

	Floyd	Dijkstra	Bellman-Ford	SPFA	Double stack_DFS
Spatial complexity	$O(N^2)$	$O(E)$	$O(E)$	$O(E)$	$O(N)$
Time complexity	$O(N^3)$	$O((N + E)\log N)$	$O(NE)$	$O(NE)$	$O(N!)$
Application	Dense graph Vertices are closely related	Dense graph Vertices are closely related	Sparse graph Edges are closely related	Sparse graph Edges are closely related	Sparse graph Edges are closely related
Usage	The optimal path of any two nodes can be obtained by executing once	Once executed, the optimal path from the first node to any node can be obtained	Once executed, the optimal path from the first node to any node can be obtained	Once executed, the optimal path from the first node to any node can be obtained	Execute once to specify all paths between two nodes

From the above Table 1, we can find that the application of different algorithms is not consistent. Since this paper is not for a specific topology, but for the data center network in the macro sense, one algorithm obviously can not adapt to all situations, and a variety of algorithms need to be called dynamically according to the conditions of edges and nodes.

In the case of dense graphs, Dijkstra algorithm can not deal with negative weight edges. Although negative weight edges are not within the scope of this paper, they can represent the excitation of a link in practice. Using Dijkstra is not conducive to subsequent expansion and program universality. And for the routing between any two nodes, the efficiency of n times Dijkstra is lower than Floyd. For sparse graphs, Bellman-Ford, SPFA and shortest path DFS have basically the same time complexity and spatial complexity, but Bellman-Ford and SPFA can only judge whether there is a negative weight loop. The shortest path DFS can run directly when there is a negative weight loop, and DFS can record all feasible paths. In this way, if the link often fails and the failed nodes are random, DFS has the shortest path priority, and can find the second path in $O(N)$ time. Therefore, Floyd and DFS algorithms are selected here, which are dynamically called by the ratio of now_nodes and now_edges. It should be noted that the implementation of the following two programs can calculate the case with negative weight, but this paper focuses on the optimal error tolerant routing with hops as the path value.

3.2 Algorithm Design

The core pseudo code of the dynamic fault-tolerant routing algorithm designed in this paper is as follows.

Begin

Count the number of now_nodes and now_edges

$\alpha = 1.4$

if now_edges/now_nodes > α

Call Floyd algorithm

Else

Call double_stack_DFS

End

The value of α is 1.4. When the edge ratio node ratio is greater than the threshold α, the topology graph is identified as a dense graph and the Floyd algorithm is called. When the ratio is less than the threshold α, the graph is identified as a sparse graph and the double_stack_DFS is called. $\alpha = 1.4$ is the best value selected after a variety of topology simulation, and its performance will be described in the experiment in the next chapter.

4 Experimental Results

4.1 Experimental Environment and Content

This paper uses plain text file to define the network topology of data center, uses Python 3.9 to implement the dynamic fault-tolerant routing algorithm, and completes the functions of topology storage, topology display, simulating network fault, detecting connectivity performance, dynamic fault-tolerant routing and so on. The experimental environment of this paper is 2.0 GHz 4-core 10th generation Intel Core i5 processor with 16 GB 3733 MHz LPDDR4X memory. The test environment parameters are shown in Table 2.

Table 2. Test environment parameter table.

Host environment	
Operating system	MacOS Catalina 10.15.7
Processor	2.0 GHz 4-core 10th generation Intel Core i5 processor
Memory	16 GB 3733 MHz LPDDR4X

At the same time, in order to verify the correctness of the algorithm and quantitatively analyze its related performance, this paper uses plain text files to define multiple topologies, including bus topology, k = 4 Fat-tree topology, DCell topology and so on. These topologies are manually input according to the description and definition of previous papers, and the third-party library Networkx [16] is used to display the topology diagram to ensure that the topology diagram is consistent with the blueprint. Its general form is shown in Fig. 9 and 10.

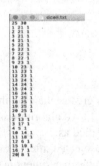
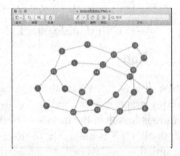

Fig. 9. Definition form of DCell network topology.

Fig. 10. DCell network topology visualization.

Finally, in order to better analyze the dynamic routing fault-tolerant algorithm, this study sets up several groups of comparative experiments:

(1) Taking Floyd algorithm as the benchmark algorithm, the accuracy of dynamic routing fault-tolerant algorithm is tested.

(2) Comparison of the time complexity of Floyd algorithm, depth first algorithm and different α value dynamic routing algorithms in the ratio of topology with different edge node ratio.

(3) Comparison of spatial complexity of Floyd algorithm, depth first algorithm and different value dynamic routing algorithms in topological graphs with different edge node ratios.

(4) Comparison of fault tolerance performance of each topology using dynamic fault-tolerant routing algorithm.

For the experimental parameter selection of the algorithm, after reading any Fat-tree or DCell topology, this paper simulates the routing fault by randomly closing the node or link, reduces the link node ratio by equal difference, and counts the time complexity and space complexity of each algorithm through the test code. Where α is set to 1.3, 1.4 and 1.5.

4.2 Algorithm Validity Test

For the effectiveness of the algorithm, this paper mainly tests two aspects: the accuracy and fault tolerance of the algorithm. The accuracy of the algorithm reflects whether the algorithm is correct or not, that is, whether the algorithm can find the shortest routing path when the topology is fixed, and the path does not include any faulty nodes or links. The fault tolerance of the algorithm reflects the reliability of the algorithm, that is, whether the algorithm can still work normally and find a feasible path in the case of as many faults as possible.

4.2.1 Accuracy of Algorithm

Here, the Flyod algorithm is used as the benchmark algorithm, a topology map is defined by text file, and the dynamic routing algorithm and benchmark algorithm are used for testing. A random function is defined to randomly send multiple source nodes and target nodes into the two algorithms, and then the obtained paths are compared. The accuracy of the algorithm is 100% after multiple tests at any closed node or link. The screenshot of the correctness test command line is shown in Fig. 11.

```
Run:    main
       ----test 98/100------
       source:1 destination:2
       result of Floyd[1, 9, 2]
       result of best_route[1, 9, 2]
       correct:98 error:0

       ----test 99/100------
       source:1 destination:8
       result of Floyd[1, 9, 17, 15, 8]
       result of best_route[1, 9, 17, 15, 8]
       correct:99 error:0

       ----test 100/100------
       source:2 destination:6
       result of Floyd[2, 9, 17, 13, 6]
       result of best_route[2, 9, 17, 13, 6]
       correct:100 error:0

       accuracy:100%
```

Fig. 11. Effectiveness test of dynamic fault tolerant routing algorithm.

4.2.2 Fault Tolerance of Algorithm

In the actual production environment, nodes or links in the network topology will fail. The original static routing algorithm will set many paths in advance and quickly switch to the next preset path in case of error in the current path. The fault tolerance of this algorithm is limited. When the damaged node or link exceeds a certain value, the routing may make an error. Dynamic fault-tolerant routing algorithm adopts the way of dynamic path acquisition, and its fault-tolerant performance actually depends on the fault-tolerant ability of the network topology itself.

In the most ideal case, the whole topology is in the form of full connection. At this time, the fault tolerance performance of the whole network is the strongest. Except for the source node and the destination node itself and the link before them, all other node or link failures will not affect the data transmission. Therefore, we define the fault tolerance of dynamic fault-tolerant routing algorithm as ftv(fault_tolerant_value), and its calculation formula is shown in Eq. 1.

$$ftv = \frac{\frac{1}{n}\sum_0^n n\_break_i}{(node - 2)} \tag{1}$$

Where n_break_i is the number of nodes deleted when there is no link between the two nodes due to random deletion after any two nodes are selected in the figure. $\frac{1}{n}\sum_0^n n\_break_i$ repeat n times and take the average value to eliminate contingency. Its value is between 0 and 1, and 1 represents the most ideal full connection. The fault tolerance of the algorithm under various topologies is tested below. The test results are shown in Table 3.

Table 3. Fault tolerance of dynamic fault-tolerant routing in various topologies.

	BUS	Fat-tree	DCell	FiConn
best_route	0.2765	0.4598	0.4778	0.5569
static_route	0.2025	0.3316	0.3219	0.3716

4.3 Algorithm Performance Test

4.3.1 Algorithm Time Consumption

In the data center network topology tested in this paper, the time consumption of each algorithm mainly depends on two parts: one is the scale of the data center network topology (mainly depends on the number of nodes and links in the topology), and the other is the ratio of link nodes (i.e. the graph is dense graph or sparse graph). This paper mainly discusses the impact of link node ratio on the performance of the algorithm under the same topology size.

Firstly, the k = 4 Fat-tree topology with 20 nodes is used to test. The Fat-tree topology has a large number of redundant links, strong fault resistance and high link node ratio.

Two benchmark algorithms and dynamic fault-tolerant routing algorithms with different values are tested to compare the time consumption of Fat-tree topology routing under the same topology scale and link node ratio. The test data are shown in Table 4.

Table 4. Time consumption of each algorithm under Fat-tree (unit: ms).

	1.15	1.20	1.25	1.30	1.35	1.40	1.45	1.50	1.55	1.60
floyd	1.764	1.822	1.922	1.775	1.781	1.946	1.962	1.863	1.843	1.870
double_stack	0.839	1.099	1.221	1.577	1.837	2.759	5.757	7.869	9.771	12.062
best_route (α = 1.3)	0.929	1.211	1.331	1.817	1.871	2.107	2.110	2.099	1.992	2.094
best_route (α = 1.4)	0.904	1.137	1.327	1.673	2.037	2.110	2.166	2.167	1.937	2.126
best_route (α = 1.5)	0.908	1.112	1.311	1.612	2.011	2.907	5.979	2.003	1.937	2.023

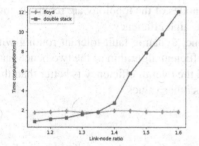

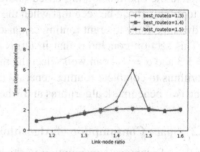

Fig. 12. Comparison of time consumption of benchmark algorithm.

Fig. 13. Comparison of time consumption between different α value routing algorithms.

As shown in Fig. 12, the two benchmark algorithms achieve different link node ratios by simulating link failures when the number of Fat-tree nodes remains unchanged (the problem scale does not change). When Fat-tree is just initialized, the link node ratio can reach 1.6, and then it is reduced to 1.15 according to the gradient equal difference of 0.05. t is obvious that the intersection of the two lines is approximately 1.35. Next, the time consumption when α is 1.3, 1.4 and 1.5 will be compared respectively.

As shown in Figs. 13, when the value is 1.5, there will be an additional period of time consumption. When the value is 1.3 and 1.4, the dynamic fault-tolerant routing algorithm can perfectly call the function with less time consumption in the two functions. Although it needs to read and judge the current node and link number before dynamic call, it will consume some additional time, It makes the time consumption of dynamic fault-tolerant routing function slightly higher, but it can ensure the efficiency of routing algorithm. It is better than the two benchmark algorithms.

The second test in this paper takes the DCell topology of 25 nodes as an example. DCell uses recursive method to ensure the reliability of the network, and its link nodes are relatively low. It tests the time consumption of two benchmark algorithms and dynamic fault-tolerant routing algorithms with different values under the same topology scale and link node ratio. The test data are shown in Table 5.

Table 5. Time consumption of each algorithm under DCell (unit: ms).

	1.00	1.04	1.08	1.12	1.16	1.20
floyd	3.902	3.835	3.889	4.414	4.097	4.307
double_stack	0.380	0.400	0.623	0.649	0.934	1.194
best_route ($\alpha = 1.3$)	0.609	0.620	0.751	0.879	1.183	1.397
best_route ($\alpha = 1.4$)	0.601	0.619	0.749	0.889	1.177	1.392
best_route ($\alpha = 1.5$)	0.609	0.620	0.750	0.881	1.219	1.401

In DCell topology, the link node ratio can only reach 1.2 when there is no link or node failure. In this case, the three dynamic fault-tolerant routing algorithms with α value will complete the optimal routing based on double stack DFS. This also exists in the later bus topology. It can be seen that when the link nodes of the topology are relatively low, the dynamic fault-tolerant routing can also have high efficiency.

This section concludes that in terms of time, dynamic fault-tolerant routing with $\alpha = 1.3$ and $\alpha = 1.4$ can well select the more efficient algorithm of the two benchmark algorithms to complete routing generation, and the overall efficiency is better than that of the two benchmark algorithms and when α is other values.

4.3.2 Space Consumption of Algorithm

The test of memory consumption in this paper is still carried out under the condition of fixed number of nodes (inconvenient problem scale). In this paper, the k = 4 Fat-tree topology with 20 nodes is used to test the memory consumption of two benchmark algorithms and dynamic fault-tolerant routing algorithms with different values under the same topology scale and link node ratio. The test data are shown in Table 6.

Table 6. Memory occupied by algorithm under Fat-tree structure (unit: MB).

	1.15	1.20	1.25	1.30	1.35	1.40	1.45	1.50	1.55	1.60
floyd	0.0492	0.0501	0.0518	0.0502	0.0504	0.0518	0.0504	0.0505	0.0502	0.0513
double_stack	0.0025	0.0024	0.0026	0.0026	0.0027	0.0026	0.0028	0.0027	0.0028	0.0028
best_route ($\alpha = 1.3$)	0.0026	0.0025	0.0026	0.0504	0.0510	0.0513	0.0502	0.0511	0.0512	0.0514
best_route ($\alpha = 1.4$)	0.0026	0.0025	0.0026	0.0026	0.0028	0.0518	0.0504	0.0510	0.0503	0.0510
best_route ($\alpha = 1.5$)	0.0026	0.0026	0.0026	0.0026	0.0027	0.0025	0.0026	0.0503	0.0503	0.0511

As shown in Fig. 14, the memory consumption of the two benchmark algorithms is compared. It can be seen that the memory consumption of the two benchmark algorithms

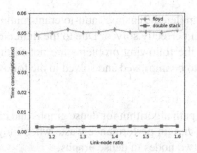

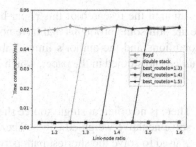

Fig. 14. Comparison of memory consumption of different benchmark algorithms.

Fig. 15. Comparison of memory consumption between different α value routing algorithms.

is independent of the link node ratio, which can be obtained from the algorithm analysis in the previous section. The spatial complexity of Floyd is fixed as $O(N^2)$, while the spatial complexity of DFS based on double stack is fixed as $O(N)$. The spatial complexity of both is only related to the size of network topology (problem scale), and under normal circumstances, the spatial complexity of Floyd is always greater than that of DFS based on double stack.

As shown in Fig. 15, the smaller the value of α, the more Floyd will be called by the dynamic fault-tolerant routing algorithm, which will increase the average memory consumption of the dynamic fault-tolerant routing algorithm. The larger the value of α, the more dynamic fault-tolerant algorithms will call double stack DFS to reduce the average memory consumption. Therefore, under the condition of ensuring the time efficiency of the algorithm, we need to increase the value of α as much as possible. At the same time, combined with the content of the previous section, when α = 1.3 and α = 1.4 can better show time efficiency, this paper selects α = 1.4 as the final threshold, which will bring lower average memory consumption.

5 Conclusion

In this paper, we propose a fault-tolerant routing algorithm based on data center in cloud environment. The dynamic routing algorithm is suitable for macro data center network topology rather than a specific type of topology. Combined with the characteristics and advantages of software defined network, the algorithm roughly distinguishes the topology into dense graph or sparse graph by using the number of links and node ratio, and call the improved Floyd and DFS based on double stack to obtain the optimal routing path. When the source node and destination node have no fault, it can achieve 100% accuracy, and the fault-tolerant performance is significantly higher than the static routing algorithm. In terms of performance, the dynamic fault-tolerant routing time consumption of α = 1.4 sensitively selects the algorithm with shorter time consumption, and reduces the average memory consumption as much as possible under the condition of ensuring the time performance, which perfectly solves the routing problem of the data center network.

Although the research of this paper has completed dynamic fault-tolerant routing, there are still some problems that have not been perfectly solved. Due to the limitation of conditions and the author's limited ability, the following problems are not further discussed and studied in the paper, which need to be improved and solved in the follow-up:

(1) There is no efficient single source shortest path algorithm for dense graphs and can solve negative weighted edges. There is a certain performance waste when Floyd is used to solve the shortest path between two nodes in dense graphs.
(2) The dynamic factor of dynamic fault-tolerant routing algorithm is only the macro selection of the global edge and node number of the graph (that is, whether the whole graph is dense or sparse), and can not be modified for fixed source nodes and destination nodes, which may lead to the degradation of some routing performance.

References

1. Rhamdani, F., Suwastika, N., Nugroho, M.: Equal-cost multipath routing in data center network based on software defined network. In: International Conference on Information and Communication Technology (ICoICT), pp. 246–249 (2018)
2. Cai, Y., Wang, C.: Software defined data center network hybrid routing mechanism. J. Commun. **37**(04), 44–52 (2016)
3. Peng, D., Lai, X.: Multi path routing algorithm for fat-tree data center network based on SDN. Comput. Eng. **44**(4), 41–45 (2018)
4. Lei, T., Lin, Z.: Software defined data center network multipath routing algorithm based on branch and bound method. Minicomput. Syst. **39**(08), 1713–1718 (2018)
5. Ya, N., Wang, X., Zhang, S.: Multipath fault-tolerance routing mechanism in data center network. In: International Symposium on Distributed Computing and Applications for Business Engineering and Science (DCABES), pp. 222–226. IEEE (2018)
6. Jiang, C., Wei, L., Xu, M.: MTR: fault tolerant routing in clos data center network with miswiring links. In: International Workshop on Local & Metropolitan Area Networks (LANMAN). IEEE (2015)
7. Ying, J.: Research on cloud computing oriented data center network architecture design. Netw. Secur. Technol. Appl. **2021**(05), 81–82 (2021)
8. Fan, W., He, J., Han, Z.: Intelligent resource scheduling based on locality principle in data center networks. IEEE Commun. Mag. **58**, 94–100 (2021)
9. Fan, W., He, J., Guo, M.: Privacy preserving classification on local differential privacy in data centers. J. Parallel Distrib. Comput. **135**, 70–82 (2020)
10. Fan, W., Xiao, F., Chen, X.: Efficient virtual network embedding of cloud-based data center networks into optical networks. Parallel Distrib. Syst. **32**, 2793–2808 (2021)
11. Arai, K.: Routing protocol based on floyd-warshall algorithm allowing maximization of throughput. Int. J. Adv. Comput. Sci. Appl. **11**(6), 436–441 (2020)
12. Banerjee, N., Chakraborty, S., Raman, V.: Improved space efficient linear time algorithms for BFS, DFS and applications. In: International Computing and Combinatorics Conference, vol. 97, pp. 119–130. Springer, Cham (2016)
13. Zhao, W., Gong, Z.: Comparative analysis of several classical shortest path algorithms. J. Chifeng Univ. (Nat. Sci. Edn.) **34**(12), 47–49 (2018)

14. Li, Y.: Improvement of Dijkstra algorithm for dealing with the shortest path of negative weight graph and determining negative ring. China New Commun. **1**(07), 166–167 (2019)
15. Gong, J., Niu, Z., Zhang, Y.: Multi Objective path planning of campus meal delivery robot based on local dimension reduction Dijkstra algorithm. J. Shandong Univ. Technol. (Nat. Sci. Edn.) **35**(04), 75–80 (2021)
16. Zhong, B., Hu, Y., Yang, J.: Research based on the Python networkx toolbox analysis of the trade network structure from an information flow perspective. J. Phys: Conf. Ser. **1646**(1), 1–6 (2020)

Forensics in Social Networks and Big Data

Social Distance Detection Using Wireless Signal in Social Networks

Chi-Yu Liu and Chia-Wei Lee(✉)

Department of Computer Science and Information Engineering, National Taitung University,
Taitung, Taiwan
cwlee@nttu.edu.tw

Abstract. Coronavirus disease 2019 (abbreviation: COVID-19) has been a topic of concern in this two years. The number of confirmed cases worldwide has continued to increase. It is a highly contagious and serious virus. In order to prevent the spread of the virus and reduce the infection rate and mortality rate, maintaining social distancing is a very important task. As the mobile phone is indispensable to modern necessities, we considered to use the mobile device to help to detect the social distance. In this paper, we provided an idea about how to use the mobile device wireless signal to detect the social distance.

Keywords: Mobile · Bluetooth · COVID-19 · Social distancing · Wireless signal

1 Introduction

In 2019, the first case of Coronavirus disease 2019 (abbreviation: COVID-19) [1] was detected in Hubei Province, China. The COVID-19 virus spread globally and quickly, and resulting in a persistent infectious epidemic. According to the statistics from the World Health Organization (WHO), as of July 20, 2021 [2]. The cumulative number of cases reported globally is now over 190 million and the number of deaths exceeds 4 million. The COVID-19 is a highly contagious and serious virus.

According to the research of public health scholars, the COVID-19 virus mainly transmitted by droplets and small airborne particles [3]. When people come into close contact with infected person, they will be infected via inhaled droplets and particles that infected people release as they breathe, talk, cough, sneeze, or sing. This is why the WHO suggested that the ways to prevent the spread of the virus are disinfect more, wear a mask, maintain social distancing, and reduce unnecessary contact.

WHO recommended that the social distance is 1.5 m indoors and one-meter outdoors [4]. Maintaining social distancing is a simple and effective way to fight COVID-19. However, it is often not valued by people. And it is not easy to determine the social distancing all the time. In order to effectively maintain social distancing and reduce the virus infection rate, we considered to use the wireless technique to help us to determine the social distance.

Mobile phones have become necessities of our life. Due to everyone will carry their mobile phone when they go outside. We consider to use the wireless technique, such

© Springer Nature Singapore Pte Ltd. 2021
L. Lin et al. (Eds.): SocialSec 2021, CCIS 1495, pp. 37–41, 2021.
https://doi.org/10.1007/978-981-16-7913-1_3

as Bluetooth, Wi-Fi, RFID (Radio Frequency IDentification), which embedded in the mobile device to determine the social distance.

The remainder of this paper is organized as follows. Section 2 reviews related work. Section 3 illustrates the main idea of detecting social distance using wireless signal. Section 4 is the conclusion and future work.

2   Related Work

The World Health Organization (WHO) has stated that there are two ways in which the spread of COVID-19 virus takes place that are respiratory droplets and physical contact. Thus, one of the research topics of prevent COVID-19 is to detect people wear face mask well or not. According to the World Health Organization (WHO), the right way to wear a mask is by adjusting the mask to cover the mouth, nose, and chin [5]. Sen and Sawant [6] presented a mask detection system that is able to detect any type of mask and masks of different shapes from the video streams for following the rules that are applied by the government. Jiang et al. [7] presented a real-time face mask detection method to detect people wear mask properly or not.

Another research topic is to maintain social distance. As prescribed by WHO, people should maintain at least 1.5 m indoors and one-meter outdoors from each other to control the spread of this disease [2, 8, 9]. Ansari and Singh [10] developed a framework that tracks humans for monitoring the social distancing being practiced. To accomplish this objective of social distance monitoring, an algorithm is developed using object detection method. Rahim et al. [11] proposed an efficient solution for real-time social distance monitoring in low light environments.

Some researchers considered the problem of detecting social distance using wireless technology. Tsai [12] proposes a method that can use wireless signal strength (RSSI) sequence to detect the proximity of movement between people. In [13], Leith and Farrel proposed a method to evaluate the potential of using Bluetooth received signal strength for proximity detection. Narvaez and Guerra [14] explored if a Bluetooth RSSI-based mobile application can be developed to detect if the social distance is met or not. In Taiwan, the Central Epidemic Command Center developed the Taiwan Social Distance app [15]. This app also used the wireless technology.

3   Detecting Social Distance

In the Taiwan Social Distance app, when an app user is confirmed to have COVID-19, the health authority will upload related data after obtaining consent from the confirmed case, and the app will automatically send alerts to app users who have come into contact with the confirmed case in the past 14 days so as to remind them to monitor their health status. This app is help the health authority to find out the coronavirus contact.

However, when people are shopping in a hypermarket, this app cannot alert the app users that they are not maintain the safety social distance immediately. Especially when someone focus on his shopping products, he cannot pay attention on the social distance issue.

In [14], Narvaez and Guerra analyzed the problems of solutions for social distancing using different technologies. In this paper, they used the Bluetooth RSSI signal to detect the social distance. And they claim that people hold their cell phones in front of them horizontally. However, people are not always hold their cell phones as if they were using it. Therefore, we try to solve the problem with the situation.

As we know, the physical obstacles also effect the transmission of Bluetooth RSSI signal. Our idea is adding some Bluetooth devices as base stations on the ceiling. This method can reduce some interferences from the physical obstacles, such as pillar, product display stands.

The customers who are in the hypermarket, the Bluetooth base stations will collect the Bluetooth signal from their cell phone. The system will determine the location for everyone according to the Bluetooth signal collection data. Then, we can evaluate the distance between each two persons met the safety social distance or not, shown as Fig. 1. If the distance is less than one meter, system will send alert to these persons who are not standing safety social distance.

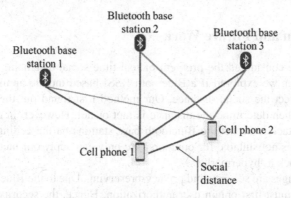

Fig. 1. The illustration of the method how to determine the social distance. The Bluetooth base stations are setting on the ceiling. System will determine the locations of cell phones and then calculate the distance between these two cell phone.

Moreover, Taiwan CDC regulated the number of people allowed in hypermarket. The number was calculated by how many people can stand in one square meter and people can maintain the social distance, shown as Fig. 2. The Bluetooth base stations also can determine the number of people in some area is a suitable number. If some area has too many persons, the system can send alert to these persons who are standing in this area.

During the epidemic, the Bluetooth signal collection data can help people to maintain the safety social distance. In the normal period, this data can help the manager of hypermarket to analyze which area is hot spot. And he can mobilize manpower to hot spot or plan the route.

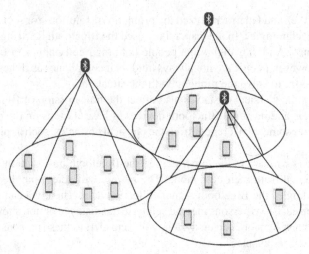

Fig. 2. The illustration of how to calculated by how many people can stand in one square meter.

4   Conclusion and Future Work

In this paper, we considered the problem of real-time social distancing detection. To address this issue, we explored if a Bluetooth RSSI-based mobile application can be developed to detect the social distance. Our method first found out the locations for each user. And then determine the distance is met or not. However, in order to avoid the physical obstacles, we set the Bluetooth base stations on the ceiling. This means that our method is not suitable for outdoors. We only can apply our method in indoor environments, such as hypermarkets.

Other challenges are security and privacy-preserving. Due to the Bluetooth technology, the system must first obtain user authorization. Hence, the security and privacy-preserving is a very important issue. If we cannot provide a safe system to protect the users' data, then fewer people want to use this application. Thus, our next research topic is to present a security mechanism.

References

1. World Health Organization (WHO): WHO corona-viruses (COVID-19). https://www.who.int/health-topics/coronavirus. Accessed 28 Sept 2021
2. World Health Organization (WHO): Who director-generals opening remarks at the media briefing on covid-19-11, March 2020. https://www.who.int/emergencies/diseases/novel-coronavirus-2019/situation-reports. Accessed 28 Sept 2021
3. World Health Organization (WHO): Modes of transmission of virus causing COVID-19: implications for IPC precaution recommendations. https://www.who.int/news-room/commentaries/detail/modes-of-transmission-of-virus-causing-covid-19-implications-for-ipc-precaution-recommendations. Accessed 28 Sept 2021
4. World Health Organization (WHO): Coronavirus Disease (COVID-19) Advice for the Public. https://www.who.int/emergencies/diseases/novel-coronavirus-2019/advice-for-public. Accessed 28 Sept 2021

5. World Health Organization (WHO) Q&A: Masks and COVID-19. https://www.who.int/eme rgencies/diseases/novel-coronavirus-2019/questionandanswers-hub/q-a-detail/q-a-on-covid-19-and-masks. Accessed 28 Sept 2021
6. Sen, S., Sawant, K.: Face mask detection for covid_19 pandemic using pytorch in deep learning. In: IOP Conference Series: Materials Science and Engineering, vol. 1070, p. 012061. IOP Publishing Ltd., Tamil Nadu (2021)
7. Jaing, X., Gao, T., Zhu, Z., Zhao, Y.: Real-time face mask detection method based on YOLOv3. Electronics 10(7), 837 (2021)
8. Setti, L., et al.: Airborne transmission route of COVID-19: why 2 meters/6 feet of inter-personal distance could not be enough (2020). PMID: 32340347
9. Sá-Caputo, D.C., Taiar, R., Seixas, A., Sanudo, B., Sonza, A., Bernardo-Filho, M.: A pro-posal of physical performance tests adapted as home workout options during the COVID-19 pandemic. Appl. Sci. 10(14), 4755 (2020)
10. Ansari, M., Singh, D.K.: Monitoring social distancing through human detection for prevent-ing/reducing COVID spread. Int. J. Inf. Technol. 13(3), 1255–1264 (2021). https://doi.org/10.1007/s41870-021-00658-2
11. Rahim, A., Maqbool, A., Rana, T.: Monitoring social distancing under various low light conditions with deep learning and a single motionless time of flight camera. PLoS ONE 16(2), e0247440 (2021)
12. Tsai, J.Y.: Proximity detection for social distancing based on wireless signal strength time series. Master Thesis of National Cheng Kung University (2020)
13. Leith, D.J., Farrell, S.: Coronavirus contact tracing: evaluating the potential of using bluetooth received signal strength for proximity detection. ACM SIGCOMM Comput. Commun. Rev. 50(4), 66–74 (2020)
14. Narvaez, A.A., Guerra, J.G.: Received signal strength indication—based COVID-19 mobile application to comply with social distancing using bluetooth signals from smartphones. Data Science for COVID-19 (2021)
15. Taiwan CDC: The Taiwan social distancing application and its contact tracing algorithm. https://github.com/ailabstw/social-distancing. Accessed 28 Sept 2021

An Efficient Adaptive Fault Diagnosis Algorithm for Highly Scalable Data Center Networks

Xiangke Wang, Yudu You, Xiao-Yan Li$^{(\boxtimes)}$, Ximeng Liu, and Yang Yang

College of Computer and Data Science, Fuzhou University, Fuzhou 350108, China
xyli@fzu.edu.cn

Abstract. The big data system based on data center network provides low-latency, high-quality services for big data applications. When server failure occurs in data center network, the security of the big data platform and the service quality of big data applications will be severely affected. A highly scalable data center network ($HSDC$) is an emerging server-centric data center network that achieves incremental scalability while ensuring low cost and energy consumption, low diameter, and high bisection width. In this paper, we determined the connectivity and diagnosability of $HSDC$. Then we firstly design an efficient adaptive fault diagnosis algorithm to diagnose the actual status of all servers in $HSDC$ with at most $m2^m + 4m(m-2)$ (resp. 9) tests, where m is the dimension of the $HSDC$ and $m \geq 3$ (resp. $m = 2$). Experimental results show that for $HSDC$, our algorithm can achieve complete diagnosis and greatly reduce the number of tests.

Keywords: Big data · Data center network · Fault diagnosis · Algorithm

1 Introduction

Nowadays, with the continuous development of big data applications, the resulting amount of data has become larger and larger, leading to the need for more storage resources and higher bandwidth requirements, as well as more efficient network systems. The big data platform based on the data center network (DCN) can provide low-latency, high-quality, non-disruptive big data services. The growing demand for big data application has led to the expansion of DSNs. Many DCNs have been proposed, which can be divided into two categories: *switch-centric* DCNs and *server-centric* DCNs. In the server-centric DCN, such as DCell [1], BCCC [2], and RCube [3], each switch only acts as a non-blocking crossbar switch. Manage network communication by placing the task of packet routing on the servers, which can reduce the number of switches used in server-centric DCN and the cost of its own construction.

Supported by the National Natural Science Foundation of China (Nos. 62002062 and 62072109).

L. Lin et al. (Eds.): SocialSec 2021, CCIS 1495, pp. 42–57, 2021.
https://doi.org/10.1007/978-981-16-7913-1_4

With the expansion of DCNs scale, failures occurs inevitably. Only by ensuring the reliability of DCN can the potential of big data services be maximized and the security of the big data platform can be ensured. Therefore, fault diagnosis is one of the key requirements for designing a big data platform. Moreover, for the server-centric DCNs, the failure of servers will have the greatest impact on the reliable communication or calculation of the entire network. If each switch in the server-centric DCN is regarded as a transparent network device, each server represents a processor in a multi-processor system, and each link between servers represents a link between processors, then the server diagnosis of the server-centric DCN is equivalent to the processor diagnosis of a multiprocessor system. Based on this, the diagnosis of faulty servers in DCell has been fully studied [4–6].

Identifying all faulty processors in a multiprocessor system (referred to as *system*) is called *system-level fault diagnosis*. If all faulty processors in a system can be determined and the number of faulty processors does not exceed t, the system is said to be *t-diagnosable*. The *diagnosability* of a system is the maximum number of faulty processors that the system allows to have, which guarantee the correctly diagnosis. In system-level diagnosis, Preparata, Metze and Chien [7] proposed the first diagnostic model called PMC model. In the PMC model, each processor can test its neighboring processors. Given a pair of adjacent processors u and v, the outcome of test v by u is represented by $r(u, v)$. If u evaluates v as faulty (resp. fault-free), $r(u, v) = 1$ (resp. 0). If u is fault-free, then $r(u, v)$ is reliable; otherwise, $r(u, v)$ is unreliable. The outcome $r(u, v) = 0$ (resp. 1) is called 0-*arrow* (resp. 1-*arrow*). Given a t-diagnosable N-processors system G, if all pre-allocated test tasks (that is, each processor is tested by at least t other processors) have been executed, and then the exact status of each processor in G can be identified by the obtained test outcomes. Obviously, due to the lack of flexibility and the need for a large number of tests (i.e. Nt tests), these reduce the efficiency of the traditional diagnosis algorithm. In [8], Nakejima proposed an adaptive diagnosis algorithm, which assigns the following test tasks according to the previous test results, thereby adaptively executing the test tasks, and determining the exact status of some processors of G in different test rounds. Therefore, reducing the number of test rounds and the total number of tests is the main goal of designing an effective adaptive diagnosis algorithm. In addition, some well-known adaptive diagnosis algorithms for interconnected network structures have been studied, such as Hypercube networks [9], hierarchical multiprocessor systems [10], and Hamiltonian networks [11].

Highly scalable data center network (*HSDC*) [12] is a server-centric DCN, which has incremental scalability and retains some of the outstanding characteristics of DCNs, such as low cost, low energy consumption, short diameter, and high bisection width. Qin et al. [13] constructed completely independent spanning trees (CISTs) for *HSDC*. CISTs have important applications in DCNs, such as fault-tolerant multi-node broadcasting, reliable broadcasting, secure message distribution and so on. In this paper, we design an efficient fault diagnosis algorithm for the *HSDC*. The main contributions of this paper are summarized as follows:

- We determined the diagnosability of $HSDC$.
- An adaptive diagnosis algorithm for $HSDC$ is first proposed to identify the exact status of all servers of $HSDC$. The maximum number of tests of the proposed algorithm is analyzed.
- Comprehensive simulations verify that our algorithm is effective and significantly reduces the number of tests compare to the traditional algorithm.

The rest of the paper is organized as follows. We introduce some basic knowledge and the formal definition of $HSDC$ in Sect. 2. Section 3 provides the formal definition and some properties of logic graph of $HSDC$. An adaptive diagnosis algorithm is proposed, and the maximum number of tests of our algorithm is analyzed theoretically in Sect. 4. Finally, we verify the performance of the proposed algorithm in Sect. 5 and conclude the paper in Sect. 6.

2   Preliminaries

In the study of the data center network, the data center network can be represented by a graph $G = (V(G), E(G))$, where each vertex $u \in V(G)$ denotes a server or a switch, and each edge $(u, v) \in E(G)$ denotes a physical link between two vertices u and v. Given a graph G, let $V(G)$ and $E(G)$ denote the vertex set and the edge set of G, respectively. Let $|V(G)|$ denote the total number of vertices of G. For any two distinct vertices u and v, if $(u, v) \in E(G)$, we say u (resp. v) is a neighbour of v (resp. v). The *connectivity* of G, denoted by $\kappa(G)$, is the number of vertices that must be removed from G to make G disconnected. A *path* is a sequence of adjacent vertices, denoted by $\langle v_0, v_1, \cdots, v_l \rangle$, where its two ends are v_0 and v_l, and all the vertices are distinct except possibly $v_0 = v_l$. A *hamiltonian path* is a path that traversed all the vertices of G only once. A *cycle* is a path with the same vertex at two ends. A *hamiltonian cycle* is a cycle that contains all the vertices of G. The set of integers from 1 (resp. n) to m is denoted by $[n]$ (resp. $[m, n]$), where $1 < m$ and $n < m$. The complete graph of m vertices is denoted by K_m.

A $HSDC$ network adopts low-cost commodity m-port switches and dual-port servers. The $HSDC$ network structure is divided into two categories: *complete* structure and *incomplete* structure. All server ports in the complete $HSDC$ network are occupied, but there are idle server ports in the incomplete $HSDC$ network. Two different types of $HSDC$ networks are defined as follows:

Definition 1 [12]. *The m-dimensional complete $HSDC$ network denoted by $HSDC_m(m)$ with the vertex set $\{x_m x_{m-1} \cdots x_1; y | x_i \in \{0, 1\}, i \in [m], y \in [0, m]\}$. For a vertex $x_m x_{m-1} \cdots x_1; y$, if $y = 0$, it is a switch; otherwise, it is a server. A switch $x_m x_{m-1} \cdots x_1; 0$ is adjacent to a server $x_m x_{m-1} \cdots x_1; y$ for any $y \in [m]$. Moreover, two servers $x_m x_{m-1} \cdots x_1; y$ and $x'_m x'_{m-1} \cdots x'_1; y'$ are adjacent if and only if $y = y' \in [m]$ and $x_y = 1 - x'_y$, $x_i = x'_i$ for any $i \in [m] \setminus \{y\}$.*

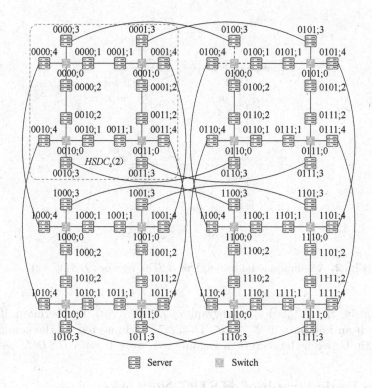

Fig. 1. A 4-dimensional complete *HSDC* network $HSDC_4(4)$.

Figure 1 shows $HSDC_4(4)$ with 16 switches and 64 servers. In $HSDC_m(m)$, a switch and its adjacent servers constitute the basic building unit called a *block*. Each $HSDC_m(m)$ contains 2^m blocks. For $HSDC_m(m)$, if we treat each block as a single vertex and connect them through the remaining edges, we can get an m-dimensional Hypercube network.

Definition 2 [12]. *One type of m-dimensional incomplete HSDC networks denoted by $HSDC_m(n)$ with $m > n$ and it has the vertex set $\{x_n x_{n-1} \cdots x_1; y | x_i \in \{0,1\}, i \in [n], y \in [0,m]\}$. For a vertex $x_n x_{n-1} \cdots x_1; y$, if $y = 0$, it is a switch; otherwise, it is a server. A switch $x_n x_{n-1} \cdots x_1; 0$ is adjacent to a server $x_n x_{n-1} \cdots x_1; y$ for any $y \in [m]$. Moreover, two servers $x_n x_{n-1} \cdots x_1; y$ and $x'_n x'_{n-1} \cdots x'_1; y'$ are adjacent if and only if $y = y' \in [n]$ and $x_y = 1 - x'_y$, $x_i = x'_i$ for any $i \in [n] \setminus \{y\}$.*

Figure 2 shows $HSDC_4(2)$ with 4 switches and 16 servers. For $HSDC_m(n)$, each block contains $m - n$ servers with an idle port. And the vertex subset $\{x_n x_n - 1 \cdots x_1; y | x_i \in \{0,1\}, i \in [n], y \in [n+1,m]\}$ of $V(HSDC_m(n))$ is a set of servers with an idle port.

Lemma 1 [12]. *$HSDC_m(m)$ composes of 2^{m-n} $HSDC_m(n)s$.*

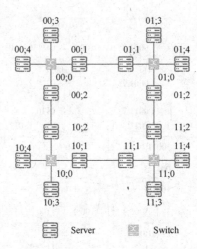

Fig. 2. A 4-dimensional incomplete $HSDC$ network $HSDC_4(2)$.

Obviously, $HSDC_m(n)$ is a subgraph of $HSDC_m(m)$. Furthermore, if each server with an idle port in 2^{m-n} $HSDC_m(n)$s is connected by the connection relationship between the servers in Definition 1, we will get a $HSDC_m(m)$.

3   The Logic Graph of *HSDC* Networks

For $HSDC_m(m)$, if we regard switches as transparent devices, each block can be abstracted as a complete graph. Focusing only on the adjacency relationship between servers, the formal definitions of the logic graph of $HSDC_m(m)$ and $HSDC_m(n)$ are as follows.

Definition 3. *A logic graph of $HSDC_m(m)$ denoted by $L\text{-}HSDC_m(m)$ with $m \geq 2$ and it has the vertex set $\{x_m x_{m-1} \cdots x_1; y | x_i \in \{0, 1\}, i \in [m], y \in [m]\}$. Two vertices $x_m x_{m-1} \cdots x_1; y$ and $x'_m x'_{m-1} \cdots x'_1; y'$ are adjacent if and only if $y \neq y'$ and $x_i = x'_i$ for any $i \in [m]$ or $y = y', x_y = 1 - x'_y$ and $x_i = x'_i$ for any $i \in [m] \setminus \{y\}$.*

Definition 4. *A logic graph of $HSDC_m(n)$ denoted by $L\text{-}HSDC_m(n)$ with $m > n$ and it has the vertex set $\{x_n x_{n-1} \cdots x_1; y | x_i \in \{0, 1\}, i \in [n], y \in [m]\}$. Two vertices $x_n x_{n-1} \cdots x_1; y$ and $x'_n x'_{n-1} \cdots x'_1; y'$ are adjacent if and only if $y \neq y'$ and $x_i = x'_i$ for any $i \in [m]$ or $y = y', y \in [n], x_y = 1 - x'_y$, and $x_i = x'_i$ for any $i \in [n] \setminus \{y\}$.*

Figure 3 shows a $L\text{-}HSDC_4(4)$. The subgragh of $L\text{-}HSDC_4(4)$ induced by a vertex set $\{0000; 1, 0000; 2, 0000; 3, 0000; 4\}$ is a complete graph K_4.

Lemma 2 [14]. *In m-dimensional Hypercube network, for any two distinct vertices u and v, there are m vertex-disjoint paths joining u and v.*

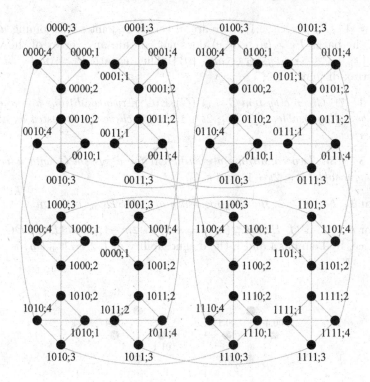

Fig. 3. A logic graph of $HSDC_4(4)$.

Lemma 3. *The connectivity of $L\text{-}HSDC_m(m)$ is m.*

Proof. Let u and v be any two distinct vertices of $L\text{-}HSDC_m(m)$. We will show how to construct m vertex-disjoint paths joining u and v as the following two cases.

Case 1. u and v are not in the same block. In $L\text{-}HSDC_m(m)$, each block can be regarded as a vertex in an m-dimensional hypercube network H_m. By Lemma 2, for any two different blocks in $L\text{-}HSDC_m(m)$, there are m block-disjoint paths. Moreover, for any block in $L\text{-}HSDC_m(m)$, it is connected to m blocks, and each of its vertices is connected to only one of the m connected blocks. Moreover, in $L\text{-}HSDC_m(m)$, each block is a K_m. In K_m, the paths from any vertex to the other $m-1$ vertices can be vertex-disjoint. Then for any block in $L\text{-}HSDC_m(m)$, the m paths from its any vertex to m connected blocks can be vertex-disjoint. Hence, for any two distinct vertices u and v in $L\text{-}HSDC_m(m)$, if u and v are not in the same block, then there are m vertex-disjoint paths joining u and v.

Case 2. u and v are in the same block. Without loss of generality, let $u = x_m x_{m-1} \cdots x_1; y$ and $v = x_m x_{m-1} \cdots x_1; y'$, where $y \neq y'$. For any vertex $P_1 = x_m x_{m-1} \cdots x_1; y_1$ and $y_1 \in [m] \setminus \{y, y'\}$, the path $P_1 = \langle u, v \rangle$ and the path $P_2 = \langle u, p_1, v \rangle$ are vertex-disjoint. Let vertex $u_1 = x_m x_{m-1} \cdots x_{y+1} x'_y x_{y-1} \cdots x_1; y$, where $x'_y = 1 - x_y$. By Case.1, there are m vertex-disjoint paths joining u_1 and v, one of the paths $P_3 = \langle u_1, \cdots, v \rangle$ does not contain any vertex of the vertex set $V_b = \{x_m x_{m-1} \cdots x_1; y_3 | y_3 \in [m] \setminus \{y\}\}$. Then a path $P_4 = \langle u, P_3 \rangle$, P_1 and P_2 are vertex-disjoint.

Lemma 4 [7]. *Given a system $G = (V(G), E(G))$, two conditions are necessary for G to be t-diagnosable: $|V(G)| \geq 2t + 1$, and each vertex is tested by at least t other vertices.*

Lemma 5 [15]. *Two conditions are sufficient for a system G with n vertices to be t-diagnosable: $n \geq 2t + 1$, and $\kappa(G) \geq t$.*

Theorem 1. *For $m \geq 2$, the diagnosability of $L\text{-}HSDC_m(m)$ is m.*

Proof. For $m \geq 2$, $|V(L\text{-}HSDC_m(m))| = m2^m > 2m+1$, and $\kappa(L\text{-}HSDC_m(m))$ is m. Hence, by Lemmas 4 and 5, the diagnosability of $L\text{-}HSDC_m(m)$ is m.

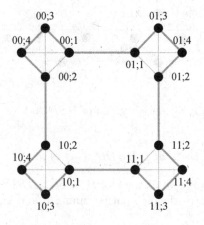

Fig. 4. A hamiltonian cycle of $L\text{-}HSDC_4(2)$, where the hamiltonian cycle consists of all blue edges and black vertices. (Color figure online)

$L\text{-}HSDC_m(2)$ contains 4 K_m's, and there exists a hamiltonian path with two ends $x_2 x_1; 1$ and $x_2 x_1; 2$ in each K_m, where $x_1, x_2 \in \{0, 1\}$. Moreover, $L\text{-}HSDC_m(2)$ contains 4 edges $(00; 1, 01; 1)$, $(10; 1, 11; 1)$, $(00; 2, 10; 2)$ and $(01; 2, 11; 2)$. Then we can construct a hamiltonian cycle with $4m$ vertices for $L\text{-}HSDC_m(2)$, as shown in Fig. 4.

4   Adaptive Diagnosis Algorithm for $HSDC$

The skeleton of the adaptive diagnosis algorithm for $L\text{-}HSDC_m(m)$ is described in **Algorithm 1**. The details of the algorithm will be described in the following subsections.

Algorithm 1: An adaptive diagnosis scheme for $L\text{-}HSDC_m(m)$ with at most m faulty vertices.

Input: A $L\text{-}HSDC_m(m)$ with at most m faulty vertices.
Output: The status of all vertices of the $L\text{-}HSDC_m(m)$.

1 Partition the $L\text{-}HSDC_m(m)$ into 2^{m-2} $L\text{-}HSDC_m(2)$s, denote by
  $X_0, X_1, \cdots, X_{2^{m-2}-1}$, respectively;

2 Construct a hamiltonian cycle for each $L\text{-}HSDC_m(2)$;

3 In the first two rounds, conduct basic tests along each hamiltonian cycle in
  parallel;

4 Evaluate the total number of suspicious cycles, denoted by f_c;

5 **if** $f_c \geq m - 1$ **then**

6 | // See subsection- 4.2

7 | Partition each suspicious cycle into path(s) by **Algorithm 2**
      Cycle-Partition in parallel, and evaluate the total number of paths f_s;

8 | Colour vertices on each path by the **Algorithm 3 Path-Colour** in parallel;

9 | The faulty vertices of all paths can be identified easily.

10 **else**

11 | // See subsetion- 4.3.

12 | For any X_i which has a suspicious cycle, the fault diagnosis process is as
      follows:

13 | Each vertex that has neighbour in the clean cycles are identified by its
      neighbour in the clean cycles;

14 | The unknown vertices can be identified by valid neighbour(s) in the same
      block. The faulty vertices of unknown block(s) can be identified easily.

15 **end**

4.1 Basic Tests of the First Two Rounds

$L\text{-}HSDC_m(m)$ with $m \geq 2$ can be divided into 2^{m-2} $L\text{-}HSDC_m(2)$s. For the convenience of discussing the adaptive diagnosis algorithm later, we denote each $L\text{-}HSDC_m(2)$ as X_i, where $i \in [0, 2^{m-2} - 1]$. As mentioned earlier, there is a hamiltonian cycle with $4m$ vertices in each X_i. For a cycle $\langle v_0, v_1, \cdots, v_{4m-1} \rangle$, in the first round, all even vertices test odd vertices in a clockwise direction (i.e., v_{2j} tests v_{2j+1}), and in the second round, all even vertices test odd vertices in a clockwise direction (i.e., v_{2j+1} tests v_{2j+2}), where $j \in [0, 2m - 1]$ and "+" means modulo $4m$ addition. If the hamiltonian cycle contains 1-arrow(s), we regarded the hamiltonian cycle as a *suspicious cycle*; otherwise, we regarded the hamiltonian cycle as a *clean cycle*. For a suspicious cycle, it contains at least one faulty vertex. Note that $4m > m$, for a clean cycle, every vertex is fault-free. Then all faulty vertices must be in these suspicious cycles, which means that these suspicious cycles need to be tested to identify their exact status. Let f_c denote the total number of suspicious cycles in $L\text{-}HSDC_m(m)$. For the convenience of analyzing the number of tests of the algorithm, we call the tests in the first and second rounds *basic tests*, and the tests required by the algorithm in the subsequent execution process are called *additional tests*.

4.2   Identifying Suspicious Cycles When $f_c \geq m - 1$

When $f_c \geq m - 1$, the following two algorithms are available for the diagnosis process of the suspicious cycles. The **Algorithm Cycle-Partition** [7] is used to partition a suspicious cycle into the path(s), where each path contains at least one faulty vertex. The **Algorithm Path-Colour** [16] colors the vertices of the path as black, white, or gray, where the black vertices are faulty, the white vertices are fault-free, and the grey vertices need additional tests to identify their exact statuses. Figure 5 (a) gives an example of executing the **Algorithm Cycle-Partitioning** in a $L\text{-}HSDC_4(2)$ with at most 4 faulty verties, and Fig. 5 (b) gives the results of executing the **Algorithm Path-Colour** on the three paths of Fig. 5 (a).

Algorithm 2: Cycle-Partition

Step 1: Choose a 0-arrow a_0 followed by a 1-arrow;
Step 2: Let a be the arrow following a_0. If a is 0-arrow, then set $a_0 = a$ and proceed **Step 2**; otherwise, go to **Step 3**;
Step 3: Mark with a label X the arrow following 1-arrow a. If it was not previously marked, set a_0 the X-marked arrow and go to **Step 2**; otherwise, delete those X-marked arrows, then the algorithm terminates.

Algorithm 3: Path-Colour

Step 1: Let m denote the maximum number of faulty vertices, s denote the number of the paths obtained by the **Algorithm Cycle-Partition**, and $q = m - s + 1$;
Step 2: If a path has more than $q + 1$ vertices and has at least one 0-arrow, then we color the head of the path with black and color $q - 1$ vertices from the tail with gray, and all vertices that are colored yet are colored white;
Step 3: If a path has at most $q + 1$ vertices, then we color all vertices in the path with gray.

Let f_s denotes the total number of paths of a $L\text{-}HSDC_m(m)$. There are at most m faulty vertices in a $L\text{-}HSDC_m(m)$, when $f_c \geq m - 1$, therefore each suspicious cycle has one or two faulty vertices. Moreover, $f_c \leq f_s \leq m$. Suppose that each suspicious cycle contains only one path after executing the **Algorithm Cycle-Partition**, i.e., $f_c = f_s$. If $f_s = m$, then only the black vertex is faulty (as shown in Fig. 6 (a)). If $f_s = m - 1$, by the **Algorithm Cycle-Partition**, there is only one gray vertex adjacent to the black vertex on each suspicious cycle. Obviously, the black vertex is faulty and the gray vertex can be tested by another fault-free neighbour (as shown in Fig. 6 (b)). Suppose that a suspicious cycle contains two paths after executing the **Algorithm Cycle-Partition**, i.e., $f_c = m - 1$, and $f_s = f_c + 1 = m$. If both paths in this suspicious cycle contain at least three vertices, then only the black vertex is faulty (as shown in Fig. 6

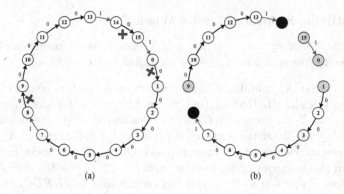

Fig. 5. (a): An example of executing the algorithm Cycle-Partition, where a red arrow indicates 1-arrow. (b): An example of executing the algorithm Path-Colour. (Color figure online)

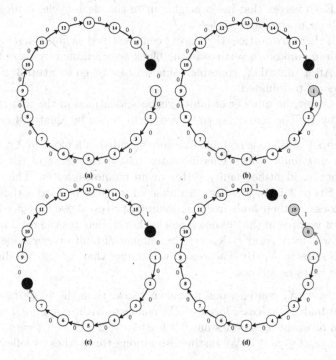

Fig. 6. Four examples of additional tests for $f_c \geq m-1$, where a green counterclockwise arrow indicates an additional test. (Color figure online)

(c)); otherwise, this suspicious cycle has a path that contains a black vertex and a path that only contains two gray vertices, one adjacent to the black vertex and the other adjacent to a fault-free neighbour (as shown in Fig. 6 (d)). Only one of these two gray vertices is faulty and can be verified by the fault-free neighbor.

4.3   Identifying Suspicious Cycles When $f_c < m - 1$

Theorem 2. *When $f_c < m - 1$, for any X_i which has a suspicious cycle, at least one faulty-free vertex in X_i can be identified by its neighbours.*

Proof. Noted that X_i contains 4 blocks, where each block is connected to the $m - 2$ same cycles in a L-$HSDC_m(m)$. When $f_c < m - 1$, for any X_i which is a suspicious cycle, X_i connects with C_i clean cycles and $m - 2 - C_i$ suspicious cycles, where $1 \le C_i \le m - 2$. On the contrary, supposing that each vertex in X_i that has a neighbour in the clean cycles is identified as faulty by its neighbour in the clean cycles. Then all suspicious cycles have at least $(m - 2 - C_i) + 4C_i = m + 3C_i - 2$ faulty vertices. By $m + 3C_i - 2 > m$, it contradicts that a L-$HSDC_m(m)$ has at most m faulty vertices.

For any X_i which has a suspicious cycle, the diagnosis process is as follows:

- **Step 1:** Each vertex that has a neighbour in the clean cycles is identified by its neighbour in the clean cycles.
- **Step 2:** If there are vertices that have been identified as faulty-free in a block, the remaining unknown vertices in the block are identified by these fault-free vertices. After that, if X_i contains unknown blocks, go to **Step 3**; otherwise, the process is terminated.
- **Step 3:** Count the number of faulty vertices identified in the first two steps, denoted by f_i. The remaining unknown vertices can be identified easily.

After **Step 1**, if there is no fault-free vertex finded in a block in X_i, the block is called an *unknown block*. This indicates that each vertex in the unknown block is either an identified faulty vertex or an unknown vertex. Therefore, the purpose of **Step 2** is to identify all unknown vertices in blocks that are not unknown blocks by their fault-free neighbours. In **Step 3**, we only need to identify unknown vertices in the unknown blocks. Let n_i denotes the total number of unknown blocks in X_i, and f_i denotes the number of faulty vertices identified in the first two steps in X_i. By Theorem 2, we can get that $n_i \le 3$. We distinguish among three cases as follows.

Case 1. $n_i = 1$. X_i contains one unknown block, then the block has at least C_i identified faulty vertices. Moreover, X_i connects with $m - 2 - C_i$ suspicious cycles. Then all suspicious cycles have at least $(m - 2 - C_i) + C_i = m - 2$ faulty vertices. Hence, $0 \le f_i \le 2$. We distinguish among three cases as follows.

Case 1.1. $f_i = 0$. Suppose u and v are two vertices in the unknown block, where $u = x_m x_{m-1} \cdots x_1; 1$, $v = x_m x_{m-1} \cdots x_2 x_1; 2$, $x_i \in \{0, 1\}$ and $i \in [m]$. By Definition 3, u and v are adjacent to vertices that are not in the unknown blocks in X_i. Moreover, $f_i = 0$, both u and v have a fault-free neighbour and u (resp. v) can be identified by the fault-free neighbour. If both u and v are identified as faulty, the remaining unknown vertices in the unknown block are fault-free; otherwise, at least one of u and v is identified as fault-free by their fault-free vertices, then the remaining unknown vertices in the unknown block can be identified by the fault-free neighbour.

Case 1.2. $f_i = 1$. Suppose u and v are two vertices in the unknown block, where $u = x_m x_{m-1} \cdots x_1 ; 1$, $v = x_m x_{m-1} \cdots x_1 ; 2$, $x_i \in \{0, 1\}$ and $i \in [m]$. By $f_i = 1$, all suspicious cycles have at least $(m - 2 - C_i) + C_i + f_i = m - 1$ faulty vertices, and at least one of u and v has a fault-free neighbour. Without loss of generality, assuming that u have a fault-free neighbour. If u is identified as faulty by this fault-free neighbour, the remaining unknown vertices in the unknown block must be fault-free; otherwise, the remaining unknown vertices in the unknown block can be identified by u.

Case 1.3. $f_i = 2$. All suspicious cycles have at least $(m - 2 - C_i) + C_i + f_i = m$ faulty vertices and each unknown vertex in the unknown block is fault-free.

Case 2. $n_i = 2$. X_i contains two unknown blocks, then the two unknown block has at least $2C_i$ identified faulty vertices. Moreover, X_i connects with $m - 2 - C_i$ suspicious cycles. Then all suspicious cycles have at least $(m - 2 - C_i) + 2C_i = m + C_i - 2$ faulty vertices.

Case 2.1. $C_i = 1$. All suspicious cycles have at least $m - 1$ faulty vertices and $0 \leq f_i \leq 1$. Consider that $f_i = 1$, the remaining unknown vertices in the two unknown blocks are fault-free. Consider that $f_i = 0$, each unknown block has at least a vertex that has a fault-free neighbour. If a vertex that has a fault-free neighbour is identified as faulty by its fault-free neighbour, the remaining unknown vertices in the two unknown blocks are fault-free; otherwise, the remaining unknown vertices in the block can be identified by the vertex.

Case 2.2. $C_i = 2$. All suspicious cycles have at least m faulty vertices and the remaining unknown vertices in the two unknown blocks are fault-free.

Case 3. $n_i = 3$. X_i contains three unknown blocks, then the three unknown block has at least $3C_i$ faulty vertices. Moreover, X_i connects with $m - 2 - C_i$ suspicious cycles. Then all suspicious cycles have at least $(m - 2 - C_i) + 3C_i = m + 2C_i - 2$ faulty vertices. By $(m + 2C_i - 2) \leq m$ and $C_i \geq 1$, then $C_i = 1$. The remaining unknown vertices in the three unknown blocks are fault-free.

4.4   Evaluating the Number of Tests for *HSDC*

Theorem 3. *Algorithm 1 takes at most* $m2^m + 4m(m - 2)$ *(resp. 9) tests to identify all faulty vertices of* $L\text{-}HSDC_m(m)$ *with at most* m *faulty vertices with* $m \geq 3$ *(resp.* $m = 2$*).*

Proof. In the first two rounds of **Algorithm 1**, each vertex is tested only once by other vertices, then the number of basic tests is $m2^m$. For a $L\text{-}HSDC_m(m)$ with $f_c = f_s = m - 1$, each suspicious path has one unknown vertex, then the total number of additional tests is $m - 1$. For a $L\text{-}HSDC_m(m)$ with $f_c = m - 1$ and $f_s = m$, there could be a path that only contains two unknown vertices that need one additional test to identify their exact statuses. For a $L\text{-}HSDC_m(m)$ with $f_c \leq m - 2$, each vertex in suspicious cycles needs at most one additional test to identify its actual status, each suspicious cycles has $4m$ vertices, then at most $4m \times f_c$ additional tests are necessary to identify the faulty vertices in the $L\text{-}HSDC_m(m)$. Since the maximum number of additional tests appears at $f_c = m - 2$, at most $m2^m + 4m(m - 2)$ additional tests are necessary to identify the $L\text{-}HSDC_m(m)$ with at most m faulty vertices. Hence, if $m \geq 3$ (resp. $m = 2$), **Algorithm 1** takes at most $m2^m + 4m(m - 2)$ (resp. 9) tests to identify all faulty vertices of $L\text{-}HSDC_m(m)$.

5   Simulation Results

In this section, we will conduct multiple experiments to verify whether our algorithm can diagnose the actual status of all vertices in $L\text{-}HSDC_m(m)$, and compare with the traditional algorithm in terms of the number of tests. We use a 3.00 GHz Intel®Core™ i5-9500 CPU and 24 GB RAM under the Windows 10 operating system. Our algorithm and related experiments are implemented by Python. Note that each data in figures and tables is the average of 1000 experiments.

5.1   Verify the Correctness and Completeness of Our Algorithm

In this subsection, our purpose is to verify the correctness and completeness of our algorithm. For $L\text{-}HSDC_m(m)$, each vertex has the same probability of being faulty, and the total number of faulty vertices is randomly selected within its diagnosability m. Moreover, the probability of the outcome of a faulty vertex test a fault-free (resp. faulty) vertex to be 1 is denoted by p_1 (resp. p_2). Then we simulated our algorithm's diagnosis of $L\text{-}HSDC_m(m)$ under four different values of p_1, p_2, where $m \in [5, 8]$.

Moreover, for $L\text{-}HSDC_m(m)$, its vertex set, fault-free vertex set and faulty vertex set are denoted by V, V_t, and V_f, respectively. Moreover, the fault-free vertex set, the faulty vertex set and the unknown vertex set derived by the algorithm are denoted by V_p, V_n, and V_u, respectively. We set $V_{tp} = V_t \cap V_p$, $V_{tn} = V_t \cap V_n$, $V_{fp} = V_f \cap V_p$, $V_{fn} = V_f \cap V_n$, and use the following four metrics to measure the performance of our algorithm: accuracy rate $AR = \frac{|V_{tp}| + |V_{fn}|}{|V_p| + |V_n|} \times 100\%$, precision rate $PR = \frac{|V_{tp}|}{|V_{tp}| + |V_{fp}|} \times 100\%$, recall rate $RR = \frac{|V_{tp}|}{|V_{tp}| + |V_{tn}|} \times 100\%$, and unknown rate $UR = \frac{|V_u|}{|V|} \times 100\%$.

The simulation results in Table 1 show that the changes in p_1 and p_2 have no effect on the diagnosis results of the algorithm and our algorithm can correctly identify the statuses of all vertices of $L\text{-}HSDC_m(m)$. Then both p_1 and p_2 are set to 0.5 for the next experiments.

5.2   Performance Comparison

In this subsection, the performance of the diagnosis algorithm is measured by the number of tests. The maximum number of tests, the average number of tests, the maximum number of additional tests, and the average number of additional tests

Table 1. The impact of different p_1 and p_2 values on AR, PR, RR and UR in L-$HSDC_m(m)$ with $m \in [5, 8]$

$p_1 = p_2 = 0.5$	$L\text{-}HSDC_5(5)$	$L\text{-}HSDC_6(6)$	$L\text{-}HSDC_7(7)$	$L\text{-}HSDC_8(8)$
AR	100%	100%	100%	0%
PR	100%	100%	100%	0%
RR	100%	100%	100%	0%
UR	100%	100%	100%	0%
$p_1 = 0.7, p_2 = 0.5$	$L\text{-}HSDC_5(5)$	$L\text{-}HSDC_6(6)$	$L\text{-}HSDC_7(7)$	$L\text{-}HSDC_8(8)$
AR	100%	100%	100%	0%
PR	100%	100%	100%	0%
RR	100%	100%	100%	0%
UR	100%	100%	100%	0%
$p_1 = p_2 = 0.3$	$L\text{-}HSDC_5(5)$	$L\text{-}HSDC_6(6)$	$L\text{-}HSDC_7(7)$	$L\text{-}HSDC_8(8)$
AR	100%	100%	100%	0%
PR	100%	100%	100%	0%
RR	100%	100%	100%	0%
UR	100%	100%	100%	0%
$p_1 = 0.7, p_2 = 0.8$	$L\text{-}HSDC_5(5)$	$L\text{-}HSDC_6(6)$	$L\text{-}HSDC_7(7)$	$L\text{-}HSDC_8(8)$
AR	100%	100%	100%	0%
PR	100%	100%	100%	0%
RR	100%	100%	100%	0%
UR	100%	100%	100%	0%

of our algorithm are denoted by adp_m, adp_a, adp_m^a, and adp_a^a, respectively. The number of tests for traditional diagnosis algorithm is usually Nt, denoted by tr, where N is the total number of vertices in a system, and t is the diagnosability of the system. The number of tests of the traditional algorithm for a L-$HSDC_m(m)$ is $m^2 2^m$, denoted by tr.

Table 2 shows the adp_m, adp_a, tr, adp_m^a and adp_a^a of L-$HSDC_m(m)$ in different dimensions. The dimension m of L-$HSDC_m(m)$ varies from 5 to 8. Table 2 shows that the number of tests of our algorithm is much smaller than that of traditional diagnosis algorithm. For example, for a L-$HSDC_8(8)$, the average number of tests of our algorithm is 13.06% of the number of tests of traditional diagnosis algorithms. Figure 7 plots the changes in the adp_m, adp_a and tr values of L-$HSDC(m)$ as the dimension m increases. It can be observed from Fig. 7 that the adp_m and adp_a of our algorithm increase logarithmically with the increase of m. Because the basic tests of our algorithm for a L-$HSDC_m(m)$ is static and the number of the basic tests is $m2^m$, so adp_a is slightly less than adp_m. Figure 8 plots the changes in the adp_m^a and adp_a^a values of L-$HSDC_m(m)$ as the dimension m increases. Figure 8 shows that adp_m^a and the adp_a^a of our algorithm increase exponentially with the increase of m, and adp_a^a is half of adp_m^a.

Table 2. The adp_m, adp_a, tr, adp_m^a and adp_a^a of $L\text{-}HSDC_m(m)$ with $m \in [5,8]$.

$p_1 = p_2 = 0.5$	$L\text{-}HSDC_5(5)$	$L\text{-}HSDC_6(6)$	$L\text{-}HSDC_7(7)$	$L\text{-}HSDC_8(8)$
adp_m	220	480	1036	2240
adp_a	191	430	964	2139
tr	800	2304	6272	16384
adp_{am}	60	96	140	192
adp_{aa}	31	46	68	91

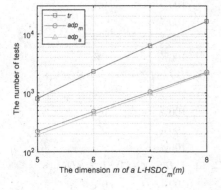

Fig. 7. The adp_m, adp_a and tr of $L\text{-}HSDC_m(m)$ for $m \in [5,8]$.

Fig. 8. The adp_a^m and adp_a^a of $L\text{-}HSDC_m(m)$ for $m \in [5,8]$.

6 Conclusion

The big data platform based on the data center network provides reliable and high-quality services for big data applications. However, when the server in the data center network fails, it will affect the service quality of the big data application and the security of the big data platform. In this paper, we prove that the connectivity and diagnosisability of m-dimensional $HSDC$ are m. Then we propose an algorithm that can completely diagnose the actual status of all servers in m-dimensional $HSDC$ with at most $m2^m + 4m(m-2)$ (resp. 9) tests if $m \geq 3$ (resp. $m = 2$). Simulation experiments show that our algorithm not only achieves complete diagnosis for $HSDC$ with faulty servers does not exceed its diagnosisability, but also greatly reduces the number of tests compared with traditional diagnosis algorithm.

References

1. Guo, C., Wu, H., Tan, K., Shi, L., Zhang, Y., Lu, S.: Dcell: a scalable and fault-tolerant network structure for data centers. In: Proceedings of the ACM SIG-COMM 2008 Conference on Data Communication, pp. 75–86. Association for Computing Machinery, New York (2008)

2. Li, Z., Guo, Z., Yang, Y.: BCCC: an expandable network for data centers. IEEE/ACM Trans. Netw. **24**(6), 3740–3755 (2016)
3. Li, Z., Yang, Y.: RCube: a power efficient and highly available network for data centers. In: 2017 IEEE International Parallel and Distributed Processing Symposium (IPDPS), pp. 718–727. IEEE, Orlando (2017)
4. Gu, M.M., Hao, R.X., Liu, J.B.: The pessimistic diagnosability of data center networks. Inf. Process. Lett. **134**, 52–56 (2018)
5. Li, X., Fan, J., Lin, C.K., Cheng, B., Jia, X.: The extra connectivity, extra conditional diagnosability and t/k-diagnosability of the data center network DCell. Theoret. Comput. Sci. **766**, 16–29 (2019)
6. Li, X., Fan, J., Lin, C.K., Jia, X.: Diagnosability evaluation of the data center network DCell. Comput. J. **61**(1), 129–143 (2017)
7. Preparata, F.P., Metze, G., Chien, R.T.: On the connection assignment problem of diagnosable systems. IEEE Trans. Electron. Comput. **EC–16**(6), 848–854 (1967)
8. Nakajima, K.: A new approach to system diagnosis. In: 19th Allerton Conference on Communication, Control and Computing, pp. 697–706 (1981)
9. Kranakis, E., Pelc, A.: Better adaptive diagnosis of hypercubes. IEEE Trans. Comput. **49**(10), 1013–1020 (2000)
10. Lai, P.L., Chiu, M.Y., Tsai, C.H.: Three round adaptive diagnosis in hierarchical multiprocessor systems. IEEE Trans. Reliab. **62**(3), 608–617 (2013)
11. Ye, L.C., Liang, J.R.: Five-round adaptive diagnosis in Hamiltonian networks. IEEE Trans. Parallel Distrib. Syst. **26**(9), 2459–2464 (2015)
12. Zhang, Z., Deng, Y., Min, G., Xie, J., Yang, L.T., Zhou, Y.: HSDC: a highly scalable data center network architecture for greater incremental scalability. IEEE Trans. Parallel Distrib. Syst. **30**(5), 1105–1119 (2019)
13. Qin, X.W., Hao, R.X., Chang, J.M.: The existence of completely independent spanning trees for some compound graphs. IEEE Trans. Parallel Distrib. Syst. **31**(1), 201–210 (2020)
14. Zhang, Y.: Node-disjoint shortest and next-to-shortest paths in n-dimensional hypercube (in Chinese). Pure Math. **7**(4), 230–235 (2017)
15. Hakimi, S., Amin, A.: Characterization of connection assignment of diagnosable systems. IEEE Trans. Comput. **C–23**(1), 86–88 (1974)
16. Araki, T.: Optimal adaptive fault diagnosis of cubic Hamiltonian graphs. In: 7th International Symposium on Parallel Architectures, Algorithms and Networks, pp. 162–167. IEEE, Hong Kong (2004)

Realization of Safety Reinforced Terminal Equipment for Secondary System of Substation

Xiaoming Wang[1](✉), Ke Zhou[1], and Congyun Wu[2]

[1] Electric Power Research Institute of Guangxi Power Grid Co., Ltd., Nanning 530023, China
[2] Guangxi Power Grid Co., Ltd., Nanning 530023, China

Abstract. With the high integration of informatization and industrialization, the degree of intelligence and automation of the secondary system of substations has been continuously enhanced. While enjoying the convenience, we also need to face the challenges and threats brought by the Internet. Given the confidentiality, integrity, and other security threats that the secondary system applications or tools may face during the calculation and transmission process, the safety reinforced terminal protection technology based on the USB interface has become a research hotspot. Although traditional safety reinforced equipment is easy to produce, the algorithms in it have been specified by the manufacturer and downloaded to the corresponding equipment. Considering that the security requirements of different scenarios are quite different, and different users have multi-level security requirements, the AVR microcontroller is programmed through the Arduino IDE platform, and a safety-reinforced terminal device with a customizable encryption algorithm is designed and implemented, which not only realizes functions such as identity authentication and content encryption, but also meets the personalized needs of users' independent choices, and improves the security and controllability of the entire secondary system. After the test, the usability and robustness of the terminal are preliminarily proved.

Keywords: Grid System · Safety reinforcement terminal · Microcontroller · Substation safety

1 Introduction

Achieving a high degree of integration of power system energy flow and communication system information flow and further creating a safe, reliable, and efficient power grid system is one of the strategic plans in the "Industry 4.0" era. As the basis for carrying information in substations, the secondary system itself includes a variety of functional applications. The control commands and parameter setting commands issued by the master station need to be executed by the secondary system. However, if the control command is stolen or tampered with, security identification and data integrity verification cannot be performed, and the illegal operation of the substation performed by the master station in the case of hijacking or personnel misoperation cannot be identified and isolated, which has a risk of causing power grid security accidents. On the other

© Springer Nature Singapore Pte Ltd. 2021
L. Lin et al. (Eds.): SocialSec 2021, CCIS 1495, pp. 58–74, 2021.
https://doi.org/10.1007/978-981-16-7913-1_5

hand, because equipment manufacturers often use personal computers, USB flash drives, and configuration tools for operation and maintenance operations, there are many problems such as unsafe on-site secondary system configuration and maintenance terminal, equipment upgrade software version and engineering configuration and backup are not controllable, and excessive reliance on the manufacturer for the correctness of management configuration, which brings great hidden dangers to the safe, reliable and stable operation of the secondary system of the substation.

Although traditional security reinforcement equipment is easy to produce and obtain, for security purposes, many operations are shielded, resulting in the inherent shortcoming of too few customizable parts. Even with the improvement of chip performance, the types of algorithms that can be loaded on hardened devices have increased, but the algorithms have been specified by manufacturers and downloaded to the corresponding devices in advance. If developers have special needs, they can only customize them to equipment manufacturers themselves. Not only will the production cycle be long, but the cost will also be greater, which will inevitably consume more human and material resources. In addition, due to the large differences in the security requirements of different scenarios in the secondary system, different users have multi-level security requirements. Although traditional security reinforcement equipment is convenient to produce, its functional limitations are no longer sufficient to satisfy users. In this paper, we use the Arduino IDE platform to program the AVR microcontroller and design and implement a security-reinforced terminal device with a customizable encryption algorithm. It not only realizes the functions of identity authentication, content encryption, etc. but also meets the personalized needs of the user's independent choice and improves the safety and controllability of the entire secondary system. In summary, we make the following contributions:

- We design and implement a terminal device that runs on the AVR microcontroller and can be used as a safety reinforcement. It can use the USB interface to ensure the security of information transmission between the computer and the interactive object.
- The device realizes the function of identity authentication and data encryption in the Microcontroller Unit (MCU), which can be called by the outside program, and includes a variety of feasible algorithms. Developers of external programs can choose to call the required functions according to their own needs to meet the personalized needs of users.
- Finally, a large number of experiments are carried out to verify the availability and effectiveness of the safety reinforcement terminal, and the performance of different functional algorithms is compared and analyzed.

The remainder of this paper is structured as follows: Sect. 2 discusses the background and related works about the safety reinforced terminal. In Sect. 3, we define the proposed approach and used methods. Section 4 introduces the simulations and numerical results. Then in Sect. 5, we conclude the paper.

2 Background

2.1 Arduino

Arduino [1] is a simpler, more user-friendly, and humanized hardware development platform designed for AVR microcontrollers. Different models of Arduino use different microcontroller models and control circuit boards, but a special programming development software that supports these models is commonly used. The Arduino UNO model used in this experiment is essentially a single-chip microcomputer control board and uses the AVR single-chip microcomputer as the control core [2, 3]. In addition to the ATmega328 minimum system circuit, the board also contains some peripheral IO chips connected to the microcontroller.

2.2 PIN Code

The so-called PIN code is generally a "password" with more than 4 digits that is easy to remember, but it generally only contains pure numbers and is only associated with the hardware that sets the PIN code. Anyone who knows the PIN code can use the device. For some devices, the PIN code has the same function as the account password, and both can access the device and even enter the logged-in account space on the device, but the PIN code generally cannot replace the account password to modify account information [4]. As a password, the PIN code does not protect the user's usage rights, but protects the usage rights of the user's device, while traditional passwords generally protect the read and write rights of the specific user data corresponding to it. At this time, the PIN code and account password realize the two-factor authentication in identity authentication.

2.3 Introduction to Cyber Security

Identity Authentication. Identity authentication is mainly used to determine whether the physical real identity of the authenticator matches the data identity [5, 6]. There are three authentication methods: (1) According to the information you know (what you know). (2) According to what you have. (3) According to the unique body (who you are).

In the case of physical identity and data identity matching, the three methods are all feasible, so for better security, two of the three are selected to complete the authentication, which is the so-called two-factor authentication [7–9].

Asymmetric Encryption Algorithm. Its asymmetry is mainly reflected in the fact that it requires two keys, a public key, and a private key, and they are not the same [10]. If one of the keys is allowed to be disclosed, then it can be called a "public key", and the other key must be kept strictly secret and cannot be disclosed to others, and is called a "private key". Specifically, if the plaintext is encrypted with a public key, the other party needs to use its paired private key to decrypt it, and the public key itself cannot be decrypted; the same is true for private keys [11]. By definition, public and private keys cannot be derived from each other. Common asymmetric encryption algorithms include the famous and most widely used RSA algorithm abroad, the elliptic curve encryption algorithm (ECC), and the domestic SM2 algorithm [12].

Symmetric Encryption Algorithm. It is called the symmetric key because the key used in the encryption and decryption process is the same and shared by both parties in communication. In fact, for the convenience of communication and key management in multi-person communication, usually, only a single key is used between multiple people. The existence of the symmetric key makes the encryption process and the decryption process very similar, and the decryption process can be regarded as the inverse operation of the encryption process. Common symmetric encryption algorithms include internationally well-known DES, 3DES (Triple-DES), AES algorithms, and national encryption algorithms SM1, SM4 [12, 13].

Hash Algorithm. It is a method of creating a digital "fingerprint" represented by a fixed character set (as long as it can be expressed as a binary string) [14]. The hash function can compress a large amount of data into a short and fixed string, also called a digest algorithm, but it cannot restore the previous data. Because small changes to the input data will also cause drastic changes in the corresponding hash, so in the case where the probability of hash collision is minimal, the hash function can be used to verify whether the input data has been tampered with, that is, it can be used to ensure the integrity of the information [15–17].

2.4 Safety Reinforced Terminal Products

Dongle. The dongle is a device that provides program security extensions for software developers. It is a tool with a built-in single-chip microcomputer or smart card with software protection functions. It provides a set of interfaces and function tools suitable for various languages for software developers to use. In the past, domestic dongle chips used general-purpose chips. The advantage is that it is cheap and easy to produce. The disadvantage is that it is too common and the possibility of being cracked is huge. The cracker can obtain the program content in the chip by analyzing and detecting the chip circuit, decompiling to learn the program logic, and dynamically debugging to obtain the program interaction information, thereby cloning an identical dongle. But now domestic dongles have begun to use foreign imported smart card chips that are difficult to crack, which greatly enhances the security performance of the equipment.

Dynamic Token. As a representative of one-time password technology, dynamic passwords are specifically designed to generate an unpredictable password, usually a combination of numbers, within a certain period through a special algorithm, and limit the use time and the number of uses of the password. The dynamic password can effectively protect the security of high-risk operations (such as payment) and user login, etc., because it is changed over time. So it also eliminates the need for users to modify the password regularly and avoids the disaster caused by password leakage. A dynamic token is a physical terminal device used to generate a dynamic password.

USB Key. As a type of safety reinforced terminal, USB Key is a hardware device that interacts with a computer through a USB interface [18, 19]. As an independent hardware device, it contains a single-chip microcomputer or smart card chip inside, has a certain user-defined storage space, and has built-in algorithms for identity authentication and even data encryption [20]. The user's private key is stored in the internal memory of the USB Key while ensuring that the key will not be stolen during the communication process and will not be tracked in the PC memory. USB Key [21] is mainly used to ensure the security of identity authentication in the process of information transmission in insecure channels such as the network [6, 7, 21].

3 System Model

3.1 Demand Analysis and Overall Design

In general, we design and implement a safety-reinforced terminal device that runs on the AVR microcontroller and can configure its algorithm. This system mainly transmits information to the outside world through the serial port of the single-chip microcomputer, realizes the identity authentication and data encryption function inside the single-chip microcomputer for the call of the program in the outside world, and adds a variety of feasible algorithms to the realization of the function.

The physical results presented at the end not only need to realize the basic functions that can be achieved by devices such as USB keys and ensure certain safety but also ensure that the developers of external programs can choose to call the required functions according to their own needs. The security effect here is mainly reflected in: the core information (such as keys, etc.) related to the algorithm that needs to be protected and does not want to be intercepted or eavesdropped on will not exist in the memory of the caller's computer, nor will it appear in the process of communication and information exchange. The overall structure of the system is shown in Fig. 1, which is divided into two parts: data encryption and identity authentication.

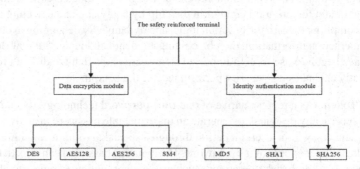

Fig. 1. The system architecture of the safety reinforced terminal.

3.2 System Module Design

We mainly design and implement the two functional modules of data encryption and identity authentication as shown below.

Data Encryption. The information interaction entity of the data encryption module mainly involves the demo calling program and the single-chip microcomputer [22, 23]. Among them, the calling program transmits instructions and data in plain text to the single-chip microcomputer. The single-chip microcomputer encrypts the plain text through related algorithms and a built-in key and then sends it back to the calling program. During the whole process, the key will not be transferred between the two, which ensures that the ciphertext returned without the key cannot be easily decrypted, and the plaintext can only be obtained after decrypting the ciphertext through the decryption function of the single-chip microcomputer. The detailed module design is shown in Fig. 2.

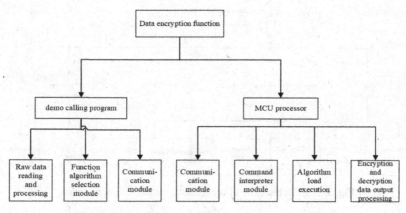

Fig. 2. The architecture of the data encryption module.

Among them, the demo calling program mainly interacts with the single-chip microcomputer through the communication module. The user must select the data and algorithm to be encrypted or decrypted before sending the request to the single-chip microcomputer to obtain the result through the communication module. After receiving the user's request through the communication module, the single-chip microcomputer obtains the content that the user needs to encrypt and decrypt and the algorithm to be used through the command interpreter module, and finally sends the result back to the caller through the communication module.

Identity Authentication. The information interaction of the identity authentication function involves the Server, the Client, and the MCU processing program [24, 25]. The Server generates a random number and sends it to the Client and then sends the random number to the MCU. The internal program of the MCU uses an algorithm to encrypt the random number and then sends it back to the Client and then sends it to the Server from the Client. The Server uses the same algorithm to verify whether the results of the random number encryption are the same and finally sends the verification information back to the Client to complete the identity verification.

The module design of this part is shown in Fig. 3. First, the Client sends a login request to the Server through the login module. After receiving the login request through the communication module, the Server generates a random number through the random number generation module and then uses the communication module to send the verification code to the Client and forwards it to the single-chip microcomputer. The single-chip microcomputer receives the random number through the communication module. After being interpreted by the interpreter module, the random number is processed by the specified algorithm, and the processed result is sent back to the Client and forwarded back to the Server. The Server also uses the same algorithm to calculate the random number, compare the result with the received one-chip computer processing result, and finally, send the verification information back to the login module of the Client.

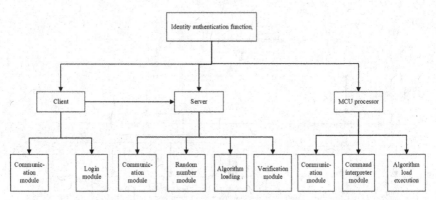

Fig. 3. The architecture of the identity authentication module.

3.3 Procedure Flow

The Demo calling program can be developed in different programming languages according to your own needs, as long as it can communicate with the microcontroller through the serial port. So here is only the program flow chart realized by the internal program of the single-chip microcomputer.

Data Encryption. Figure 4 is the program flow chart of the data encryption function of the system.

From top to bottom, PIN code detection is performed first. The PIN code and the key stored in the device (required by each algorithm) form the two-factor authentication. After the PIN code is verified, it will wait for the user to continue to enter the command. When the command is received, the command will be explained, including the choice of algorithm, encryption, or decryption [26, 27]. Finally, the corresponding algorithm is selected to encrypt and decrypt the data block that has been passed in, and then the result is sent back to the caller.

Identity Authentication. Figure 5 is the program flow chart of the identity authentication function of the system. From top to bottom, PIN code detection is performed first.

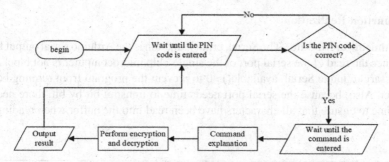

Fig. 4. The program flow chart of the data encryption function of the system.

The PIN code and the key used by the algorithm stored in the single-chip microcomputer form a two-factor authentication. The identity authentication process is relatively simple, just encrypting the random number obtained, here you can use the HMAC series digest algorithm [28]. By mixing the secret key and the random number to perform the digest, it can prevent the attacker from being able to easily perform identity authentication cheating when the random number is intercepted and the digest algorithm is learned. The use of random numbers is to prevent replay attacks so that the information required for each authentication will change with the change of the random number. Intercepting a certain transmission of identity authentication information will not take effect after the random number is changed.

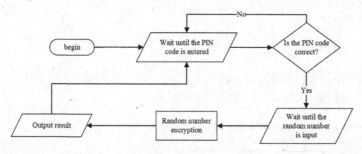

Fig. 5. The program flow chart of the identity authentication function of the system.

3.4 Function Realization

Communication Module. The Serial. print() function is the Arduino serial output function. Since the read of the serial port of the single-chip microcomputer is not blocked, it is necessary to judge Serial. available()>0 to prevent the program from running before and after. Also, because the serial port needs time to transmit bit by bit, there needs a delay time to ensure that all characters have been read into the buffer when reading.

```
while(Serial.available()>0&&verify==1){
      delay(100);
      Serial.readBytes(in,16);
}// accept external input
```

PIN Code Verification Module. In this part, the user can customize the global variable PIN value in the MCU code and then verify whether the input value in and the global variable PIN are equal through the verifyPIN function.

```
byte PIN[8]={0x31,0x32,0x33,0x34,0x35,0x36,0x37,0x38};
bool verifyPIN(byte PIN[8],byte in[8]){
for(int i=0;i<8;i++){
  if(in[i]!=PIN[i])
    return 0;
  }
  return 1;
}
if(verifyPIN(PIN,check)){
  Serial.println("right");verify=1;}
else {
  Serial.println("error");
  return 0;}
```

Encryption and Decryption Module. The system realizes and integrates four encryption algorithms: DES, AES128, AES256, and SM4. Taking the SM4 algorithm as an example, the implementation process is given.

```
unsigned char key[16] =
  {0x01,0x23,0x45,0x67,0x89,0xab,0xcd,0xef,0xfe,0xdc,0xba
,0x98,0x76,0x54,0x32,0x10};
unsigned char input[16] =
  {0x01,0x23,0x45,0x67,0x89,0xab,0xcd,0xef,0xfe,0xdc,0xba
,0x98,0x76,0x54,0x32,0x10};
unsigned char output[16];
sm4_context ctx;
//encrypt standard testing vector
sm4_setkey_enc(&ctx,key);
sm4_crypt_ecb(&ctx,1,16,input,output);
printnArray(output,16);
//decrypt testing
sm4_setkey_dec(&ctx,key);
sm4_crypt_ecb(&ctx,0,16,output,output);
printnArray(output,16);
```

The key is built into the code of the single-chip microcomputer, input is the result from the calling program obtained by the single-chip microcomputer, and output is the calculation result of the algorithm that the single-chip microcomputer is ready to output to the outside world. After setting the key and input, call the library function sm4_crypt_ecb to get the SM4 result, and finally output it.

Summary Module. The system we proposed includes three modules: MD5 digest, SHA1 digest, and SHA256 digest. Taking the SHA256 digest module as an example, the specific implementation process is as follows:

```
Serial.begin(9600);
uint8_t* hash;
uint32_t a;
unsigned long ms;
Serial.begin(9600);
Seri-
al.println("Expect:ba7816bf8f01cfea414140de5dae2223b00361
a396177a9cb410ff61f20015ad");
Serial.print("Result:");
ms = micros();
Sha256.init();
Sha256.print("abc");
printHash(Sha256.result());
Serial.print(" Hash took : ");
Serial.print((micros() - ms));
Serial.println(" micros");
Serial.println();
```

Initialize the SHA256 object first, then pass the string to be digested into the SHA256 object for mapping. Finally, use the output function printHash to output the result.

4 Experiment and Discussion

The finished physical picture is shown in Fig. 6. At present, the USB interface has been used to connect with the host, ready for system testing.

Fig. 6. The Physical objects of the safety reinforced terminal.

The purpose of the system test is to verify whether the functions realized by the overall design meet the requirements, and a series of demo calling programs need to be designed and developed to call the functions realized by the single-chip microcomputer. The demo program here is developed using Python to simulate the call of a normal program to the single-chip microcomputer. After the functional test is completed, we also conduct some tests on the performance of the entire system, such as the execution time of the algorithm, and compare and analyze the results.

4.1 Data Encryption Module Integration Test

The method to verify the function of the data encryption module is to re-decrypt the ciphertext obtained after encrypting the same string to determine whether the original string can be obtained. At the same time, it can also be compared with the result obtained from an online encryption and decryption website on the network. The original text data used for the test is '12345678abcdefghaaaaaaaaahhhhhhhh', and the test data encryption result is shown in Fig. 7.

The first part is the verification part of the PIN, which proves that the function is normal. The remaining three parts are the encryption results of the three strings of b'12345678abcdefgh', b'aaaaaaaaahhhhhhhh', b'aaa\x00\x00\x00\x00\x00\x00\x00\x00\x00\x00\x00\x00\x00' respectively. Compare them with the online encryption of the website to prove that the results are correct.

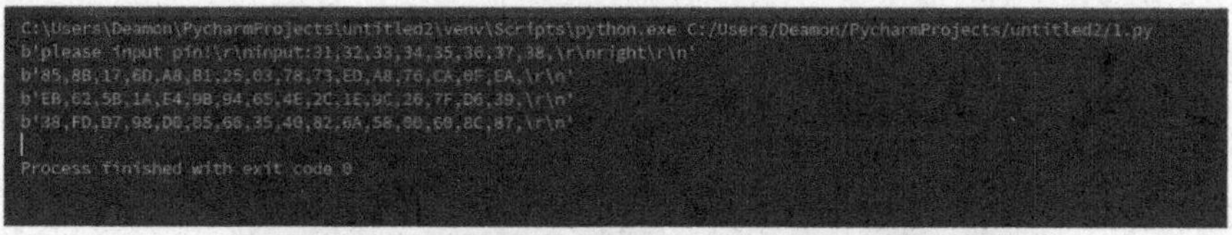

Fig. 7. Data encryption module integration test results.

4.2 Identity Authentication Module Integration Test

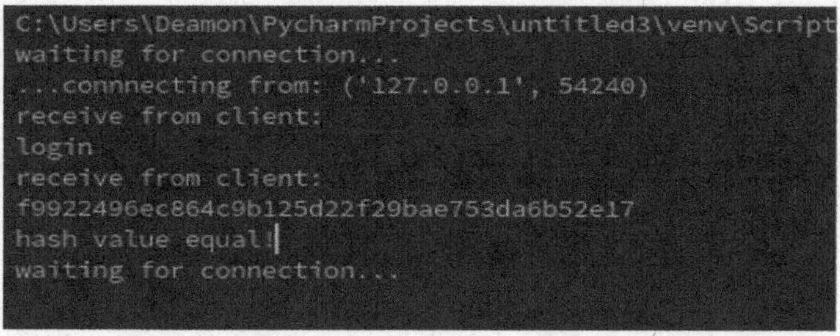

Fig. 8. Server-side identity authentication module integration test results.

The Server-side service program result is shown in Fig. 8. Clint's login request and the hash value of the random number from the single-chip microcomputer are successfully received. Finally, after calculation, it is found that the hash function value calculated by the server itself is equal to the passed value, and the login success string is sent to the client.

As shown in Fig. 9, the Client receives the verification code '1970' from the server, sends it to the MCU, and MCU sends the result back to the client after calculation. The client receives the hash value after the hash operation of the MCU, then sends the hash value to the server. The server compares the self-calculated hash value with the received hash value, and finally finds that the hash calculations are equal, then it can send the 'login success' string to the client to show that the identity authentication has passed. As a result, the entire identity authentication function test passed.

4.3 Algorithm Performance Test

Digest algorithm. As shown in Fig. 10, a single SHA256 takes 32116 μs, a single SHA1 takes 30052 μs, and MD5 takes only 1600 μs. It can be found that the runtime difference between SHA1 and SHA256 is not obvious, but both are significantly longer than MD5. In other words, MD5 is more efficient when digesting short strings such as "abc".

Data Encryption Algorithm. For the same data, five algorithms (DES, Triple-DES, AES128, AES256, and SM4) are used for encryption and decryption experiments. The runtime statistical analysis is shown in Table 1.

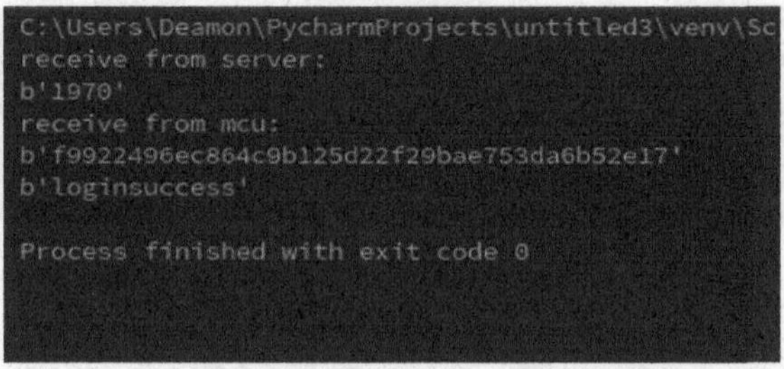

Fig. 9. Client-side identity authentication module integration test results

(a) The SHA256 digest algorithm performance test results.

(b) The SHA1 digest algorithm performance test results

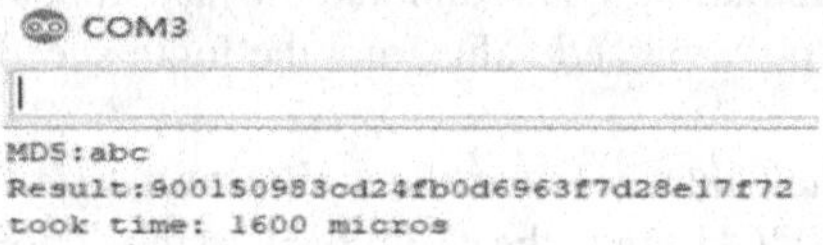

(c) The MD5 digest algorithm performance test results

Fig. 10. Digest algorithm performance test results

Table 1. Encryption and decryption algorithms time-consuming statistics table

Algorithm name	Time
DES	35748 μs
Triple-DES	107240 μs
AES128	69680 μs
AES256	69680 μs
SM4	70580 μs

In general, Triple-DES takes the longest time, and the time taken for a single DES is exactly about half of that of AES and SM4. Compared with the SM4 algorithm, the conventional DES encryption algorithm is 64-bit [29], while the SM4 algorithm, as a grouping algorithm, has a data block length of 128 bits and a key length of 128 bits. Therefore, it is reasonable to reduce the time of the single DES by half compared with the SM4 algorithm. For the AES algorithm, as an asymmetric key algorithm, 128, 192, or 256-bit keys can be used, and 128-bit data blocks are used to encrypt and decrypt data [30]. In the experiments carried out in this article, the encryption and decryption of AES128 and AES256 take the same time. It may be because the length of the data to be encrypted is the same so that AES128 and AES256 have similar encryption processing. That is, AES256 does not perform additional 4 round key generation processes and corresponding SPN operations [13].

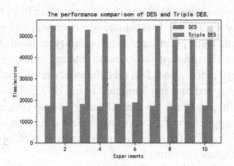

Fig. 11. Performance comparison between single DES and Triple-DES.

For a further comparative analysis of the single DES algorithm and the Triple-DES algorithm, as shown in Fig. 11. The time required to encrypt a DES algorithm is 17,872 μs, and the time required for triple DES is 53612 μs. There is an obvious three-fold relationship.

As shown in Fig. 12, through experiments by changing the input data to 16 bytes, we found that SM4, AES256, AES128, and DES take about the same time for 16-byte plaintext input.

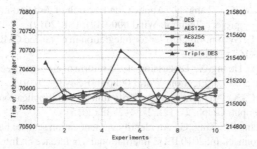

Fig. 12. Algorithm performance comparison when the input is 16 bytes of data.

5 Conclusion

With the continuous expansion of substation construction and the further improvement of automation systems, a large number of intelligent terminal equipment, applications, and tools have been put into the field application of substations. However, the intrinsic safety and trustworthiness technology of these devices has not been developed simultaneously with the spread of device applications. They are likely to be monitored or even tampered with within the process of use, which further leads to more prominent security vulnerabilities of their ontology, and provides more possibilities for malicious intrusion [31]. Information security needs to ensure the confidentiality, integrity, and availability of information [32]. For software that stores information that needs to interact with the outside world, if the encryption protection technology is also included in its code, it is easy to be debugged, analyzed, decompiled, and finally cracked. How to ensure the security of information transmission between interactive objects has now become a difficult problem that urgently needs technical improvement and resolution. However, cryptography-based data encryption technology, identity authentication, data signature, and other technologies can prevent information leakage, identity counterfeiting, and data tampering to a large extent. Based on this, the safety reinforced terminal protection technology that we designed and implemented based on USB interface hardware has low cost, good versatility, and can also meet the user's personalized security needs. For the secondary system application function-level safety detection system, it has certain practical significance to realize the safety reinforcement of AVC operation instructions, intelligent alarms, and other functions.

Acknowledgment. Our work is supported by China Southern Power Grid Science and Technology Project: Research and Application of Key Technologies of Intrinsic Safety Substation Measurement and Control and PMU Device (GXKJXM20200242).

References

1. An, Y., Zhao, B., Li, Y.: Research on software protection method based on USBKey. In: 19th IEEE International Symposium on Asynchronous Circuits and Systems, pp. 210–213. IEEE, Wuhan (2014)
2. Lang, Q.-Y., Wu, M.-C., Zhang, N.: Application research of Arduino in the development of pressure monitoring project. Technol. Wind **000**(012), 181 (2019)
3. Ayoub, L., Lado, F.: System-on-chip sensor integration in advanced CMOS technology. ECS Trans. **85**(8), 151–162 (2018)
4. Sun, L.-J., Long, Y., Huang, X.: Discussion on the reform of electronic technology experiment teaching based on arduino. Electron. World **000**(003), 34–35 (2019)
5. Liu, Y.-H., Shen, C.-X.: An information security function and application model. J. Comput.-Aided Design Comput. Graph. **27**(12), 2734–2738 (2015)
6. Liu, Z., Gu, L., Yang, Y., Xing, G.: An identity authentication scheme based on USB key for trusted network connect. In: 2010 IEEE International Conference on Information Theory and Information Security, pp. 203–207. IEEE, Beijing (2010)
7. Yang, J., Zhou, J.: Analysis on the security threats of ID authentication and threat defense measure. Netinfo Secur. **10**(11), 83–84 (2010)

8. Jayaraman, C.: USB based dynamic authentication alert system for computers. Int. J. Comput. Appl. **107**(6), 17–20 (2014)
9. Yu, J., Zhang, C.-F.: Design and analysis of a USB-Key based strong password authentication scheme. In: 2010 International Conference on Computational Intelligence and Software Engineering, pp. 1–4. IEEE, Wuhan (2010)
10. Zhao, D., Luo, W.: One-time password authentication scheme based on the negative database. Eng. Appl. Artif. Intell. **62**(06), 396–404 (2017)
11. Gao, M.: Talking About the application of symmetric encryption algorithm and asymmetric encryption algorithm. Electron. World **37**(15), 59–60 (2015)
12. Cai, M.: Analysis on the application of data encryption technology in computer network communication security. Telecom World **26**(05), 92–93 (2019)
13. Fernando, E., Agustin, D., Irsan, M., Murad, D.-F., Rohayani, H., Sujana, D.: Performance comparison of symmetries encryption algorithm AES and DES with raspberry Pi. In: 2019 International Conference on Sustainable Information Engineering and Technology, pp. 353–357. IEEE, Mataram (2019)
14. Wu, Z.-H., Zhao, J.-N., Zhu, Y.: Comparative study on application of Chinese cryptographic algorithms and international cryptographic algorithms in vehicle microcotrollers. Netinfo Secur. **19**(08), 68–75 (2019)
15. Saxena, S., Kishore, N.: PRDSA: effective parallel digital signature algorithm for GPUs. IJ Wirel. Microw. Technol. **7**(5), 14–21 (2017)
16. Li, A., Zhang, Y., Zhang, J., Zhu, G.: A token strengthened encryption packer to prevent reverse engineering PE files. In: 2015 International Conference on Estimation, Detection and Information Fusion, pp. 307–312. IEEE, Harbin (2015)
17. Agnihotri, D., Ahmed, S., Darekar, D., Gadkari, C., Jaikar, S., Pawar, M.: A secure document archive implemented using multiple encryption. In: 2020 International Conference on Smart Electronics and Communication, pp. 765–770. IEEE, Shenzhen (2020)
18. Wu, K., Zhang, Y., Cui, W., Jiang, T.: Design and implementation of encrypted and decrypted file system based on USBKey and hardware code. AIP Publishing LLC **1839**(1), 020215(1–8) (2017)
19. Meng, Y.-X., Dong, J.-Y., Yin, Y.-H., Qi, L.: Transparent encryption technique for Word documents based on USB Key in manufacturing system. Trans Tech Publications Ltd **252**(1), 323–326 (2013)
20. Gelbart, O., Leontie, E., Narahari, B., Simha, R.: A compiler-hardware approach to software protection for embedded systems. Comput. Electr. Eng. **35**(2), 315–328 (2009)
21. Liu, J.-D., Tian, Y., Wang, S.-H.: A fast new one-way cryptographic hash function. In: 2010 IEEE International Conference on Wireless Communications, Networking and Information Security, pp. 302–306. IEEE, Beijing (2010)
22. Guo, J.: Smartphone-Powered electrochemical biosensing dongle for emerging medical IoTs application. IEEE Trans. Industr. Inf. **14**(6), 2592–2597 (2017)
23. Abu, P.: A power-efficient multiband planar USB dongle antenna for wireless sensor networks. Sensors **19**(11), 2568 (2019)
24. Son, T.-T., Burton, A., Le-Minh, H., Hien, D.-Q.: Experimental study of pc-to-pc over a visible light channel using Li-Fi USB dongle. In: 26th International Conference on Telecommunications, pp. 215–219. IEEE, Hanoi (2019)
25. Wen, H., Chen, Q.-A., Lin, Z.: Plug-N-Pwned: comprehensive vulnerability analysis of ODB-II dongles as a new over-the-air attack surface in automotive IoT. In: 29th USENIX Security Symposium (USENIX Security 20), Boston, USA, pp. 949–965 (2020)
26. Hu, W., Wu, Q.-H., Liu, S.-L.: Design of secure eID and identity authentication agreement in mobile terminal based on the state secret algorithm and blockchain. Netinfo Secur. **18**(07), 7–15 (2018)

27. Zhang, P., Chen, C.-S., Hu, H.-G.: Working mode of authentication and encryption based on block cipher. Netinfo Secur. **14**(11), 8–17 (2014)

28. Li, M., Shi, G.-Z., Lou, J.-P.: USB key identity authentication scheme based on password service platform. Comput. Appl. Softw. **35**(9), 288–291 (2018)

29. Xu, H.-B., Li, Y.-H.: The application of DES encryption algorithm to protect data security in the file transfer. Netinfo Secur. **9**(06), 24–26 (2009)

30. Zhang, J.-H., Guo, X.-B., Fu, X.: AES encryption algorithm analysis and the application in information security. Netinfo Secur. **11**(05), 31–33 (2011)

31. Cui, G.-Y.: To build international market security made in China – decoding the international exploration and practice of flying integrity. China Inf. Secur. **9**(10), 74–76 (2018)

32. Yang, X., Hou, Y., Ma, J., He, H.: CDSP: A solution for privacy and security of multimedia information processing in industrial big data and internet of things. Sensors **19**(3), 556 (2019)

Modeling Dynamics of Covid-19 Infected Population with PSO

Guangdong Huang[1]([⊠]) and Aihua Li[2]

[1] China University of Geosciences in Beijing, Beijing, China
gdhuang@cugb.edu.cn
[2] Montclair State University, Montclair, USA
lia@montclair.edu

Abstract. This study focuses on the Covid-19 spreading dynamics in Bergen County, New Jersey, USA. Due to limited covid-19 testing capacity, it was difficult to assess the real data about the virus spreading in New Jersey counties. Our study is based on the available incomplete daily data from March 15 to July 15 of 2020. In order to capture an overall picture of the local dynamics of the infected population and predict reasonable future situations, we perform several traditional dynamic modeling methods. A region-stage-modified-SEIR model (denoted MSEIR) and a SEIRH model are constructed to describe the dynamics of the infected population. Particle Swarm Optimization (PSO) is used to identify the parameters of the developed models. In order to predict the cumulative number of the infected individuals, the produced models are used to simulate the dynamics of the population in four epidemiological groups respectively: susceptible, exposed, infected, and recovered groups. By this process, we obtain a better picture of the COVID-19 infected individuals in the target county.

Keywords: COVID-19 · PSO · MSEIR · SEIRH

1 Introduction

Tollowing the pioneering work by Kermack and McKendrick [1], mathematical modeling on infectious diseases has become a powerful tool in helping understanding infectious disease transmission. This area of research is interdisciplinary and is gaining increasing interests [2–4]. The well-known SIR model has been an effective method in predicting the outbreak periods for a large series of infectious diseases in many countries around the world [1]. After the SIR model, Aron proposed the SEIR model in 1981. SEIR model gives more consideration on the presence of incubation periods in infectious diseases compared with the SIR model. Evam introduced the time series with the SEIR model to well simulate the spread of measles in 2000.

Since 1926, Mckendrick used random methods to describe the epidemic process of infectious diseases and proposed the malaria transmission model. Based

© Springer Nature Singapore Pte Ltd. 2021
L. Lin et al. (Eds.): SocialSec 2021, CCIS 1495, pp. 75–89, 2021.
https://doi.org/10.1007/978-981-16-7913-1_6

on the introduction of random model, the concept of "basic reproductive rate" was proposed, and Ross-Mckendrick model was established [5–8] in 1950. In 1957 Bartle et al. demonstrated that stochastic models could be used to deal with possibly periodic ones Epidemic diseases, which marked the beginning of the application of stochastic models to the study of disease transmission models, and Bailey, Anderson et al. are all good works in this respect [9–12]. With the aim of being more realistic and predictive, the network structure of contacts on the disease transmission has been considered in several publications recently [13–16]. As COVID-19 spreads around the world, tens of millions people were infected and hundreds of thousands people died. The world economy is in the doldrums. Mathematical approaches are widely used to infer critical epidemiological transitions and parameters of COVID-19. Methods such as epidemic curve fitting, surveillance data during the early transmission, and other epidemic models are frequently applied to generate forecasts of COVID-19 pandemic across the world [17–19]. As the research on COVID-19 deepens, some scholars have also begun to study the transmission model of COVID-19 with isolation and immunity [20–22]. The previous studies mainly focus on big cities with complete susceptible (S), infected (I) and immune or recovered (R) individuals and the time series built upon them. Using these time series, one can calculate the model parameter and the propagation rules and predict the future propagation trend. However, in most of small and medium-sized cities in the United States, the accessible data sets are incomplete and some of them are inaccurate. It is a less studied situation. When investigating small cities, it is more challenging to identify the model parameters, to reverse the daily variation patterns of different populations, and to formulate the disease transmission propagation rules. In this paper, we apply a combination of methods, such as SEIR model and PSO, to study the transmission pattern of COVID-19 in Bergen, New Jersey. We first develop MSEIR and SEIRH models by modifying the SEIR model. Then we divided the Bergen COVID-19 period into four stages. Applying the particle swarm optimization algorithm and data on Bergen COVID-19 accumulated infected population, we identify the model parameters and simulate daily data $S(t)$, $E(t)$, $I(t)$, $R(t)$ (in Table 5) through different periods. Finally by comparing errors in every stage of the simulation, we choose the optimization model and use it to predict daily cumulative infected population of Bergen County from July 16 to August 31 with the 95% confidence interval.

2   Methodology

2.1   The SEIR and MSEIR Models

In an SEIR model, a population of size N is divided into 4 epidemiological groups: susceptible, exposed, infected, and recovered respectively, denoted S, E, I, R, with $S + E + I + R = N$. We need to consider simultaneously three processes: new incubation, new infections, and removal of hosts. The first of these processes is the only one that affects susceptible hosts. We set $\frac{dS}{dt} = -\alpha SI$, where α is the infection rate. This process, which involves αSI, also contributes to $\frac{dE}{dt}$. In an SEIR-model, removal occurs as a result of recovery from the disease with permanent immunity or of deaths from the disease. Removal of hosts is the only process that affects R because only hosts in I are candidates for removal and in none of these scenarios can hosts ever leave the R-compartment. Thus $\frac{dR}{dt}$ is proportional to the number of infectious hosts, that is, $\frac{dR}{dt} = \gamma I$, where γ is the rate of removal. Since removal of hosts decreases I, the process also contributes a term $-\gamma I$ to $\frac{dI}{dt}$. We obtain the following model:

$$\frac{dS}{dt} = -\alpha SI \tag{1}$$

$$\frac{dE}{dt} = \alpha SI - \beta E \tag{2}$$

$$\frac{dI}{dt} = \beta E - \gamma I \tag{3}$$

$$\frac{dR}{dt} = \gamma I \tag{4}$$

The exposed individuals of COVID-19 is less infectious than that of infection, but it is still highly infectious. If we use the SEIR model directly, there is a risk of overestimating the rate of transmission. Thus, we need to make modifications. The first of the modification processes is the only one that affects susceptible hosts. We set $\frac{dS}{dt} = -\alpha S \cdot (I + \theta E)$, where θ is the infection rate incubation to infection. The process also contributes a term $\alpha S \cdot (I + \theta E)$ to $\frac{dE}{dt}$. We obtain the following model (named as MSEIR model):

$$\frac{dS}{dt} = \frac{-\alpha S \cdot (I + \theta E)}{N} \tag{5}$$

$$\frac{dE}{dt} = \frac{\alpha S \cdot (I + \theta E)}{N} - \beta E \tag{6}$$

$$\frac{dI}{dt} = \beta E - \gamma I \tag{7}$$

$$\frac{dR}{dt} = \gamma I \tag{8}$$

In the middle stage, researchers take isolation measures against infectious diseases. Note that SEIR and MSEIR do not consider isolation and hospitalization, so they could not well simulate the variation pattern of COVID-19 spreading. Here we establish a more realistic differential equation model with isolation, hospitalization, and death consideration to analyze the daily $S(t)$, $E(t)$, $I(t)$, $R(t)$ variation pattern. We stratified the population as susceptible (S), exposed (E), infectious with symptoms (I), hospitalized (H), and recovered (R) compartments. A further classification will include quarantined susceptible (S_q) and isolated exposed (E_q) compartments (see Fig. 1) [22]. With contact tracing, a proportion q of individuals exposed to the virus is quarantined. The quarantined individuals can either be moved to the compartment E_q or S_q depending on whether they are effectively infected or not. While the other proportion $1 - q$ of individuals consists of those who were exposed to the virus but missed from the contact tracing and those individuals who were once effectively infected and would be moved to the exposed compartment E, or otherwise would stay in compartment S. Note that the probability of infection is α, the contact rate is ρ (the effective contact coefficient), and the effective contact is ρc. The rate of susceptible people S converting to isolated susceptible people S_q, isolated contacts E_q and contacts E are $(\rho c) q (1 - \alpha)$, $(\rho c) \alpha q$, and $(\rho c) \alpha (1 - q)$. At the same time the infected individuals I and the exposed individuals E have impact on the susceptible individuals, which may force the isolated susceptible S_q to change into susceptible individuals S again (see Fig. 1). Thus a system of differential equations representing the modified SEIR model for COVID-19 outbreaks is as follows (Denoted SEIRH model) [28,29]:

$$\frac{dS}{dt} = - \left((\rho c) \alpha + (\rho c) q (1 - \alpha) \right) S (I + \theta E) + \lambda S_q \tag{9}$$

$$\frac{dE}{dt} = (\rho c) \alpha (1 - q) S (I + \theta E) - \sigma E \tag{10}$$

$$\frac{dI}{dt} = \sigma E - (\delta_I + b + \gamma_I) I \tag{11}$$

$$\frac{dS_q}{dt} = (\rho c) q (1 - \alpha) S (I + \theta E) - \lambda S_q \tag{12}$$

$$\frac{dE_q}{dt} = (\rho c) \alpha q S (I + \theta E) - \delta_q E_q \tag{13}$$

$$\frac{dH}{dt} = \delta_I I + \delta_q E_q - (b + \gamma_H) H \tag{14}$$

$$\frac{dR}{dt} = \gamma_I I + \gamma_H E_q. \tag{15}$$

In the above system, θ is the infection rate incubation to infections and λ is the isolation release rate. σ is the conversion rate from an incubation to an infected person, b is the fatality rate, δ_I is the rate of infected individuals to isolation infected individuals, δ_q is the conversion rate of the isolated incubation to the isolated infected individuals, γ_I is the recovery rate of the infected, and γ_H is the recovery rate of isolated infected individuals.

2.2   The Model Parameter Identification

In the study of development of infectious diseases using mathematics models, the time-dependent numbers $S(t)$, $E(t)$, $I(t)$, and $R(t)$ play important roles in identifying the parameters of the model. But in many cities of the United States, accessible data are scarce and incomplete. For example, only the data on cumulative infected population are available for many cities. It is challenging to use such limited data to study transmission patterns.

For a certain region, the actual number of cumulative infected individuals is denoted $\overline{CI}(t)$ at time t. Suppose we use SEIR-model to simulate the real situation. For a set of reasonable parameters of the model, corresponding theoretical

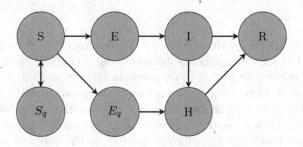

Fig. 1. Modified SEIR dynamic model

solution to $S(t)$, $E(t)$, $I(t)$, $R(t)$ can be obtained. Let $CT(t) = I(t) + R(t)$, which measures the theoretical accumulative infected individuals. We expect that the resulting $CT(t)$ is close to the actual amount $\overline{CI(t)}$. We perform the method of least-squares approximation to minimizes the sum of squared residuals, that is, the error between $CI(t)$ and $\overline{CT(t)}$, to determine the model parameters α, β, γ. The corresponding mathematical model provides the minimum value point of the error function:

$$\min_{\alpha,\beta,\gamma} \sum \left\{ f(\alpha,\beta,\gamma) = \left(CI(t) - \overline{CT(t)} \right)^2 \right\}. \tag{16}$$

Based on the above ideas, optimization algorithms are developed to obtain the model parameters for Bergen County of New Jersey in each infection stage.

2.3 PSO Algorithm

Particle swarm optimization (PSO) is an optimization algorithm based on evolutionary computation technique. The basic PSO is developed from research on swarm such as fish schooling and bird flocking. It was first introduced in 1995 [23] and then a modified PSO was introduced in 1998 to improve the performance of the original PSO. A new parameter called inertia weight is added [24]. This is a commonly used PSO where inertia weight is linearly decreasing during iteration in addition to another common type of PSO which is reported by Clerc [25,26]. In PSO, instead of using genetic operators, individuals are evolved by cooperation and competition among themselves through generations. A particle represents a potential solution to a problem. Each particle adjusts its flying according to its own flying experience and its companion flying experience and is treated as a point in a D-dimensional space. The ith particle is represented as $X_i = (x_{i1}, x_{i2}, \cdots, x_{iD})$. The best previous position (giving the minimum fitness value) of any particle is recorded and represented as $P_i = ((p_{i1}, p_{i2}, \cdots, p_{iD})$, this is called p best. The index of the best particle among all particles in the population is represented by the symbol g, called as g best. The velocity for the particle i is represented as $V_i = ((v_{i1}, v_{i2}, \cdots, v_{iD})$. The particles are updated according to the following equations:

$$V_{id}^{n+1} = w\dot{V}_{id}^n + c_1 \cdot [\text{rand}(*)](P_{id}^n - X_{id}^n) + c_2 \cdot [\text{rand}(*)](P_{gd}^n - X_{id}^n) \tag{17}$$

$$X_{id}^{n+1} = X_{id}^n + V_{id}^{n+1} \qquad (18)$$

where c_1 and c_2 are two positive constant. While rand(*) is a random function between 0 and 1, and n represents iteration. Equation 17 is used to calculate particle's new velocity according to its previous velocity and the distances of its current position from its own best experience (position) and the group's best experience. Then the particle flies toward a new position according to Eq. 17. The performance of each particle is measured according to a pre-defined fitness function (performance index), which is related to the problem to be solved. Inertia weight, w is brought into Eq. 18 to balance between the global search and local search capability [24] and it can be a positive constant or even positive linear or nonlinear function of time. It has been also shown that PSO with different number of particles (swarm size) has reasonably similar performances [27]. Swarm size of 10–50 is usually selected. The process of model parameter identification in each infectious stage is shown in Fig. 2.

3   Case Study

3.1   Data Analysis

On March 4, 2020, Governor Phil Murphy and Lieutenant Governor Sheila Oliver issued a joint statement, announcing that the first confirmed case in New Jersey was a 30-year-old male hospitalized in Bergen County. Affected by the epidemic, on March 8, some school districts announced closures or revised schedules. On March 9, Governor Phil Murphy declared state of emergency in New Jersey. On March 14 a curfew was declared in the city of Hoboken through July 15 when the cumulative number of infection is 176,392 and the cumulative number of deaths is 15,642. The COVID-19 data of the 21 New Jersey counties from the middle of March to the middle of August 2020 were obtained from internet https://1point3acres.com/ which included the cumulative number of infection, the new infections, the cumulative number of deaths, the new deaths, and the recovered individuals. However the data were not accurate and were incomplete, especially the data on recovered individuals. Figure 3 shows all NJ infected cases and deaths from March 13 to August 20. We used the cumulative number of infection $CI(t)$ as the only real data. We choose Bergen county as a example and collect the cumulative number of infected individuals from March 15 to July 15 for the study and we assume other counties have the similar situation.

3.2   The Bergen Case Model

Bergen is a county in New Jersey and it is very close to New York City by sharing the Hudson River with NYC. The first confirmed case in New Jersey was in Bergen County which made it one of the counties hardest hit by COVID-19. Thus, it is of great significant to study Bergen's COVID-19 situation. Figure 4 shows the number of infected individuals in Bergen and Fig. 5 shows the daily increased infected individuals. From Fig. 5 we can see that the infection period

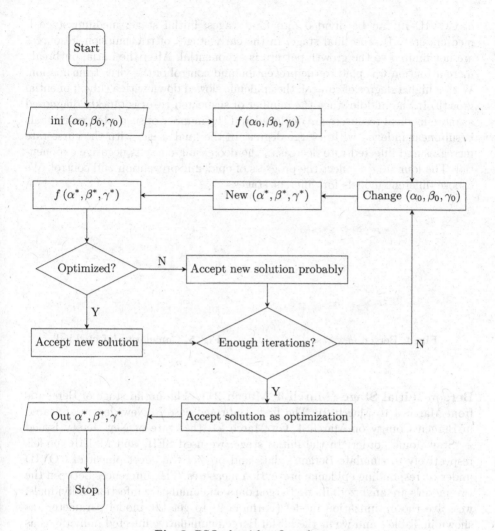

Fig. 2. PSO algorithm flow chart

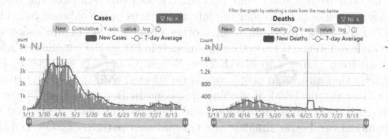

Fig. 3. NJ case and deaths data

of COVID-19 can be divided into four stages: initial stage, medium stage I, medium state II, and final stage. In the early stages of transmission, resources are not limited so the growth pattern is exponential. After the initial outbreak, more attention was paid to the prevention and control of the virus transmission. With a higher degree of control, the epidemic slowed down with a subexponential growth. In the middle stage the number of suspected cases is quickly diagnosed as more medical resources are deployed and the number of suspected individuals is sublinear indexed with a large degree. In the final stage, with the curse rate increases and infected rate decreases, the decreasing curve is negative exponential. The four stages reflect the progress of epidemic prevention and control. We choose different models for different stages.

Fig. 4. Bergen new case

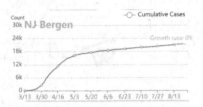

Fig. 5. Cumulative infected ind.

Bergen Initial Stage (March 4–March 21). The initial stage of Bergen is from March 4 to March 21. The first confirmed case in New Jersey appeared in Bergen County on March 4. On March 21, the state of New Jersey issued a "Stay-Home" order. In the initial stage, we used SEIR and MSEIR models respectively to simulate Bergen's data and predict the development of COVID under corresponding epidemic prevention measures. The differences between the two models are analyzed. Using Bergen data on cumulative infection individuals, we solve the optimization model (Formula 9) to get the model parameters as shown in Table 1 and we fit the initial Bergen cumulative infected individuals as shown in Fig. 6. By putting these parameters into both SEIR and MSEIR models we predict the future development trend of COVID-19 as shown in the Fig. 7. It can be seen from Table 1 that the SEIR model overestimates the infection rate because it does not consider the infection status of the exposed individuals. Figure 7 also verifies this result from another point of view. Figure 5 shows that there is little difference between the two models in fitting the cumulative infected individuals from March 4 to March 21 in Bergen County. In contrast to Fig. 5, Fig. 7 shows that almost all people would be infected with the COVID-19 about 50 days after the outbreak if nothing was done in Bergen County. There is a big difference between the actual data and the predicted data. In summary, the MSEIR model can better simulate the transmission pattern of COVID-9 in the initial stage of the infection.

Table 1. SIR and SEIR parameters of Bergen county

SEIR	α	β	γ	MSEIR	α	β	γ	θ
	1.0895	0.394	0.07		0.63	0.2	0.06	0,8

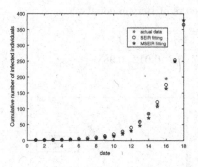

Fig. 6. Initial fitting of Bergen   **Fig. 7.** Initial prediction of Bergen

Bergen Middle Stage I (March 21–April 7). The middle stages of Bergen are from March 22 to May 2 before the golf courses and parks were re-opened gradually in Bergen from May 2. Based on the growth trend of the epidemic, we divide the middle term into the accelerating and decelerating growth periods. The accelerating parts is named as meddle stage I (March 21–April 7) and the decelerating part is the middle stage II (April 7–May 2).

In this section, we modify the SEIR and SEIRH models to simulate and predict the daily numbers of $S(t), E(t), I(t), R(t)$ in Bergen County. Let $\lambda = \frac{1}{14}$ (the duration of isolation was 14 days), $\sigma = \frac{1}{7}$ (the incubation period is 7 days), $\delta_q = 0.13$, $b = 0.000235$, and $\delta_I = 0.13$ (adopted from an internet source) in the SEIRH model. Using data on Bergen cumulative infected individuals (March 21–April 7) and the PSO Algorithm we establish the optimization model to obtain the model parameters. The MSEIR parameters are shown in Table 2 and the SEIRH parameters are in Table 3. In comparison with Table 1, Table 2 shows that each of α and β in the middle I stage is less than that in the initial state but each γ or θ is bigger than that in the initial period. This indicates that the infection rate in the middle phase is lower than that in the early phase and the cure rate in the middle phase is higher than that in the early phase.

The MSEIR and SEIRH fittings are shown in Fig. 8 and the prediction is shown in Fig. 9. Figure 8 shows that there is little difference between the two models in fitting the cumulative infected individuals from March 21 to April 7 in Bergen County. Figure 9 shows that using the MEIR model the cumulative infected individuals would stabilize at 883,500 about 110 days after the outbreak and correspondingly the cumulative infected individuals using SEIRH model would stabilize at 100,000. It indicates that the SEIRH model gives more accurate predictions compared to other models.

Table 2. Middle I MSEIR parameters of Bergen county

MSEIR	α	β	γ	θ
–	0.1634	0.13	0.1	1

Table 3. Middle I SEIRH parameters of Bergen county

SEIRH	pc	α	q	γ_I	γ_H	θ
–	4.8	4.73e−08	2e−07	0.2	0.012	0.98

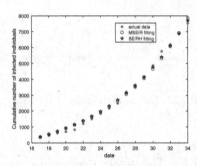

Fig. 8. Middle I fitting   **Fig. 9.** Middle I prediction

Bergen Medium Stage II (April 7–May 2). Similar as in the middle stage I, we assign $\lambda = \frac{1}{14}$ (the duration of isolation was 14 days), $\sigma = \frac{1}{7}$ (the incubation period is 7 days), $\delta_q = 0.13$, $b = 0.000235$, and $\delta_I = 0.13$. Using PSO and the data on Bergen cumulative infected individuals of the middle stage II, we obtain the SEIRH parameters as shown in Table 4 and the SEIRH parameters as shown in Table 5. In addition, Table 4 shows that the parameters α, β, θ of the MSEIR model in the middle II is less than that in the Middle I stage but γ of the MSEIR model in the middle II stage is bigger than that in the middle I stage. This indicates that the infection rate in the middle II is lower than that in the middle I stage but the cure rate in the middle II phase is higher than that in the middle I phase. Table 5 shows that the parameters pc and α of SEIRH in the middle II is bigger than that in the middle I. This means that the epidemic prevention effect of the middle II phase is better than that of the middle I. By applying these parameters in the MSEIR and SEIRH models, we can fit the Bergen data on cumulative infected individuals (shown in Fig. 10) and predict the future development trend of COVID-19 as shown in Fig. 11.

Figure 10 also shows that MSEIR's simulation is very close to the real data, while SEIRH overestimates the number of infected individuals in the early phase and underestimates the number of infected individuals in the later phase. It maybe because the growth curve of the accumulative infected individuals in the middle II phase is very close to linear, while the growth curve of SEIRH follows exponential curvature. Figure 11 shows that the cumulative infected individuals using the MSEIR model would stabilize at 220,000 about 110 days after the outbreak but the cumulative infected individuals would stabilize at 150,000 using the SEIRH model about 55 days after the outbreak. So the MSEIR model gives more accurate predictions compared to the SEIRH models.

Table 4. Middle II MSEIR parameters of Bérgen county

SEIR	α	β	γ	θ
–	0.039	0.0771	0.2587	0.8

Table 5. Middle II SEIRH parameters of Bergen county

SEIRH	pc	α	q	γ_I	γ_H	θ
–	2	2.81E−9	1E−7	0.01	0.32	0.8

Bergen: Final Stage (May 2–July 15). Similar as in 3.2.3 for Bergen middle stage II, we set $\lambda = \frac{1}{14}$ (the duration of isolation was 14 days), $\sigma = \frac{1}{7}$ (the incubation period is 7 days), $\delta_q = 0.13$, $b = 0.000235$, and $\delta_I = 0.13$. Using PSO and data on Bergen cumulative infected individuals of the final stage we obtain the MSEIR parameters as shown in Table 6 and the SEIRH parameters in Table 7. From Table 6 we see that in the final stage, the parameters α and β of MSEIR are less than that in the middle II stage but θ and γ are bigger than that is in the middle II stage. It concludes that the infection rate in the final stage is lower than that in the middle II stage but the cure rate in the middle II phase is higher than that in the middle I phase. Table 7 shows that the parameters pc and θ of SEIRH in the final stage is bigger than that in the middle II state. This means that the epidemic prevention effect in the final stage is worse than that the middle II stage. It has an obvious reasoning: in the final stage, the economy has restarted and people's per capita contact rate has increased.

By applying the above parameters into MSEIR and SEIRH models, we can fit the Bergen County data on cumulative infected individuals (see Fig. 12) and predict the future development trend of COVID-19 as shown in Fig. 13. Similar as the other stages, Fig. 12 shows that there is little difference between the two models in fitting the cumulative infected individuals from May 2 to July 15 in Bergen County. Furthermore, Fig. 13 shows that the cumulative infected individuals described in the MSEIR model would stabilize at 20,000, but the cumulative infected individuals using the SEIRH model would not stabilize. In conclusion, the MSEIR model gives more accurate predictions.

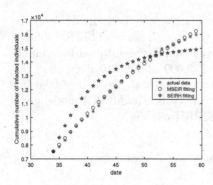

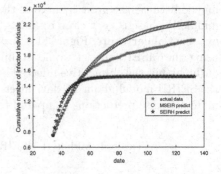

Fig. 10. Medium II fitting   **Fig. 11.** Medium II prediction

Table 6. Final stage: MSEIR parameters

MSEIR	α	β	γ	θ
–	0.0148	0.0365	0.3	0.8857

All Stages in Bergen (March 4–July 15). After evaluating the performances of different models, we select the MSEIR model in the first stage, the SEIRH model in the middle I stage, and the MSEIR model in the middle II stage and the final stage. Using this combination of mixed models and its corresponding model parameters, we achieved a better fitting to the COVID-19 infection data from March 4 to July 15 and used it to predict the infection situation from July 16 to August 31. We give the corresponding simulation error and the 95% confidence interval by simple calculations. The simulation and prediction graphs are demonstrated in Fig. 14 and the error curve between the actual data and the predicted data are shown in Fig. 15. It can be seen that from Figs. 14 and 15 that the simulation results of the mixed model are relatively close to the real situation.

Table 7. Final stage: SEIRH parameters

SEIRH	pc	α	q	γ_I	γ_H	θ
–	9.9958	1.9E−8	9.99E−6	0.2612	0.39982	0.9

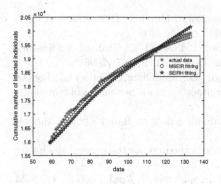

Fig. 12. Final stage: infection fitting

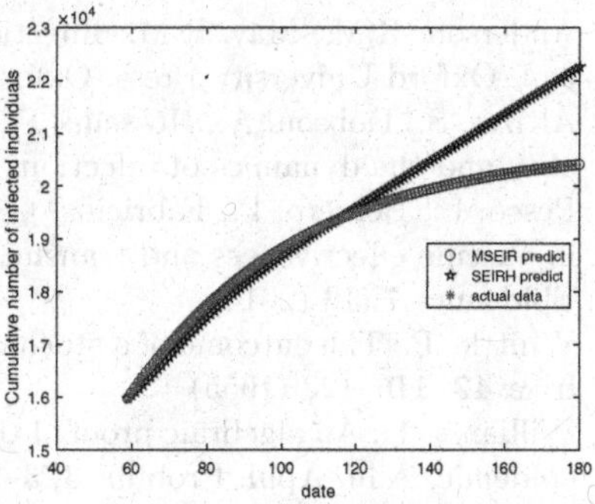

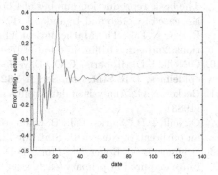

Fig. 13. Final stage: infection prediction

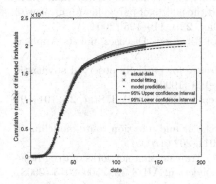

Fig. 14. Infection fitting & prediction

Fig. 15. Infection prediction error

4 Conclusion

In this research, we first break down the considered COVID-9 period of Bergen County into four stages based on the performances of different models. Secondly we identify the model parameters by the PSO optimizing algorithm and use SEIR, MSEIR and SEIRH models to simulate the values of $S(t), E(t), I(t), R(t)$. Thirdly, we perform a comparison study and select a better-fitting model for each stage and build a mixed model. Finally, we apply the mixed model and its corresponding model parameters to fit the COVID-19 infection data from March 4 to July 15 and predict the infection situation from July 16 to August 31. The corresponding simulation error and the 95% confidence interval are provided which confirm that the simulation results of the mixed model are relatively accurate.

References

1. Kermack, W.O., McKendrick, A.G.: A contribution to the mathematical theory of epidemics. Proc. R. Soc. Lond. Ser. A **115**, 700–721 (1927)

2. Anderson, R.M., May, R.M.: Infectious Diseases of Humans: Dynamics and Control. Oxford University Press, Oxford (1991)

3. Altizer, S., Dobson, A., Hosseini, P., Hudson, P., Pascual, M., Rohani, P.: Seasonality and the dynamics of infectious disease. Ecol. Lett. **9**, 467 (2006)

4. Pesco, P., Bergero, P., Fabricius, G., Hozbor, D.: Modelling the effect of changes in vaccine effectiveness and transmission contact rates on pertussis epidemiology. Epidemics **7**, 13 (2014)

5. Whittle, P.: The outcome of a stochastic epidemic-a note on Bailey's paper. Biomefrika **42**, 116–122 (1955)

6. Williams, T.: An algebraic proof of the threshold theorem for the general stochastic epidemic. Adu. Appl. Probub. **3**, 3–22 (1971)

7. Ridler-Rowe, C.J.: On a stochastic model of an epidemic. J. Appl. Probab. **4**, 19–33 (1967)

8. Chowel, G., Hengartner, N.W., Castillo-Chavez, C., Fenimore, P.W., Hyman, J.M.: The basic reproduction number of Ebola and the effects of public health measures: the case of Congo and Uganda. J. Theor. Biol. **229**, 119–126 (2004)

9. Bailey, N.T.J.: The Mathematical Theory of Infectious Diseases and its Applications, 2nd edn. Griffin, London (1975)

10. O'Neill, P.D., Roberts, G.O.: Bayesian inference for partially observed stochastic epidemics. J. R. Stat. Soc. Ser. A **162**, 121–129 (1999)

11. Becker, N.G.: Analysis of data from a single epidemic. Austral. J. Stat. **25**, 191–197 (1983)

12. O'Neill, P.D., Marks, P.J.: Bayesian model choice and infection route modeling in an outbreak of Norovirus. Stat. Med. **24**, 2011–2024 (2005)

13. Brenner, B.G., Roger, M., Moisi, D.D., et al.: Transmission networks of drug resistance acquired in primary/early stage HIV infection. AIDS **22**, 2509–2015 (2008)

14. Yerly, S., Junier, T., Gayet-Ageron, A., et al.: The impact of transmission clusters on primary drug resistance in newly diagnosed HIV-1 infection. AIDS **23**, 1415–1423 (2009)

15. Kouyos, R.D., von Wyl, V., Yerly, S., et al.: Molecular epidemiology reveals long-term changes in HIV type 1 subtype B transmission in Switzerland. J. Infect. Dis. **201**, 1488–1497 (2010)

16. Keeling, M.J., Eames, K.T.: Networks and epidemic models. J. R. Soc. Interface **2**, 295–307 (2005)

17. Kucharski, A.J., et al.: Early dynamics of transmission and control of COVID-19: a mathematical modeling study. Lancet Infect. Dis. (2020). https://doi.org/10.1016/S1473-3099(20)30144-4

18. Liu, Y., Gayle, A.A., Wilder-Smith, A., Rocklv, J.: The reproductive number of COVID-19 is higher compared to SARS coronavirus. J. Travel Med. (2020)

19. Pirouz, B., Shaffiee, H.S., Shaffiee, H.S., Piro, P.: Investigating a serious challenge in the sustainable development process: analysis of confirmed cases of COVID-19 (new type of coronavirus) through a binary classification using artificial intelligence and regression analysis. Sustainability **12**(6), 2427 (2020)

20. Toshikazu, K.: Prediction of the epidemic peak of coronavirus disease in Japan. J. Clin. Med. **9**, 789 (2020)

21. Saghazadeh, A., Rezaei, N.: Immune epidemiological parameters of the novel coronavirus - a perspective. Expert Rev. Clin. Immunol. **16**, 465–470 (2020)

22. Tang, B., Bragazzi, N.L., Li, Q., Tang, S.: An updated estimation of the risk of transmission of the novel coronavirus (2019-nCov). Infect. Dis. Model. **5**, 248–255 (2020)

23. Kennedy, J., Eberhart, R.C.: Particle swarm optimization. In: Proceedings of the IEEE International Conference on Neural Networks (Perth, Australia), Piscataway, NJ, pp. IV: 1942–1948. IEEE Service Center (1995)

24. Shi, Y.H., Eberhart, R.C.: A modified particle swarm optimizer. In: IEEE International Conference on Evolutionary Computation, Anchorage, Alaska (1998)

25. Eberhart, R.C., Shi, Y.H.: Comparing inertia weights and constriction factors in particle swarm optimization. In: Proceedings of the 2000 Congress on Evolutionary Computation, vol. 1, pp. 84–88 (2000)

26. Clerc, M.: The swarm and the queen: towards a deterministic and adaptive particle swarm optimization. In: Proceedings of the Conference on Evolutionary Computation, pp. 1951–1957 (1999)

27. Shi, Y.H., Eberhart, R.C.: Fuzzy adaptive particle swarm optimization. In: Proceedings of the Congress on Evolutionary Computation, Seoul, Korea (2001)

28. Cao, S., Feng, P., Shi, P.: Modified SEIR infectious disease dynamics model for Hubei Province 2019 coronavirus disease (COVID-19) outbreak prediction and assessment. J. Zhejiang Univ. (Medi. Sci.) 178–184 (2020)

29. Tang, B., et al.: Estimation of the transmission risk of the 2019-nCoV and its implication for public health interventions. J. Clin. Med. 9, 462 (2020)

Privacy Protection in Social Networks

Privacy-Enhanced Federated Learning with Weighted Aggregation

Jiale Guo[1]([⊠]), Ziyao Liu[1]([⊠]), Kwok-Yan Lam[1], Jun Zhao[1], and Yiqiang Chen[2]

[1] Nanyang Technological University, Singapore, Singapore
{jiale001,ziyao002}@e.ntu.edu.sg, {kwokyan.lam,junzhao}@ntu.edu.sg
[2] University of Chinese Academy of Sciences and Peng Cheng Laboratory,
Beijing, China
yqchen@ict.ac.cn

Abstract. The pervasive adoption of machine learning (ML) techniques by social network operators has led to a growing concern in the personal data privacy of their customers. ML inevitably accesses and processes users' personal data, which could potentially breach the relevant privacy protection regulations if not performed carefully. In this backdrop, Federated Learning (FL) is an emerging area that allows ML on distributed data without the data leaving their stored location. Typically, FL starts with an initial global model, with each datastore uses its local data to compute the gradient based on the global model, and uploads their gradients (instead of the data) to an aggregation server, at which the global model is updated and then distributed to the local datastores iteratively. However, depending on the nature of the services operated by social networks, data captured at different locations may carry different significance to the business operation, hence a weighted aggregation will be highly desirable for enhancing the quality of the FL model. Furthermore, to prevent the data leakage from aggregated gradients, cryptographic mechanisms are needed to allow secure aggregation of FL. As such, this paper proposes a privacy-enhanced FL scheme, based on cryptographic mechanisms that allow both the data significance evaluation and weighted aggregation of local models in a privacy-preserving manner. Experimental results show that our scheme is practical and secure.

Keywords: Federated learning · Secure aggregation · Data significance evaluation · Homomorphic encryption · Zero-knowledge proof

1 Introduction

Machine learning (ML) has been widely adopted by social network services in order to enhance user experiences and improve revenue opportunities by providing personalized recommendations to the social network users. On the other hand, ML inevitably accesses and processes users' personal data, which could

J. Guo and Z. Liu—Both authors contributed equally to this research.

potentially breach the relevant privacy protection regulations if not performed carefully. The situation is exacerbated by the cloud-based implementation of social network when user data are captured and stored in distributed locations, hence aggregation of the user data for ML could be a serious breach of privacy regulations. Such a scenario where multiple data stores (or custodians) jointly solve a machine learning problem while complying with privacy regulations has attracted tremendous attention from academia and industry. Privacy-preserving techniques such as differential privacy (DP), fully homomorphic encryption (FHE), and secure multi-party computation (MPC) are widely believed to be promising approaches to achieve this goal. However, it is well known that DP requires a tradeoff between data usability and privacy [1], while MPC and HE offer cryptographic privacy with high communication or computation overheads. In this backdrop, Federated Learning (FL) is an emerging area that allows ML on distributed data without the data leaving their stored location [2]. Typically, FL starts with an initial global model, with each data store (in the respective data center) uses its local data to compute the gradient based on the global model, and uploads their gradients (instead of the data) to an aggregation server, at which the global model is updated and then distributed to the local datastores iteratively.

However, depending on the nature of services operated by the social network, data captured at different locations may exhibit disparity. Hence a weighted aggregation scheme will be highly desirable for enhancing the quality of the FL-learned model. In this case, the central server is required to evaluate the significance across all local datasets in order to compute the weightings, and then aggregate all the users' locally trained models according to their weights. To calculate the weight, data significance evaluation (DSE) on data size and data quality are widely adopted. For example, in FedAvg [3], the locally trained models from users are weighted by the percentage of their data size in the total training data. Based on FedAvg, the authors in [4] further evaluate users' label quality by calculating the mutual cross-entropy between data and models of both the central server and users. Although approaches in previous works resulted in improved accuracy of the global FL model, they did not address the privacy guarantee for users' data.

Furthermore, from the angle of privacy protection, social network operators need to address the information leakage from the gradients from which one can derive the users' local training data [5]. Secure[1] aggregation schemes [6,7] aim to deal with this issue. However, during the FL process, the distributed data stores and the central server may still receive fraudulent messages due to insider frauds. For example, a dishonest participant may send fraudulent messages during DSE so as to obtain a manipulated weight. In other cases, a FL participant may upload a fraudulent model to affect the distribution of the global FL model in the current FL round in order to manipulate its weight in the next FL round [8]. Note that such an issue regarding fraudulent messages can be generalized to any FL system.

---

[1] We use the terms secure and privacy-preserving interchangeably.

In order to address the aforementioned issues, we propose a privacy-enhanced FL scheme with weighted aggregation. To summarize, our contributions are:

- We propose a general privacy-enhanced FL scheme with secure weighted aggregation, which can deal with both the data significance difference, data privacy, and dishonest participants (who send fraudulent messages to manipulate the computed weights) in FL systems.
- We give a detailed example application of our proposed scheme with performance evaluation.
- Compared to existing FL schemes, experimental results show the practicality of our proposed scheme that achieves privacy-enhanced FL with weighted aggregation while providing an additional security guarantee against fraudulent messages with an affordable 1.2 times of run time overheads and 1.3 times communication costs.

Related Works. There have been several schemes proposed to perform privacy-preserving and dropout-resilient aggregation. The main idea of these schemes is to integrate FL with privacy-preserving techniques such as DP, HE, and MPC. For example, the authors in [9] propose a DP-based FL scheme that a level of noise is added to each user's locally trained model before aggregation, which involves the trade-off between model performance and privacy. For HE-based aggregation schemes, each user's locally trained model is encrypted before uploading. Then the central server aggregates the users' model in ciphertext using HE operations and publishes the result for decryption. To deal with dropped participants, the private key is distributed among all participants [10]. Such HE-based schemes incur infeasible overhead for a large-scale FL system as the underlying threshold crypto-system involve expensive protocols. A more efficient and dropout-robust aggregation scheme is based on MPC, as proposed in [6]. In this scheme, each user's locally trained model is masked that the seeds for generating masks are secretly shared among all users using a threshold secret sharing scheme to handle the dropout users. The improved version [7] upon [6] replaces the complete communication graph in [6] with a k-regular graph to further reduce the communication overheads. Another variant TurboAgg [11] divides users into multiple groups and follows a multi-group circular structure for communication. NIKE [12] adopts a non-interactive key exchange protocol relying on non-colluding servers. Nevertheless, all of the schemes mentioned above focus on achieving FL from a privacy-preserving perspective, issues still exist that both the central server and users may send fraudulent messages to each other.

Organisation of the Paper. The rest of the paper is organized as follows. In Sect. 2, we introduce the preliminaries and supporting protocols. In Sect. 3, we describe the rationales for our proposed scheme together with a high-level overview, and the threat model. Then we describe a detailed example of the application of our proposed scheme, and discuss its privacy and security in Sect. 4. Experimental results are presented in Sect. 5 followed by the conclusions in Sect. 6.

2   Preliminaries and Supporting Protocols

This section briefly describes the preliminaries of data significance evaluation, secure aggregation, and related cryptographic protocols used in this work. The participants in our system are divided into two classes: a server S and K users[2] $\mathcal{U} = \{u_1, u_2, \ldots, u_K\}$ that each user $u_i \in \mathcal{U}$ holds a local dataset $\mathcal{D}_i = \{(x_i^j, y_i^j) | j = 1, \ldots, n_i\}$ with size n_i, where x_i^j and y_i^j are the j-th sample and corresponding label in $\mathcal{D}_i$ respectively.

2.1   Data Significance Evaluation

Data significance evaluation scheme is essential for weighted aggregation of users' models in FL. In this work, we adapt the label quality evaluation scheme proposed in [4] to illustrate how to construct an interactive evaluation scheme in a privacy-preserving manner. Note that this scheme can be generalized to any data significance evaluation scheme for federated learning.

By maintaining a small set of benchmark dataset $\mathcal{D}_s$, the central server S is allowed to quantify the credibility C_i of each local dataset $\mathcal{D}_i$ by computing the mutual cross-entropy E_i. In specific, E_i evaluates both the performance of the global model $\mathcal{M}$ on the local dataset $\mathcal{D}_i$, i.e., LL_i, and the performance of the local model of the user $\mathcal{M}_i$ on the benchmark dataset $\mathcal{D}_s$, i.e., LS_i, which is given by:

$$E_i = LS_i + LL_i$$

$$LS_i = - \sum_{(x_s, y_s) \in \mathcal{D}_s} y_s \log P(y \mid x_s; \mathcal{M}_i)$$

$$LL_i = - \sum_{(x_u, y_u) \in \mathcal{D}_i} y_u \log P(y \mid x_u; \mathcal{M})$$

Then the weight of user i's model can be defined as: $w_i = \frac{n_i C_i}{\sum_{j=1}^{K} n_j C_j}$ where $C_i = 1 - \frac{e^{\alpha E_i}}{\sum_{j=1}^{K} e^{\alpha E_j}}$. Here α is a hyper-parameter for normalization. These weights can be used in subsequent weighted aggregation to obtain the new global model as $\sum_{i=1}^{K} w_i \mathcal{M}_i$.

2.2   Secure Aggregation

Assume there is a set of client $\mathcal{U}$, and let each client $u \in \mathcal{U}$ holds a vector $\boldsymbol{x}_u$, Secure aggregation scheme [6,7] enables a server S to calculate a sum $z = \sum \boldsymbol{x}_u$ while preserving the privacy of $\boldsymbol{x}_u$. In secure aggregation scheme, a pairwise additive mask is added to $\boldsymbol{x}_u$ (assume a total order on clients) and the client u uploads $\boldsymbol{y}_u$ to the central server instead of $\boldsymbol{x}_u$, i.e. $\boldsymbol{y}_u = \boldsymbol{x}_u + \sum_{u<v} \text{PRG}(\boldsymbol{s}_{u,v}) - \sum_{u>v} \text{PRG}(\boldsymbol{s}_{v,u})$. Here pseudorandom generator (PRG) is able to generate a sequence of random numbers using the seed $\boldsymbol{s}_{u,v}$ which is agreed between client

---

[2] We use the terms user and client interchangeably.

u and client v. It is straightforward to observe that when aggregating all the $\boldsymbol{x}_u$, the masks will be canceled such that

$$z = \sum_{u \in \mathcal{U}} \boldsymbol{y}_u = \sum_{u \in \mathcal{U}} \left(\boldsymbol{x}_u + \sum_{u<v} \mathrm{PRG}(\boldsymbol{s}_{u,v}) - \sum_{u>v} \mathrm{PRG}(\boldsymbol{s}_{v,u}) \right) = \sum_{u \in \mathcal{U}} \boldsymbol{x}_u$$

Furthermore, the seeds are shared among the clients using standard Shamir secret sharing (n,t) scheme [13] to handle dropout clients. Specifically, we omit some details and summarize the illustrative secure aggregation protocol $z \leftarrow \pi_{SecAgg}(\mathcal{U}, \{\mathcal{M}_i\}, t)$ as follows.

Mask Generation $(\{R_i\}_{u_i \in \mathcal{U}_1}, \mathcal{U}_1) \leftarrow \pi_{MG}(t, \mathcal{U})$. Each user $u_i \in \mathcal{U}$ generates a random matrix R to mask the local model $\mathcal{M}$. The set of alive users after mask generation is denoted as $\mathcal{U}_1$.

Masked Model Aggregation $(y, \mathcal{U}_2) \leftarrow \pi_{MMA}(\{\mathcal{M}\}_{u \in \mathcal{U}_1}, \{R_i\}_{u_i \in \mathcal{U}_1}, \mathcal{U}_1, t)$. Each user $u_i \in \mathcal{U}_1$ computes its masked model $y_u = \mathcal{M} + R$ and uploads it to the server. Then the server collects all masked models from the set of alive users, denoted as $\mathcal{U}_2 \subseteq \mathcal{U}_1$, and computes the sum $y = \sum_{u \in \mathcal{U}_2} y_u$.

Model Aggregation Recovery $z \leftarrow \pi_{MAR}(y, \mathcal{U}_1, \mathcal{U}_2, t)$. The users $u_i \in \mathcal{U}_2$ send information according to $\mathcal{U}_2 \setminus \mathcal{U}_1$ to the server to recover the masks of dropout users $u \in \mathcal{U}_2 \setminus \mathcal{U}_1$. Then the server can compute the sum of models of the alive users $z = \sum_{u_i \in \mathcal{U}_2} \mathcal{M}$.

2.3 Cryptographic Tools

We now introduce the cryptographic tools used in our proposed scheme.

Homomorphic Encryption. A homomorphic crypto-system is a form of encryption scheme that allows computation to be performed on encrypted data directly. It can be denoted as a tuple of algorithms, i.e. $\mathsf{HE} = (\mathsf{KeyGen}, \mathsf{Enc}, \mathsf{Dec})$, where KeyGen is a key generation algorithm, Enc and Dec are used for encryption and decryption, respectively.

In this paper, we adopt Paillier [14] crypto-system which consistsof following algorithms:

- $\mathsf{HE.KeyGen}(p, q)$: For large primes p and q that $gcd(pq, (p-1)(q-1)) = 1$, compute $n = p \cdot q$ and $\lambda = lcm(p-1, q-1)$. Then, select a random integer $g \in \mathbb{Z}_{n^2}^*$ that ensure $gcd(n, L(g^\lambda \bmod n^2)) = 1$, where function L is defined as $L(x) = \frac{x-1}{n}$ and $\lambda = \varphi(n)$. Finally, output a key pair (sk, pk) where the public key is $pk = (n, g)$ and the private key is $sk = (p, q)$.
- $\mathsf{HE.Enc}(pk, m, r)$: For message $m \in \mathbb{Z}_N$, taking the public key pk and a random number $r \in \mathbb{Z}_N^*$, output a ciphertext $c = \mathsf{Enc}(m) = g^m r^n \pmod{n^2}$.
- $\mathsf{HE.Dec}(sk, c)$: For a ciphertext $c < n^2$, taking private key sk, output the plaintext message $m = \mathsf{Dec}(c) = \frac{L(c^\lambda (\bmod\ n^2))}{L(g^\lambda (\bmod n^2))}$.

Paillier supports two types of operations over ciphertext: (i) homomorphic addition between two ciphertext such that $\mathsf{Enc}(m_1) \cdot \mathsf{Enc}(m_2)(\bmod\ n^2) = \mathsf{Enc}(m_1 + m_2\ (\bmod\ n^2))$, and (ii) homomorphic multiplication between a plaintext and a ciphertext such that $(\mathsf{Enc}(m_1))^{m_2}\ (\bmod\ n^2) = \mathsf{Enc}(m_1 m_2\ (\bmod\ n))$. For simplicity, we sometimes abuse the notation Enc and Dec instead of $\mathsf{HE.Enc}(pk, m,\ r)$ and $\mathsf{HE.Dec}(sk, c)$ when the context is clear. Note that we denote $\boxplus$ with the homomorphic addition between two ciphertexts, and $\boxtimes$ with the homomorphic multiplication between a ciphertext and a plaintext. In addition, Paillier crypto-system provides semantic security against chosen-plaintext attacks (IND-CPA) such that an adversary will be unable to distinguish pairs of ciphertexts based on the message they encrypt [14].

Zero Knowledge Proof of Plaintext Knowledge. A zero-knowledge proof of plaintext knowledge (ZKPoPK) algorithm enables a prover to prove the knowledge of a plaintext m of some ciphertext $C = Enc(m)$ to a verifier in a given public encryption scheme, without revealing anything about message m. Pailler provides the algorithm PZKPoPKoZ as given in Algorithm 1 for ZKPoPK of Zero. As such, the prover with a key pair (pk, sk) can prove the knowledge of zero of a ciphertext $u = \mathsf{HE.Enc}(pk, 0, v) \in \mathbb{Z}_{n^2}$ to the honest verifier. The correctness and security proof of Algorithm 1 can be found in [15].

Algorithm 1. Paillier-based ZKPoPK of Zero $b \leftarrow \mathsf{PZKPoPKoZ}(n, u, pk, sk, v)$

Public input: n, u, pk.
Private input of the prover: $sk, v \in \mathbb{Z}_n^*$, such that $u = \mathsf{HE.Enc}(pk, 0, v)$.
Output: β

1: The prover randomly chooses $r \in \mathbb{Z}_n^*$ and sends $a = \mathsf{HE.Enc}(pk, 0, r)$ to the verifier.
2: The verifier chooses a random e and sends it to the prover.
3: The prover sends $z = rv^e \bmod n$ to the verifier.
4: The verifier checks that u, a, z are prime to n and that $\mathsf{HE.Enc}(pk, 0, z) = au^e \bmod n^2$. If and only if these requirements satisfy, output $\beta = 1$; otherwise, output $\beta = 0$.

---

3   Proposed Scheme

To evaluate the quality of each user's locally trained model hence the data significance, the standard method is to have the central server keeping a benchmark dataset and having the access to users' models and datasets, which enables computing the weights using some evaluation algorithms [7]. However, a privacy-preserving FL requires that both the user's data and locally trained models cannot be learned by any other participant. As such, the intuitive method is to have the server evaluating the weight using HE based on the encrypted dataset and model of the user. After that, the server and users can jointly aggregate the weighted model using secure aggregation protocol.

In this case, the FL scheme inevitably involves the interaction between the user and the server where participants may send fraudulent messages to manipulate the computed weight. Recall that the user can (i) publish the fraudulent weight (as we use HE for privately computing the weight, thus the decryption is on the user-side, we will explain this in detail later), and (ii) upload the fraudulent locally trained model. Therefore, a verification protocol is needed to guarantee the correctness of both computed weights and users' locally trained models. Our security definition follows the Universal Composability (UC) framework [16]. Active malicious participants can send fraudulent messages. Besides, we assume authenticated channels and signature schemes to ensure the confidentiality and integrity of messages sent by participants.

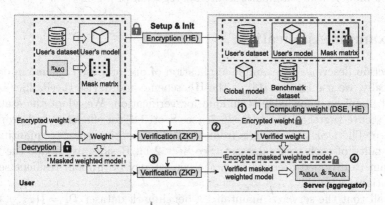

Fig. 1. Privacy-enhanced federated learning scheme with weighted aggregation.

High-Level Overview. As shown in Fig. 1, before proceeding to computing the weight, each user u_i uploads its encrypted dataset $Enc(\mathcal{D}_i)$, encrypted locally trained model $Enc(\mathcal{M}_i)$, and encrypted mask matrix $Enc(R_i)$ to the server S. Note that the encrypted datasets are uploaded only once at the very beginning of FL. After that, the server S calculates the weight $Enc(w_i)$ following a DSE algorithm for each user u_i using HE operations based on the received encrypted dataset $Enc(\mathcal{D}_i)$, encrypted model $Enc(\mathcal{M}_i)$ from each user u_i, public global FL model $\mathcal{M}$, and benchmark dataset $\mathcal{D}_s$. Then the server S sends encrypted weight $Enc(w_i)$ to the user u_i and the user decrypts the weight and publishes w_i to the all participants. Note that the user holds the private key, and the decryption of weight is on the user-side. Thus, the user may perform fraudulent decryption of the weight. ZKP is adopted here to guarantee the correctness.

However, the user may still upload fraudulent masked weighted model $w_i\mathcal{M}_i + R_i$ to the server for its benefit. Addressing such issue is not trivial as the solution may involve complicated incentive mechanisms. Luckily, since the real encrypted user's model $Enc(\mathcal{M}_i)$ and encrypted mask $Enc(R_i)$ have already been uploaded to the server at the very beginning, and the verified (real) weight of each user is public, the ZKP technique can be adopted here to guarantee the correctness. In specific, the server can obtain the real masked weighted model in ciphertext by computing $w_i \mathsf{Enc}(\mathcal{M}_i) + \mathsf{Enc}(R_i)$ using HE operations, and then asks the user to upload its weighted model $w_i \mathcal{M}_i + R_i$ for aggregation. In this case, by having both the plaintext and ciphertext of the masked weighted model, the server can require each user to prove the plaintext knowledge of its masked weighted model. Note that as the scheme requires users to upload the encrypted model $\mathsf{Enc}(\mathcal{M}_i)$ and encrypted mask matrix $\mathsf{Enc}(R_i)$ at the very beginning of each round of FL, the users will not deviate from the protocol as they do not know how to design $\mathcal{M}_i$ or R_i to manipulate their weights for benefits without knowing the information of their weights and locally trained models in the current round [8]. After that, the server and users can jointly aggregate the verified weighted models using standard secure aggregation protocol.

4   Example Application

This section describes an example application of our proposed scheme in detail. Specifically, we use Paillier [14] as the HE scheme and devise the Paillier based ZKP of plaintext knowledge technique for verification. We adopt the state-of-the-art secure aggregation scheme [6,7] (see Sect. 2.2) for efficiency and dropout-resilience. The DSE algorithm is from [4] that allows the server to quantify the label quality of each user's dataset (See Sect. 2.1). Besides, we adapt the DSE algorithm to dropped users to keep the consistency of dropout-resilient secure aggregation protocol.

Recall that the server S maintains a benchmark dataset $\mathcal{D}_s = \{(x_s, y_s)|s = 1, 2, \ldots, n_s\}$ and a global FL model $\mathcal{M}$, and the user u_i holds a local dataset $\mathcal{D}_i = \{(x_u, y_u)|u = 1, 2, \ldots, n_i\}$ and a locally trained model $\mathcal{M}_i$ as well as a Paillier key pair (sk_i, pk_i). Before proceeding to the data significance evaluation (computing the weight), each user u_i uses its pk_i to encrypt its dataset and locally trained model as $\mathsf{Enc}(\mathcal{D}_i) = \{(\mathsf{Enc}(x_u), \mathsf{Enc}(y_u))| u = 1, 2, \ldots, n_i\}$ and $\mathsf{Enc}(\mathcal{M}_i)$ respectively, and uploads them to the server. After that, the server is able to compute the weight using HE operations.

4.1   Data Significance Evaluation

The privacy-preserving data significance evaluation works as follows (see Sect. 2.1 for the version over plaintext). First, the server computes and sends the mutual cross entropy E_i in ciphertext $\mathsf{Enc}(E_i)$ to the user i as:

$$\mathsf{Enc}(E_i) = \mathsf{Enc}(LS_i) \boxplus \mathsf{Enc}(LL_i) \tag{1}$$

$$\mathsf{Enc}(LS_i) = -\sum\nolimits_{(x_s, y_s) \in \mathcal{D}_s} y_s \boxtimes \log P\left(y \mid x_s; \mathsf{Enc}(\mathcal{M}_i)\right) \tag{2}$$

$$\mathsf{Enc}(LL_i) = -\sum\nolimits_{(x_u, y_u) \in \mathcal{D}_i} \mathsf{Enc}(y_u) \boxtimes \log P\left(y \mid \mathsf{Enc}(x_u); \mathcal{M}_s\right) \tag{3}$$

Note that the computation of LS_i and LL_i involves calculating non-linear functions which cannot be directly evaluated using HE operations. A common method to address this issue is to replace these non-linear functions with polynomials. For instance, for logistic regression model $l = \sigma(\boldsymbol{\theta} \cdot \boldsymbol{x})$ where θ is the hyper-parameter and σ is the sigmoid function $\sigma(x) = \frac{1}{1+e^{-x}}$, in terms of a good tradeoff between efficiency and accuracy, the sigmoid function can be approximated by a cubic polynomial $\sigma(x) = s_0 + s_1 x + s_2 x^2 + s_3 x^3$, and thus the y in Eq. 2 and 3 can be calculated by $y = \sigma(l) = s_0 + s_1 l + s_2 l^2 + s_3 l^3$. Since in our scheme, either one of $\boldsymbol{\theta}$ and $\boldsymbol{x}$ is in ciphertext, the server can only obtain $\mathsf{Enc}(l)$, which means that the n-th power of l cannot be calculated using Paillier as it does not support multiplication of ciphertext. Therefore, one more round of communication is needed to compute y. Specifically, the server chooses a random value $r \in 2^\kappa$ to mask l as $z = l + r$ where κ is the security parameter, and sends $\mathsf{Enc}(z) = \mathsf{Enc}(l) \boxplus \mathsf{Enc}(r)$ to the user. Then the user decrypts $\mathsf{Enc}(z)$, computes $\mathsf{Enc}(z^2)$ and $\mathsf{Enc}(\sigma(z))$ from z and sends $(\mathsf{Enc}(z^2), \mathsf{Enc}(\sigma(z)))$ to the server. Since $y = \sigma(l) = \sigma(z - r) = \sigma(z) - \sigma(r) + (s_0 + 3s_3 r^3) - 3s_3 r z^2 - (2s_2 r - 3s_3 r^2) l$, the $\mathsf{Enc}(y)$ can be calculated by

$$
\begin{aligned}
\mathsf{Enc}(y) = \mathsf{Enc}(\sigma(z)) &\boxplus \mathsf{Enc}(-r) \boxplus \mathsf{Enc}(s_0 + 3s_3 r^3) \\
&\boxplus ((-3s_3 r)\mathsf{Enc}(z^2)) \boxplus ((-2s_2 r + 3s_3 r^2)\mathsf{Enc}(l)).
\end{aligned}
\tag{4}
$$

Note that since $l = \boldsymbol{\theta} \cdot \boldsymbol{x}$ is masked by r, the user has no information of how to design fraudulent $(\mathsf{Enc}(z^2), \mathsf{Enc}(\sigma(z)))$ for its benefit. In addition, there is a difference between the computation of $\mathsf{Enc}(LS_i)$ and $\mathsf{Enc}(LL_i)$ as the former involves multiplication of plaintext while the latter involves multiplication of ciphertext. This means that Eq. 2 can be directly evaluated using Paillier and Eq. 3 needs one more round for computation. Specifically, let $\mathsf{Enc}(h) = \log P(y \mid \mathsf{Enc}(x_u); \mathcal{M}^s)$ in Eq. 3, the server first sends $\mathsf{Enc}(h)$ to the user for decryption. To protect h which may leak information of x against the server, the user decrypts $\mathsf{Enc}(h)$ and masks h using a randomly chosen value r then sends $h + r$ to the server. Following that, the server computes $\mathsf{Enc}(y_u h + y_u r) = \mathsf{Enc}(y_u) \boxtimes (h + r)$. Assume that $\mathsf{Enc}(y_u r)$ has been uploaded to the server, the server is able to compute $\mathsf{Enc}(y_u h) = \mathsf{Enc}(y_u h + y_u r) \boxplus \mathsf{Enc}(-y_u r)$. Note that r is secure even if the server holds $\mathsf{Enc}(y_u)$ and $\mathsf{Enc}(y_u r)$. Such security is provided by the IND-CPA property of Paillier. In addition, for computing the cross-entropy after sigmod function, we can further simplify the polynomial replacement of their combined function using the similar above mentioned method.

After that, each user i decrypts $\mathsf{Enc}(E_i)$ and publishes E_i. Finally, all participants can compute the credibility C_i and weight w_i for each user i following:

$$
w_i = \frac{n_i C_i}{\sum_{k=1}^{K} n_k C_k} = \frac{n_i e^{\alpha RE_i}}{\sum_k n_k e^{\alpha RE_k}}, \text{ such that } \sum_i w_i = 1
\tag{5}
$$

where $C_i = \frac{e^{\alpha RE_i}}{\sum_k e^{\alpha RE_k}}$, $RE_i = \frac{1}{E_i}$. Here Eq. 5 is the adapted version of that in [4] in order to handle dropped users by simply adjusting the denominator of w_i in Eq. 5 on server-side during subsequent weighted aggregation (see Sect. 4.2).

As discussed in Sect. 3, since the user i may deviate from the protocol by publishing fraudulent decryption of E_i, a verification scheme is needed to guarantee the correct decryption of E_i on the user-side. To address this issue, we construct a variant of the ZKPoPK of Zero algorithm given in Sect. 2.3 to enable a user u_i with a key pair (pk_i, sk_i) to convince the server S the fact that a message m is the correct decryption of ciphertext c. To do so, given the message m, the server can compute $c' = c - \mathsf{Enc}(m)$ and then requires the user to prove the knowledge of zero of the ciphertext c' following Algorithm 1. The detail of this algorithm is given in Algorithm 2.

Assume that the server receives a message E_i' which is the decryption of $\mathsf{Enc}(E_i)$ from the user u_i. Following Algorithm 2, the server S and the user u_i get $\beta \leftarrow \mathsf{PPoPK}(\mathsf{Enc}(E_i), E_i', pk_i, sk_i)$. The server accepts E_i' as the plaintext of $\mathsf{Enc}(E_i)$ if and only if $\beta = 1$, which means the user u_i honestly decrypts $\mathsf{Enc}(E_i)$. Otherwise, the server refuses the message E_i' and removes the user u_i from the user set for aggregation. Similar approach can be adopted to guarantee the correct decryption of h.

Algorithm 2. Paillier-based PoPK $\beta \leftarrow \mathsf{PPoPK}(c, m, pk_i, sk_i)$

Public input: $c, m, pk_i = (n, g)$.
Private input for the user u_i: $sk_i = (p, q)$
Output: β

1: The server randomly chooses $r_s \in \mathbb{Z}_n^*$, and computes $c' = c - \mathsf{HE.Enc}(pk_i, m, r_s)(\mathrm{mod}\, n^2)$. The server sends c' to the user.
2: The user computes $r' = c'^d \bmod n$, where $d = n^{-1} \bmod \varphi(n)$.
3: The server and the user jointly follow Algorithm 1 to get $\beta \leftarrow \mathsf{PZKPoPKoZ}(n, c', pk_i, sk_i, r')$.

The correctness is proved as follows. If the message m provided by the user is the decryption of c, $c' = c - \mathsf{HE.Enc}(pk_i, m, r_s)(\bmod n^2)$ should be the ciphertext of zero with respect to r' that $c' \bmod n^2 = (c')^{n \cdot d} \bmod n^2 = (r')^n \bmod n^2 = \mathsf{HE.Enc}(pk_i, 0, r')$. Therefore, the output β of the algorithm PZKPoPKoZ in step 3 is 1. Similarly, if m is not the decryption of c, the algorithm PZKPoPKoZ outputs $\beta = 0$.

Theorem 1 (Security against malicious users). *The Paillier-based Proof of Plaintext Knowledge is secure against malicious users. If there exists a probabilistic polynomial time (PPT) adversary $\mathcal{A}$ with Paillier key pair (sk, pk) providing a fraudulent plaintext m' as the decryption of c that $\mathsf{HE.Dec}(sk, c) \neq m'$. The probability of the server accepting the fraudulent decryption $\Pr[1 \leftarrow \mathsf{PPoPK}_{\mathcal{A}}(c, m', pk, sk)] \leqslant 2^{-k/2}$ where k is the bit length of n as the Paillier public key.*

Proof. Assume that a PPT adversary $\mathcal{A}$ with key pair (sk, pk) provides a fraudulent decryption m' of a ciphertext c, while $\mathsf{HE.Dec}(sk, c) = m$ and $m \neq m'$, the server accepts m' only if $1 \leftarrow \mathsf{PPoPK}(c, m', pk, sk)$. Given the Algorithm 2, the server randomly chooses $r_s \in \mathbb{Z}_n^*$ to compute $c' = c - \mathsf{HE.Enc}(pk_i, m', r_s)(\bmod n^2) = \mathsf{Enc}(m - m')$ and sends c' to the adversary

$\mathcal{A}$. To make the server accept m', the adversary $\mathcal{A}$ has to prove that c' is a ciphertext of zero. Therefore, the security of PPoPK follows from the security of PZKPoPKoZ such that the probability of the adversary make the server accept the fraudulent decryption m' is less than $2^{-k/2}$ where k is the bit length of n as the Paillier public key.

4.2 Weighted Aggregation

After obtained the verified weights, we can proceed to the weighted aggregation where the server can securely aggregate user's locally trained models to update the global FL model $\mathcal{M}$ according to their corresponding weights w, i.e. $\mathcal{M} = \sum_{u_i \in \mathcal{U}'} w_i \mathcal{M}_i$ such that $\sum_{u_i \in \mathcal{U}'} w_i = 1$, where w_i and $\mathcal{M}_i$ are the weight and local model of user u_i, and $\mathcal{U}'$ is the selected user set in the current round of FL.

Let the numerator of w_i in Eq. 5 be $\omega_i = n_i e^{\alpha RE_i}$, we can rewrite Eq. 5:

$$\mathcal{M} = \frac{1}{\sum_{u_j \in \mathcal{U}'} n_j e^{\alpha RE_j}} \sum_{u_i \in \mathcal{U}'} \omega_i \mathcal{M}_i \qquad (6)$$

Therefore, the server can deal with dropped users by adjusting $\mathcal{U}'$ and aggregates the models from alive users.

To prevent users from uploading fraudulent weighted models to the server, as we discussed in Sect. 3, the server first computes

$$\mathsf{Enc}(y_i) = \omega_i \boxtimes \mathsf{Enc}(\mathcal{M}_i) \boxplus \mathsf{Enc}(R_i) \qquad (7)$$

Then the server can verify if the user uploads its real masked weighted model relying on the Algorithm 2 with zero knowledge by checking the equality between y_i and uploaded masked weighted model y_i'.

Note that the $\mathsf{Enc}(R_i)$ should be uploaded at the very beginning of each FL round according to the analysis in Sect. 3 to prevent the user from manipulating R_i for their benefits. Besides, since verified weight ω_i is a public value and $\mathsf{Enc}(\mathcal{M}_i)$ has been uploaded during data significance evaluation, the server can calculate y_i' using Pallier HE operations. The detailed description of this example of our proposed scheme for one FL round is given in Protocol 4.1. Note that the **Setup** step is only performed once at the very beginning of federated learning. Step 0 to step 4 are performed in every FL round.

4.3 Discussion on Privacy and Security

First, we give the discussion from the angle of privacy protection. Since both the user's dataset $\mathcal{D}_i$ and locally trained model $\mathcal{M}_i$ are encrypted in step Setup and step 1, then uploaded to the server, the server learns nothing from the ciphertext. After that, during computing the weight in step 1, HE operations are applied, and thus additions between ciphertexts do not leak any information. For computing a polynomial $f(l)$ which consists of multiplication between ciphertexts where the server keeps $\mathsf{Enc}(l)$, a trick is adopted as described in Sect. 2.1. The main idea is to use a random r to mask l to enable the computation $f(l + r)$ over plaintext, then deduct the redundant terms of $f(l + r)$ to obtain the encryption of $f(l)$ using HE. The security of the trick is based on that the user does not know the value of r. The privacy of the public masked weighted model $w_i \mathcal{M}_i + R_i$ in step 3 and step 4 is protected by the mask R_i randomly chosen by the user u_i. Therefore, there is no information leakage of both user's dataset and model during the execution of our proposed protocol.

Next, we discuss from the angle of security against fraudulent messages. Since the server has the encryption of the real user's model y_i, real mutual cross-entropy E_i, and real mask R_i after step setup, step 0, and step 1, while zero-knowledge proof is adopted in step 2 to ensure the correct decryption of E_i, both the server and user can compute real w_i, hence the encryption of real masked weighted model $w_i \mathcal{M}_i + R_i$, which can be used for the zero-knowledge proof in step 3. Therefore, our scheme guarantees security against fraudulent messages regarding both the users' datesets, models, and the computed weights.

5   Performance Analysis

System Setting. Our prototype is tested over two Linux workstations with an Intel Xeon E5-2603v4 CPU (1.70 GHz) and 64 GB of RAM, running CentOS 7 in the same region. The average latency of the network is 0.207 ms, and the average bandwidth is 1.25 GB/s. The central server runs in multi-thread on one workstation, while the users are running in parallel in the other workstation. In our experiments, the ring size N for Paillier is set to be a 1024-bit integer, and the security parameter κ is set to be 80. We use AES-GCM with 128-bit keys for authenticated channels, and adopt SecAgg+ scheme [7] for dropout-resilient aggregation. The performance is evaluated on several datasets from UCI repository from which each user randomly chooses samples of the same size to construct its local dataset. The details are given in Table 1.

As seen in Fig. 2, the accuracy of the global FL model before and after using our scheme shows a consistent tolerance of fraudulent messages. We can observe that sending fraudulent weights (assign $E_i = 1$) results in much fewer effects than sending fraudulent models. This indicates the difficulty of detecting fraudulent weights and the significant adverse impact of sending fraudulent models, hence the necessity of our proposed scheme. In addition, Fig. 3 shows the convergence performance when fraudulent messages exist in the FL system with and without our scheme. We should note that the tolerance of fraudulent messages on the performance of the FL model varies from datasets and models.

We also evaluate the scalability of our proposed scheme with respect to the number of parties and dropout rate, compared to the model aggregation counterpart of SecAgg [6] and the improved version SecAgg+ [7]. Note that we treat the users who do not pass PoKE and PoKM as dropout users as demonstrated in Protocol 4.1. In specific, we consider the "worst-case" dropout scenario where the users drop out during PoKE in the first phase as the server has already completed the calculation of the weights, or PoKM in the second phase as the users have already uploaded their weighted models. In Table 2, we can observe

---

Protocol: Secure Weighted Aggregation

Private inputs: Each user u_i has a dataset $\mathcal{D}_i$, a locally trained model $\mathcal{M}_i$, and a Paillier key pair (sk_i, pk_i). Sever has a benchmark dataset $\mathcal{D}_s$.
Public inputs: Each user u_i's Paillier public key pk_i. The global FL model $\mathcal{M}$, the selected user set $\mathcal{U}' \subseteq \mathcal{U}$, and a threshold t for Shamir secret sharing scheme.
Outputs: The weighted aggregation of all local models from the alive users $\sum_i w_i \mathcal{M}_i$.

- **Setup - Uploading Encrypted Dataset (performed only once):**
  User u_i:
  1. Uses pk_i to encrypt and send $\mathsf{Enc}(\mathcal{D}_i) = \{(\mathsf{Enc}(x_u), \mathsf{Enc}(y_u))\}$ to the server.
  Server:
  1. Receives $\mathsf{Enc}(\mathcal{D}_i)$ from user $u_i \in \mathcal{U}$.
- **Step init - Initialization (Init) :**
  User u_i:
  1. Computes the matrix R_i according to π_{MG}, such that $(\{R_i\}_{u_i \in \mathcal{U}_1}, \mathcal{U}_1) \leftarrow \pi_{MG}(t, \mathcal{U})$, where the output $\mathcal{U}_1$ is the set of alive users.
  2. Uses the local dataset $\mathcal{D}_i$ to train the local model $\mathcal{M}_i$.
  3. Encrypts R_i, $\mathcal{M}_i$, and then sends $\{\mathsf{Enc}(R_i), \mathsf{Enc}(\mathcal{M}_i)\}$ to the server.
  Server:
  1. Collects $\{\mathsf{Enc}(R_i), \mathsf{Enc}(\mathcal{M}_i)\}$ from the set of alive users denoted as $\mathcal{U}_2 \subseteq \mathcal{U}_1$.
- **Step 1 - Computing Mutual Cross-entropy (CompE) :**
  Server:
  1. For each user $u_i \in \mathcal{U}_2$, computes the mutual cross-entropy $\mathsf{Enc}(E_i)$ of the user u_i based on Eq. 1, 2 and 3, and then sents it to user u_i.
- **Step 2 - Proof of Knowledge of Mutual Cross-entropy (PoKE) :**
  1. The user u_i decrypts $\mathsf{Enc}(E_i)$ to get E'_i and sends it to the server.
  2. Computes $\beta_E \leftarrow \mathsf{PPoPK}(\mathsf{Enc}(E_i), E'_i, pk_i, sk_i)$ following Alg. 2.
  3. If $\beta_E = 0$, the server removes u_i from $\mathcal{U}_2$. Denote the rest of alive users as $\mathcal{U}_3$. Else both the user u_i and the server compute ω_i in Eq. 6.
- **Step 3 - Proof of Knowledge of Masked Weighted Model (PoKM) :**
  User u_i:
  1. Uploads $\underline{y'_i = w_i \mathcal{M}_i + R_i}$ to the server.
  Server:
  1. Receives y'_i from the set of current alive users denoted as $\mathcal{U}_4$. For each user $u_i \in \mathcal{U}_4$, computes $\mathsf{Enc}(y_i) = \omega_i \boxtimes \mathsf{Enc}(\mathcal{M}_i) \boxplus \mathsf{Enc}(R_i)$ according to Eq. 7.
  2. Computes $\beta_M \leftarrow \mathsf{PPoPK}(\mathsf{Enc}(y_i), y'_i, pk_i, sk_i)$ following Alg. 2
  3. If $\beta_M = 0$, the server removes u_i from $\mathcal{U}_4$, denote the rest of alive users as $\mathcal{U}_5$.
  4. Computes the aggregation of masked weighted models such that $y = \sum_{u_i \in \mathcal{U}_5} y_{u_i}$ following π_{MMA} protocol.
- **Step 4 - Weighted Aggregation (WAgg) :**
  Server:
  1. Publishes the alive user set $\mathcal{U}_5$, and cooperates with clients $u_i \in \mathcal{U}_5$ to jointly compute and output the final weighted aggregation $\mathcal{M}$ according to the protocol π_{MAR}, such that $\mathcal{M} \leftarrow \pi_{MAR}(y, \mathcal{U}_1, \mathcal{U}_5, t)$.

Protocol 4.1. Detailed description of proposed privacy-enhanced FL scheme. The participants may deviate from the protocol in the underlined operations.

that dropout users cause a significant increasement in the total run time because of the high cost of dealing with dropout users in the underlying secure aggregation scheme. As shown in Fig. 4, the experimental results show that our scheme provides an additional security guarantee against fraudulent messages with affordable overheads compared to the previous works. In particular, our scheme achieves around 1.2 times in run time and 1.3 times in communication cost upon the state-of-the-art secure aggregation scheme SecAgg+, which indicates the practicality of our scheme.

Table 1. Datasets used in our experiments. The number of clients is fixed to 100.

Dataset	#Attributes	#total samples	#Training samples per client	#Sample of benchmark dataset
ADULT [17]	14	48842	200	15060
CREDIT [18]	24	30000	240	10000
BK [19]	17	45211	350	9042
RFID-AC [20]	6	75128	400	10497

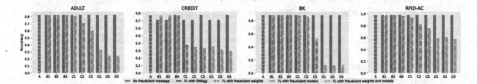

Fig. 2. FL performance over different fraudulent messages. Note that the meaning of x-axis labels are A: no fraudulent message; B1, B2, B3: the fraction of clients sending fraudulent weights 10%, 20%, 30% (similar setting of SecAgg [6]); C1, C2, C3: the fraction of clients sending fraudulent models 10%, 20%, 30%; D1, D2, D3: the fraction of clients sending both fraudulent weights and models 10%, 20%, 30%.

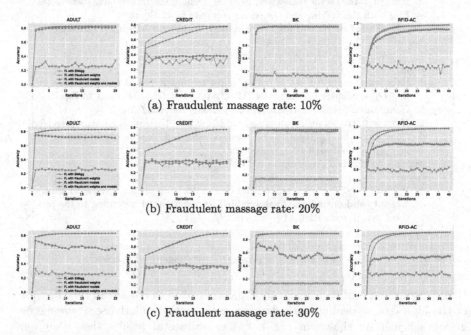

(a) Fraudulent massage rate: 10%

(b) Fraudulent massage rate: 20%

(c) Fraudulent massage rate: 30%

Fig. 3. The convergence performance of FL with different fraudulent message rate. The number of clients is fixed to 100.

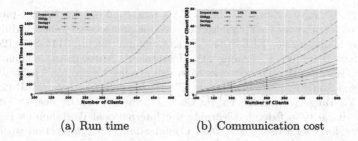

(a) Run time   (b) Communication cost

Fig. 4. The performance of our proposed scheme SWAgg compared with SecAgg [6] and SecAgg+ [7] with different dropout rate.

Table 2. The run time (s)/communication costs (MB) of the user (each) and the server (with all users) for each step of our proposed scheme in one FL round. The number of users is set to be 500. R_1 and R_2 are the fractions of dropout users in PoKE and PoKM, respectively.

	R_1	R_2	Init	ComE	PoKE	PoKM	WAgg	Total
User	0	0	0.93/0.48	5.65/1.02	0.01/0.01	0.02/0.01	0.04/0.02	6.65/1.54
Server	0	0	1.22/240	10.97/512	0.04/3	0.13/6	67.31/10	79.67/771
Server	10%	0	1.24/240	10.92/513	0.04/3	0.12/6	173.27/11	185.59/773
Server	0	10%	1.24/240	10.92/513	0.04/4	0.13/5	172.80/12	185.13/774
Server	5%	5%	1.24/240	10.95/513	0.04/3	0.12/5	172.16/13	184.51/774
Server	30%	0	1.23/241	10.92/512	0.04/3	0.10/4	351.78/14	364.07/774
Server	0	30%	1.24/240	10.95/512	0.04/4	0.12/4	354.40/15	366.75/775
Server	15%	15%	1.23/240	10.92/513	0.04/3	0.11/3	349.07/15	361.37/775

6   Conclusion

In this paper, we proposed a privacy-enhanced FL scheme for supporting secure weighted aggregation. Our scheme is able to deal with both data disparity, data privacy, and dishonest participants (who send fraudulent messages to manipulate the computed weights) in FL systems. Experimental results show that our scheme is practical and secure. Compared to existing FL approaches, our scheme achieves secure weighted aggregation with an additional security guarantee against fraudulent messages with affordable runtime overheads and communication costs.

References

1. Zhao, Y., et al.: Local differential privacy based federated learning for Internet of Things. IEEE Internet Things J. **8**(11), 8836–8853 (2021)

2. Yang, H., Zhao, J., Xiong, Z., Lam, K.Y., Sun, S., Xiao, L.: Privacy-preserving federated learning for UAV-enabled networks: learning-based joint scheduling and resource management. IEEE J. Sel. Areas Commun. **39**(10), 3144–3159 (2021)
3. McMahan, B., Moore, E., Ramage, D., Hampson, S., Arcas, B.A.: Communication-efficient learning of deep networks from decentralized data. In: Artificial Intelligence and Statistics, Fort Lauderdale, FL, USA, pp. 1273–1282. PMLR (2017)
4. Chen, Y., Yang, X., Qin, X., Yu, H., Chen, B., Shen, Z.: Focus: dealing with label quality disparity in federated learning. In: International Workshop on Federated Learning for User Privacy and Data Confidentiality in Conjunction with IJCAI 2020 (2020)
5. Zhu, L., Liu, Z., Han, S.: Deep leakage from gradients. In: Advances in Neural Information Processing Systems, Vancouver, BC, Canada, pp. 14774–14784. NeurIPS (2019)
6. Bonawitz, K., et al.: Practical secure aggregation for privacy-preserving machine learning. In: Proceedings of the 2017 ACM SIGSAC Conference on Computer and Communications Security, Dallas, TX, USA, pp. 1175–1191. ACM (2017)
7. Bell, J.H., Bonawitz, K.A., Gascón, A., Lepoint, T., Raykova, M.: Secure single-server aggregation with (poly) logarithmic overhead. In: Proceedings of the 2020 ACM SIGSAC Conference on Computer and Communications Security, Virtual Event, USA, pp. 1253–1269. ACM (2020)
8. Blanchard, P., El Mhamdi, E.M., Guerraoui, R., Stainer, J.: Machine learning with adversaries: Byzantine tolerant gradient descent. In: Proceedings of the 31st International Conference on Neural Information Processing Systems, Long Beach, CA, USA, pp. 118–128. NIPS (2017)
9. McMahan, H.B., Ramage, D., Talwar, K., Zhang, L.: Learning differentially private recurrent language models. In: International Conference on Learning Representations, BC, Canada (2018)
10. Rastogi, V., Nath, S.: Differentially private aggregation of distributed time-series with transformation and encryption. In: Proceedings of the 2010 ACM SIGMOD International Conference on Management of Data, Indianapolis, Indiana, USA, pp. 735–746. ACM (2010)
11. So, J., Güler, B., Avestimehr, A.S.: Turbo-aggregate: breaking the quadratic aggregation barrier in secure federated learning. IEEE J. Sel. Areas Inf. Theory **2**(1), 479–489 (2021)
12. Mandal, K., Gong, G., Liu, C.: Nike-based fast privacy-preserving highdimensional data aggregation for mobile devices. Technical report, CACR Technical Report, CACR 2018–10, University of Waterloo, Canada (2018)
13. Shamir, A.: How to share a secret. Commun. ACM **22**(11), 612–613 (1979)
14. Paillier, P.: Public-key cryptosystems based on composite degree residuosity classes. In: Stern, J. (ed.) EUROCRYPT 1999. LNCS, vol. 1592, pp. 223–238. Springer, Heidelberg (1999). https://doi.org/10.1007/3-540-48910-X_16
15. Damgård, I., Jurik, M., Nielsen, J.B.: A generalization of Paillier's public-key system with applications to electronic voting. Int. J. Inf. Secur. **9**(6), 371–385 (2010)
16. Canetti, R.: Universally composable security: a new paradigm for cryptographic protocols. In: Proceedings 42nd IEEE Symposium on Foundations of Computer Science, Las Vegas, Nevada, USA, pp. 136–145. IEEE (2001)
17. Kohavi, R.: Scaling up the accuracy of Naive-Bayes classifiers: a decision-tree hybrid. In: Proceedings of the Second International Conference on Knowledge Discovery and Data Mining, Portland, Oregon, USA, pp. 202–207. AAAI (1996)

18. Yeh, I.C., Lien, C.: The comparisons of data mining techniques for the predictive accuracy of probability of default of credit card clients. Expert Syst. Appl. **36**(2), 2473–2480 (2009)

19. Moro, S., Cortez, P., Rita, P.: A data-driven approach to predict the success of bank telemarketing. Decis. Support Syst. **62**, 22–31 (2014)

20. Torres, R.L.S., Ranasinghe, D.C., Shi, Q., Sample, A.P.: Sensor enabled wearable RFID technology for mitigating the risk of falls near beds. In: 2013 IEEE International Conference on RFID (RFID), pp. 191–198. IEEE (2013)

Graph Matching Based Privacy-Preserving Scheme in Social Networks

Hongyan Zhang[1,2], Xiaolin Li[1], Jiayu Xu[1], and Li Xu[1(✉)]

[1] College of Computer and Cyber Security, Key Laboratory of Network Security and Cryptology, Fujian Normal University, Fuzhou 350117, Fujian, People's Republic of China
xuli@fjnu.edu.cn
[2] Concord University College Fujian Normal University, Fuzhou 350117, Fujian, People's Republic of China

Abstract. The increasing popularity of social networks has inspired recent research to explore social graphs for data mining. Because social graph data contains sensitive information about users, publishing the graph data directly will cause privacy leakage of users. In this paper, we assume that attackers might re-identify targets with 1-neighborhood graph attacks. To prevent such attacks, we propose a Graph Matching based Privacy-preserving Scheme, named GMPS, to anonymize the social graphs. We utilize Jensen-Shannon Divergence to compute node structure similarity to improve the accuracy of node clustering. And then, utilize the graph modification to achieve k-anonymity and use graph matching to measure the similarity of graphs. The experiment results on HepTh and Facebook show that the proposed approach achieves k-anonymity with low information loss and high data utility.

Keywords: Social networks · 1-neighborhood attack · Jensen-Shannon Divergence · Graph matching · Privacy preserving

1 Introduction

The growing popularity of social networks has prompted recent research to explore social graph data to understand its structure for advertising, data mining and so on. The large amount of personal data that users share on social networks makes them a desirable target for attackers [1]. Releasing social graph data directly will compromise users' privacy, resulting the risk of uses' property and personal safety. Therefore, preserving the privacy of users has become a challenges for social graph data publishing [2].

Social networks use nodes and edges to model social relations with graph structure, where nodes represent users and edges represent relations between users [3]. Normally, data owners may release their data after Navïve anonymization, which just remove nodes' identities before data publishing. However, Navïve

© Springer Nature Singapore Pte Ltd. 2021
L. Lin et al. (Eds.): SocialSec 2021, CCIS 1495, pp. 110–118, 2021.
https://doi.org/10.1007/978-981-16-7913-1_8

anonymization cannot protect users' privacy sufficiently, while adversaries may have some background knowledge about users, i.e., degree, the 1-neighborhood graphs. Based on background knowledge, there exist re-identification or de-anonymization attacks [4–6] against graph structure, the attacks can be divided into degree attacks [7], neighborhood graph attacks [8], subgraph attacks [9]. To defend de-anonymous attacks, k-anonymity technique has been utilized by many researchers. The k-anonymity technique used in graph data publishing is implemented by adding or deleting nodes and edges to make that there are other $k - 1$ 1-neighborhood graphs isomorphic to one node. In this paper, we consider the adversary has the background with the 1-neighborhood graphs of users, because it is more difficult for an attacker to collect the information beyond a one-hop neighborhood [10].

The main contributions of this paper are summarized as follows:

1. To achieve k-anonymity, we divided nodes into several clusters in which the sizes are between $[k, 2k)$. We utilize Jensen-Shannon Divergence to compute node structure similarity to improve the accuracy of node clustering.
2. To measure graph anonymity, we use graph matching algorithm the accuracy to obtain the distance of 1-neighborhood graphs of each pair of nodes.
3. The experiment results on HepTh and Facebook show that the proposed approach achieves k-anonymity with low information loss and high data utility.

The rest of the paper is organized as follows. The notions, terminologies and the problem description are introduced in Sect. 3. The strategies are elaborated in Sect. 4. Section 5 gives the experimental analysis on our scheme respectively. The validation results are presented in this section as well. We conclude this paper in Sect. 6.

2   Related Works

To de-anonymous attacks, Campan and Truta [11] proposed a k-anonymity model, in which each node should be similar to at least $k - 1$ nodes based on both structural information and nodes attributes, therefore, the anonymized nodes cannot be re-identified with the probability larger than $1/k$. Due to this reason, k-anonymity has become the most popular method to protect individuals privacy in social network data publishing problem [12]. To achieve k-anonymity, existing approaches can be classified into clustering-based and graph modification approaches [10].

For clustering-based models, similar nodes and edges into groups to form super nodes, a super node represent a subgraph which incorporates certain similar nodes and the edges between them, the edges between super nodes represent the relationship between subgraphs. Since a clustered graph only contains super nodes and super edges, by making the size of each cluster at least k, the probability to reidentify a user can be bounded to be at most $1/k$. Campan and Truta [11] discussed how to implement clustering method when consider the lost of both node labels and structure information. Zheleva and Getoor [13] developed a clustering method to prevent the sensitive link leakage. Cormode et al. [14] introduced (k, l)-clustering for bipartite graphs and interaction graphs, respectively.

Graph modification aims to alter graph structure to achieve k-anonymity for privacy preservation. Liu and Terzi [7] proposed a approach to make node degree achieve k-anonymity, that is, each node has at least other $k - 1$ nodes with the same degree. Zhou and Pei [8] proposed a scheme to against the 1-neighborhood attack. For each vertex v, its 1-neighborhood graph is isomorphic 1-neighborhood graphs to $k - 1$ other nodes. Zou, Chen and Ozsu [9] proposed a k-automorphism scheme to preserve privacy. Cheng, Fu and Liu [15] proposed two targets of attacks, NodeInfo and LinkInfo. Then they proposed a scheme to form k pairwise isomorphic subgraphs. Yuan et al. [16] defined a k-degree-l-diversity anonymity model to protect not only the sensitive labels of individuals but also the structural information. Li et al. [17] proposed a graph based framework to preserve privacy in data publication. Based on the features of the graph, they quantified the privacy and utility measurements of the anonymous datasets. Liu et al. [10] first proposed a kind of attack named weighted 1*-neighborhood attack, which assume that attackers have some background knowledge about both individuals' 1-neighborhood graphs and the degrees of its neighbor nodes and edge weights between nodes. They proposed a heuristic indistinguishable group anonymous scheme to achieve k-anonymity. In the anonymous social graph has high graph utility. Huang et al. [18] proposed a privacy preserving approach based on the differential privacy model, which combined clustering and randomization algorithms. Moreover, they also proposed a privacy measure algorithm against graph structure and degree attacks. Ding et al. [12] proposed a new utility measurement with a new information loss matrix, based on which a k-decomposition algorithm and a privacy preserving framework are developed.

In general, existing researches about privacy preserving can protect the privacy of users for social graph data publishing. However, privacy protection needs a trade-off between privacy and data utility. In our approach, we focus on 1-neighborhood graph attack, and we can achieve better data utility meanwhile guarantee k-anonymity.

3　Preliminaries

In this paper, we use an undirected graph $G = (V, E)$ to model the social network, where V is a set of nodes, $E \subseteq V \times V$ is a set of edges. The nodes represent the users, the edges represent the relationships between users such as friendship. The cardinalities of V and E are denoted by $|V|$ and $|E|$ respectively, We assume that $|V| = n, |E| = m$.

Due to the small world phenomenon of social networks,the diameters of social networks are small, it is difficult to collect information of d-hop neighbors. We focus on 1-Neighborhood Graph attack, the adversary have knowledge about one node's edge-neighborhood graph.

Definition 1. *(1-Neighborhood Graph)* [8] $G(v) = <V(v), E(v)>$, *where* $V(v)$ *is the set of neighborhood nodes of* v *and* $V(v) = \{u | (u, v) \in E\} \cup \{v\}$. $E(v)$ *is the set of edges between the nodes in* $V(v)$, *and* $E(v) = \{(u, v) | u, v \in V(v) \wedge (u, v) \in E\}$.

4 The Proposed Approach

4.1 Node Clustering

In this section, we use k-anonymity to preserve the identities privacy of users. In order to achieve k-anonymity, the processing is divided into three steps: (1) Cluster initializing: for given nodes, according to the node degree and local cluster coefficient, we cluster the nodes in graph G into several clusters. (2) Cluster reshaping: for all clusters, compute the degree distribution similarity(DDS) between each two nodes, according to DDS, reshaping the clusters, s.t. every cluster has $[k, 2k)$ nodes. (3) Modify the 1-neighborhood graph of nodes in every cluster, s.t. the 1-neighborhood graph of nodes in the same cluster probabilistic indistinguishability.

Cluster Initializing. For a given graph $G = <V, E>$, we initially cluster nodes $v \in V$ by the following metrics: $d(v)$, $lc(v)$. Here, $d(v)$, $lc(v)$ denote the degree of the node v and the local clustering coefficient, respectively.

Definition 2. *Local clustering coefficient* $lc_v = \mu_G(v)/\omega_G(v)$, *where* $\mu_G(v)$ *and* $\omega_G(v)$ *are the numbers of triangles and triples in* $G(v)$, *respectively.*

We group nodes into a cluster if $|d(v_i) - d(v_j)| < \delta_1$ and $|lc(v_i) - lc(v_j)| < \delta_2$, δ_1, δ_2 are two pre-defined parameters, and then we obtain several clusters $C_1^1, C_2^1 \dots C_{M_1}^1$.

Although after the above processing, the nodes are grouped into several clusters, not all the sizes of the clusters are greater than or equal to k. In reality, during the empirical study, the size of clusters follow the power-law distribution, that is, the cardinalities of most clusters are small, a small number of the clusters have thousands of members. Therefore, we execute a cluster combination process to make sure that the sizes of all clusters will be larger than k.

First, we sort all the clusters in descending order of the cardinality of the clusters, $C_1^2, C_2^2 \dots C_{M_1}^2$. For each cluster of a size smaller than k, we incorporate the nodes in C_{i+1}^2 into C_i^2, the processing continues until every cluster has a size larger than k. Algorithm 1 shows the processing of Cluster Initializing.

Cluster Reshaping

Definition 3 *(JensenCShannon Divergence [19]). Suppose that we have two sets of discrete values* x_i *and* y_i *with the corresponding probability distribution,* $p(x_i)$ *and* $p(y_j)$. *The relative entropy between these two distributions is defined as* $R[p(x)||p(y)] = \sum_{i=1}^{n} p(x_i)\frac{p(x_i)}{p(y_i)}$.

Suppose that there are M_1 clusters after cluster initializing, we sort the clusters in the descending order of the maximal node degree of the members in the clusters, the sorted clusters are denoted as $C_1', C_2', \ldots C_{M_1}'$, $|C_i'| = n_i'$. For each cluster C_i' which size is larger than $2k$, we perform cluster splitting to enable the size of each cluster to be $[k, 2k)$. We utilize the degree distribution similarity as the metric to slip the clusters. In order to obtain the degree distribution similarity of all the other nodes in the same cluster, first, construct the 1-neighborhood graph of nodes in the same cluster. Then, for each node $v \in C_i'$, obtain the degree distribution $P(v)$ of its 1-neighborhood graph. Compute the degree distribution similarity of the these nodes, for node $v \in C_i'$, compute the degree distribution similarity with all the other nodes u in C_i', $sim_{uv} = 1 - \frac{R_{uv}}{R_{max}}$. Then, select the $k-1$ most similar nodes of node v, add these nodes and v into the same cluster.

In order to compute the degree distribution similarity of two nodes in social networks, the processing is divided into three steps: (1) compute the nodes' degree distribution. (2) compute the relative entropy of two nodes. (3) compute the similarity of two nodes.

(1) Compute the nodes' degree distribution

Graph $G = <V, E>$, where $V = \{v_1, v_2, \cdots, v_n\}$, $E = \{e_1, e_2, \cdots, e_m\}$. $G(v_i) = <V(v_i, E(v_i))>$ is the 1-neighborhood graph of node v_i, let $N_i = |V(v_i)|$. $D_{v_i} = \{d_{i1}, d_{i2}, \ldots, d_{iN_i}\}$, D_{v_i} represent the degree sequences of nodes in $G(v_i)$, including v_i. $P_i = \{p_{i1}, p_{i2}, \ldots, p_{iN_i}\}$, where $p_{ij} = \frac{d_{ij}}{D_i}$, $D_i = \sum_{i=1}^{N_i} d_{ij}$.

(2) Compute the relative entropy of two nodes

Suppose two nodes v_i and v_j, the degree distribution of the two nodes are $P_i = \{p_{i1}, p_{i2}, \ldots, p_{iN_i}\}$, $P_j = \{p_{j1}, p_{j2}, \cdots, p_{jN_j}\}$. Even if $N_i \neq N_j$, without loss of generality, let $N_i > N_j$, we could add $|N_i - N_j|$ 0s into P_j. The relative entropy between v_i and v_j is

$$r_{ij}[P_i||P_j] = \sum_{k=1}^{N_i} p_{ik} \frac{p_{ik}}{p_{jk}}.$$

(3) Compute the similarity of two nodes

Due to the asymmetry of the relative entropy, we also need to compute $r_{ji}[P_j||P_i] = \sum_{k=1}^{N_i} p_{jk} \frac{p_{jk}}{p_{ik}}$. Let $R_{ij} = r_{ij} + r_{ji}$, $R_{max} = max(R_{ij})$, $1 \leq i, j \leq n$, the similarity of each pair of nodes can be defined as follows:

$$sim_{ij} = 1 - \frac{R_{ij}}{R_{max}}.$$

4.2   Graph Modification

After node clustering, we need to modify the graph to achieve $k-$anonymous. Suppose that there are M clusters, $C_1, C_2, \ldots C_M$, the size of each cluster is about $[k, 2k)$. We sort the clusters in descending order of the maximal node degree, and the new ordered clusters are denoted as $\widehat{C_1}, \widehat{C_2}, \ldots \widehat{C_M}$. Then, for each pair of nodes u and v in the same cluster, we compute distance between the l-neighborhood graphs of each pair of nodes to determine whether they are structure similar. If the 1-neighborhood of all nodes in the same cluster are inexact matching, then, we achieve k-anonymity.

We use the Munkres's algorithm [20] to find the minimum cost $cost(G(u), G(v))$. If $cost(G(u), G(v)) \geq \alpha$, Find the optimal edit path $p = p_1, p_2, \ldots p_{n+m}$ of the integers $1, 2, \ldots, n + m$ which minimizes $\sum\limits_{i=1}^{n+m} C_{ip_i}$. Then, modify the graph structure to achieve structure similarity. The process is given as Algorithm 1.

Algorithm 1. Graph Modification

Input: Graph G, α
Output: Anonymity Graph $\widetilde{G}$
1: Sort $C_i, i = 1, 2, \ldots M$ with descending order of maximal node degree
2: obtain $\widehat{C_i}, i = 1, 2, \ldots M$
3: **for** each $\widehat{C_i}$ **do**
4:     choose the first node suppose u as the seed
5:     **for** each node v in $\widehat{C_i} - \{u\}$ **do**
6:         construct 1-neighborhood graphs of $G(u)$ and $G(v)$
7:         compute $Cost(G(u), G(v))$
8:         **if** $Cost(G(u), G(v)) \geq \alpha$ **then**
9:             find the optimal edit path $p = p_1, p_2, \ldots p_{n+m}$
10:             modify $G(v)$ similar to $G(v)$
11: **return** $\widetilde{G}$

---

5   Validation Experiment

In this section, All the experiments were conducted in Python on a server running the Ubuntu 20.04.1 LTS operating system. To demonstrate the effectiveness of our scheme, we validate the performance of the proposed scheme on two real datasets: CA-HepTh and Facebook. Details of graph characteristics are shown in Table 1.

Table 1. Details of Social Networks

Dataset	Nodes	Edges	AVD	ACC	APL
HepTh	9877	25998	5.3	0.4714	7.4
Facebook	4039	88234	44	0.605	4.7

To explore the utility of the anonymized graph $\widetilde{G}$, we test the following two metrics:

1. *Average degree(AVD)*: The AVD of G can be calculated as $\sum_{v \in V} d_v/|V|$;
2. *Average clustering coefficient(ACC)*: The ACC of G can be calculated as $\sum_{v \in V} C_v/|V|$, where C_v is the local clustering coefficient of v;

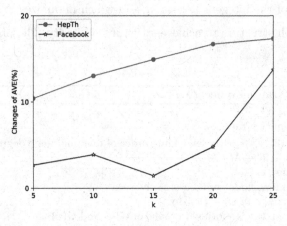

Fig. 1. AVE

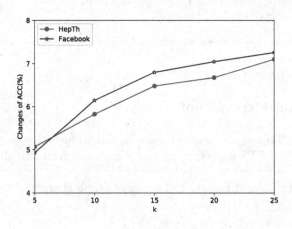

Fig. 2. ACC

Average Degree (AVE). The AVE of G can be calculated as $\sum_{v \in V} d_v/|V|$. Figure 1 shows the change of average degree of HepTh and Facebook. We can see that as k increase, change of AVE increases. The AVE change in the Facebook is small, while HepTh is the larger. As k increase from 5 to 25, the percentage of AVE changes from 0.112 to 0.176 in Hepth, while from 0.026 to 0.137 in Facebook. The result may be caused by the ACC, the larger the ACC, the smaller the percentage of AVE changes.

Average Clustering Coefficient (ACC). Clustering coefficient is the degree of clustering between the nodes of a graph. The ACC of G can be calculated as $\sum_{v \in V} C_v / |V|$, where C_v is the local clustering coefficient of v. Figure 2 is the ACC of datasets, as k increase changes of ACC increase in both dataset. In Hepth, the change is from 5.12 to 6.93, from 4.98 to 7.05 in Facebook. Therefore, the ACC changes nearly in both datasets.

6   Conclusions

Although graph anonymization can reduce the risk of privacy disclosure, malicious attackers might have background knowledge about 1-neighborhood graph of targets, and they may re-identity the users in anonymous social graphs. In this paper, we propose a Graph Matching based Privacy-preserving Scheme, named GMPS, in Social Networks to realize social graph anonymization. We utilize JensenCShannon Divergence to compute node structure similarity to improve the accuracy of node clustering. And then, utilize the graph modification to achieve k-anonymity and use graph matching to measure the similarity of graphs. The experiment results on HepTh and Facebook show that the proposed approach achieves k-anonymity with low information loss and high data utility.

Acknowledgments. The authors would like to thank the National Science Foundation of China (Nos. U1905211, 61771140, 61702100, 61702103), Fok Ying Tung Education Foundation (No. 171061), Natural Science Foundation of Fujian Province (No. 2020J01167), Educational Research Project for Young and Middle-aged Teachers in Fujian Province (Science and Technology) (No. JAT200968).

References

1. Rathore, S., Sharma, P.K., Loia, V., Jeong, Y.-S., Park, J.H.: Social network security: issues, challenges, threats, and solutions. Inf. Sci. **421**, 43–69 (2017)
2. Kleinberg, J.M.: Challenges in mining social network data: processes, privacy and paradoxes. In: Proceedings of the 13th ACM SIGKDD International Conference on Knowledge Discovery and Data Mining, San Jose, California, USA, pp. 4–5. ACM (2007)
3. Wang, Q., Zhang, Y., Lu, X., Wang, Z., Qin, Z., Ren, K.: Real-time and spatio-temporal crowd-sourced social network data publishing with differential privacy. IEEE Trans. Dependable Secure Comput. **15**(4), 591–606 (2018)
4. Narayanan, A., Shmatikov, V.: De-anonymizing social networks. In: 30th IEEE Symposium on Security and Privacy, Oakland, California, USA, pp. 173–187. IEEE (2009)

5. Ji, S., Mittal, P., Beyah, R.: Graph data anonymization, de-anonymization attacks, and de-anonymizability quantification: a survey. IEEE Commun. Surv. Tutor. **19**(2), 1305–1326 (2017)
6. Li, H., Chen, Q., Zhu, H., Ma, D., Wen, H., Shen, X.S.: Privacy leakage via de-anonymization and aggregation in heterogeneous social networks. Trans. Dependable Secure Comput. **17**(2), 350–362 (2020)
7. Liu, K., Terzi, E.: Towards identity anonymization on graphs. In: Proceedings of the ACM SIGMOD International Conference on Management of Data, Vancouver, BC, Canada, pp. 93–106. ACM (2008)
8. Zhou, B., Pei, J.: Preserving privacy in social networks against neighborhood attacks. In: 24th International Conference on Data Engineering, Mexico, pp. 506–515. IEEE (2008)
9. Zou, L., Chen, L., Ozsu, M.: K-automorphism: a general framework for privacy preserving network publication. Proc. VLDB Endow. **2**(1), 946–957 (2009)
10. Liu, Q., Wang, G., Li, F., Yang, S., Wu, J.: Preserving privacy with probabilistic indistinguishability in weighted social networks. IEEE Trans. Parallel Distrib. Syst. **28**(5), 1417–1429 (2017)
11. Campan, A., Truta, T.: A clustering approach for data and structural anonymity in social networks. In: 2nd ACM SIGKDD International Workshop Privacy Security Trust in KDD, USA, pp. 33–54. ACM (2008)
12. Ding, X., Wang, C., Choo, K.K.R., Jin, H.: A novel privacy preserving framework for large scale graph data publishing. IEEE Trans. Knowl. Data Eng. **33**(2), 331–343 (2021)
13. Zheleva, E., Getoor, L.: Preserving the privacy of sensitive relationships in graph data. In: Bonchi, F., Ferrari, E., Malin, B., Saygin, Y. (eds.) PInKDD 2007. LNCS, vol. 4890, pp. 153–171. Springer, Heidelberg (2008). https://doi.org/10.1007/978-3-540-78478-4_9
14. Cormode, G., Srivastave, D., Yu, T., Zhang, Q.: Anonymizing bipartite graph data using safe grouping. VLDB Endow. 833–844 (2008)
15. Cheng, J., Fu, A., Liu, J.: K-isomorphism: privacy preserving network publication against structural attacks. In: ACM SIGMOD International Conference on Management of Data, Indianapolis, Indiana, USA, pp. 459–470. ACM (2010)
16. Yuan, M., Chen, L., Yu, P.S., Yu, T.: Protecting sensitive lables in social network data anonymization. IEEE Trans. Knowl. Data Eng. **25**(3), 633–647 (2013)
17. Li, X.Y., Zhang, C., Jung, T., Qian, J., Chen, L.: Graph-based privacy-preserving data publication. In: IEEE INFOCOM 2016-The 35th Annual IEEE International Conference on Computer Communications, San Francisco, CA, USA, pp. 1–9. IEEE (2016)
18. Huang, H., Zhang, D., Xiao, F., Wang, K., Gu, J., Wang, R.: Privacy-preserving approach PBCN in social network with differential privacy. IEEE Trans. Netw. Serv. Manag. **17**(2), 931–945 (2020)
19. Tsai, S., Tzeng, W., Wu, H.: On the Jensen-Shannon divergence and variational distance. IEEE Trans. Inf. Theory **51**(9), 3333–3336 (2005)
20. Riesen, K., Bunke, H.: Approximation graph edit distance computation by means of bipartite graph matching. Image Vis. Comput. **27**(7), 950–959 (2009)

Anonymizing Global Edge Weighted Social Network Graphs

Jiaru Wang[1], Ziyi Wan[1,3], Jiankang Song[1,3], Yanze Huang[1,2] (iD), Yuhang Lin[1,3],
and Limei Lin[1,3(✉)] (iD)

[1] College of Computer and Cyber Security, Fujian Normal University,
Fuzhou 350117, Fujian, People's Republic of China
`linlimei@fjnu.edu.cn`
[2] School of Computer Science and Mathematics, Fujian University of Technology,
Fuzhou 350118, Fujian, People's Republic of China
[3] Key Laboratory of Network Security and Cryptology, Fujian Normal University,
Fuzhou 350117, Fujian, People's Republic of China

Abstract. Privacy protection of individual users in social networks is becoming more and more important, thus it requires effective anonymization techniques. In this paper, we use Kruskal and Prim algorithms to model the linear programming of the minimum spanning tree. Finally, we execute the experiments on the number of anonymity solutions and time with different edge weights to analyze the Kruskal algorithm and Prim algorithm to verify their anonymity feasibility.

Keywords: Privacy protection · Edge weight anonymization · Social network

1 Introduction

Social networks are growing very fast in human society nowadays, and they are attracting the interest of researchers from many disciplines. In social networks, the data might contain sensitive information of individuals, which should not be released. However, disclosing information is a voluntary act for individuals, while they do not know who can access their data and how their data will be used. Thus the data needs to be anonymized before publication to protect the privacy of individuals. There has been increasing concerns on the privacy of individuals in social networks. Siddula et al. [1] proposed a scheme for k-anonymity by using an enhanced equi-cardinal clustering method. In 2020, Huang et al. [2] gave a differential privacy protection scheme based on clustering and noise in social networks. In 2021, Safi et al. [3] provided a framework for privacy protection by public broadcast and attribute-baed encryptions in mobile social networks.

In social networks, individuals can link to or make friends with each other. Moreover, there are rich interactions in social networks, such as joining communities or groups of common interest. Thus we can view a social network as a graph, where individuals are treated as nodes, and the links represent the social ties between individuals. For edge weighted social networks, the weights of edges represent the closeness of social ties

---

The original version of this chapter was revised: The sections Introduction, Preliminary and References have been revised and updated. The correction to this chapter is available at https://doi.org/10.1007/978-981-16-7913-1_14

© Springer Nature Singapore Pte Ltd. 2021, corrected publication 2022
L. Lin et al. (Eds.): SocialSec 2021, CCIS 1495, pp. 119–130, 2021.
https://doi.org/10.1007/978-981-16-7913-1_9

between individuals, which should be protected by methods such as anonymization. Das et al. [4, 5] proposed a scheme for protecting the weighted social networks based on linear programming. Also, Zhang and Zhu [6] explored the centrality and cumulative degree distribution of skeletons for weighted social network. The privacy in k-anonymity of shortest paths by modifying edge weights are studied in [7, 8], respectively. Liu et al. [9] proposed an anonymization scheme based on probabilistic indistinguishability, while Dou et al. [10] used weighted noise injection to preserve privacy in multimedia recommendation for social networks. In order to boost the accuracy of differentially private, Wang and Long [11] designed an algorithm for each sub-network of original weighted social network. Moreover, Walia et al. [12] used weighted graph to propose a secure multimodal cancelable biometric system. Furthermore, Zhao et al. [13] gave secure outsourcing schemes based on untrusted cloud server for the min-cut of undirected edge-weighted graphs. Besides, Yin et al. [14] designed local Bayesian differential privacy, and proposed a hybrid method for federal learning.

In this paper, we focus on the anonymization of edge weights. We model the edge weighted graph by preserving the required key property, and replace the original edge weights by other edge weights satisfying the model. In [4, 5], the authors did not give the experimental steps for specific algorithms. On this basis, we first give specific experimental steps, and then further propose anonymous schemes under different algorithms. The contributions of this paper are listed as follows.

- We use the Kruskal and Prim algorithms to model the linear programming of the minimum spanning tree.
- We execute the experiments on the number of anonymity solutions and time with different edge weights to analyze the Kruskal algorithm and Prim algorithm to verify their anonymity feasibility.

2 Preliminary

Das et al. [4, 5] proposed an abstract modeling technique based on linear programming problems as follows. For an algorithm whose key attributes are expressed as linear combinations of edge weights, it makes decisions based on the actual values w_i's of edge weights and uses variables x_i to model the decisions. In its execution, each step is be expressed by inequalities involving edge weights, which lead to a system of linear inequalities:

$$\begin{bmatrix} p_{11} & p_{12} & \ldots & p_{1m} \\ p_{21} & p_{22} & & p_{2m} \\ \vdots & & \ddots & \vdots \\ p_{nm} & p_{nm} & \cdots & p_{nm} \end{bmatrix} \begin{bmatrix} x_1 \\ x_2 \\ \vdots \\ x_m \end{bmatrix} \leq \begin{bmatrix} q_1 \\ q_2 \\ \vdots \\ q_n \end{bmatrix} \tag{1}$$

$$P = \begin{bmatrix} p_{11} & p_{12} & \ldots & p_{1m} \\ p_{21} & p_{22} & & p_{2m} \\ \vdots & & \ddots & \vdots \\ p_{nm} & p_{nm} & \cdots & p_{nm} \end{bmatrix} \tag{2}$$

$$X^T = [x_1, x_2, \ldots, x_n],$$
$$Q^T = [q_1, q_2, \ldots, q_n]$$

(3)

When the edge weights are replaced by any solution of (1), the properties of the graph will be preserved under the modeled algorithm. In general, the model is formulated as a linear programming problem by the above expressions (1), (2) and (3) as follows.

Minimize (or Maximize) $F(x_1, x_2, \ldots, x_m)$

subject to $PX \leq Q$

(4)

where F is a linear objective function. The model can be obtained by changing the set of inequalities (4) for different algorithms that correspond to different series of inequalities and objective functions. In the following, we use the Kruskal algorithm and Prim algorithm models based on the minimum spanning tree.

3 Anonymizing Scheme

Given the original weighted graph $G = (V, E, W)$, we use w_i to represent the original weight of the positive edge, where each w_i corresponds to the edge $i = (u, v) \in E$. We use x_i to represent the anonymization edge weight in anonymity edge weighted graph $M = (V, E, X)$, and the component in the matrix X, where V and E do not change, and only the edge weight is anonymized.

In order to implement anonymizing models of different algorithms, a concrete original edge weighted graph $G = (V, E, W)$ is described as follows (Fig. 1).

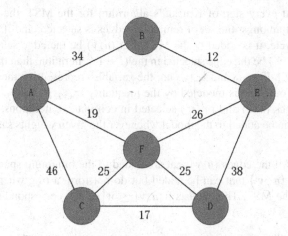

Fig. 1. A concrete original edge weighted graph G.

$$V = \{A, B, C, D, E, F\},$$

$$E = \{(A, B), (B, E), (A, F), (F, E), (A, C), (F, C), (F, D), (E, D), (C, D)\},$$

$$W = \{w_1, w_2, w_3, w_4, w_5, w_6, w_7, w_8, w_9\} = \{34, 12, 19, 26, 46, 25, 25, 38, 17\}$$

For subsequent verification of the anonymizing model, the minimum spanning trees of the original edge weighted graph G based on the Kruskal algorithm and Prim algorithm are respectively listed as follows (Fig. 2):

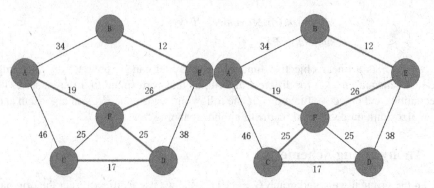

Fig. 2. Two minimum spanning tree based on the original edge weighted graph.

3.1 An Anonymity Model of Edge Weight Based on Kruskal Algorithm

A. Abstract model based on Kruskal algorithm

Constraint I: At every step of Kruskal's algorithm for the MST, the edge with the minimum weight amongst the set of remaining edges is selected, and if this edge does not result in a cycle, it is added to the MST. Let (u, v) be the edge selected in the ith iteration, and (u', v') be the edge selected in the $(i + 1)^{th}$ iteration, then this implies that $w[u, v] \le w[u', v']$. If $x_{(u,v)}$ and $x_{(u',v')}$ are the variables representing these edges in the model, then this outcome is modeled by the inequality $x_{(u,v)} \le x_{(u',v')}$. Therefore, for every pair of edges (u, v) and (u', v') selected in consecutive iterations, the inequality $x_{(u,v)} \le x_{(u',v')}$ can be added to the model whenever the given weights satisfy $w[u, v] \le w[u', v']$.

Constraint II: All the edges (u, v) that are added to the minimum spanning tree, and the minor edges (u', v') that can be added but do not form a ring when the last edge is not added to the MST. There exists $w[u, v] \le w[u', v']$, correspondingly there is a constraint $x_{(u,v)} \le x_{(u',v')}$.

Objective function:

$$Minimize \ F(x_1, x_2, \ldots, x_m) = c_1 x_1 + c_2 x_2 + \ldots + c_m x_m,$$
$$Num_{c_m=1} = n - 1, Num_{c_m=0} = m - n + 1 \tag{5}$$

where $Num_{c_m=1}$ represents the number of $C_m = 1$ and $Num_{c_m=0}$ represents the number of $C_m = 0$.

Based on the Kruskal algorithm, we establish a concrete anonymity model as follows:

First, add the edge (B, E) with the smallest edge weight, whose edge weight is x_2. Second, add edge (C, D) with edge weight is x_9, then $x_2 \leq x_9$. If edge (A, F) is added, whose edge weight is x_3, then $x_9 \leq x_3$. Fourth, add edge (C, F) with edge weight is x_6, then $x_3 \leq x_6$. Finally, add edge (E, F) with edge weight is x_4, then $x_6 \leq x_4$.

Therefore:

$$P = \begin{bmatrix} 0 & 1 & 0 & 0 & 0 & 0 & 0 & 0 & -1 \\ 0 & 0 & -1 & 0 & 0 & 0 & 0 & 0 & 1 \\ 0 & 0 & 1 & 0 & 0 & -1 & 0 & 0 & 0 \\ 0 & 0 & 0 & -1 & 0 & 1 & 0 & 0 & 0 \end{bmatrix} \tag{6}$$

$$X^T = [x_1, x_2, \ldots, x_9],$$
$$Q^T = [q_1, q_2, \ldots, q_n] = [0, 0, \ldots, 0] \tag{7}$$

Based on constraint II, for any x_i, $1 \leq x_9 \leq 38$.

Based on the above constraints, the linear model is solved. Assume that the publisher further restricts the edge weight to $10 \leq x_9 \leq 38$. By the exhaustive method, it is found that there are 53,130 anonymity solutions for the publisher to choose. The time taken to solve the linear model is 62.003 s.

B. Validation based on Kruskal specific model

In this subsection, we choose one solution for verifying the anonymity as follows (Fig. 3).

Scheme I: $x_2 = 16, x_3 = 21, x_4 = 27, x_6 = 26, x_9 = 19$.

The anonymity graph is listed as follows:

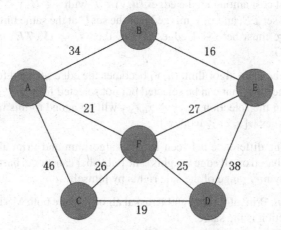

Fig. 3. Anonymity graph based on Scheme I.

Through the Kruskal algorithm, a minimum spanning tree of the anonymity graph of Scheme I is obtained as follows, where the red edges represent the edges of the anonymity graph spanning tree (Fig. 4).

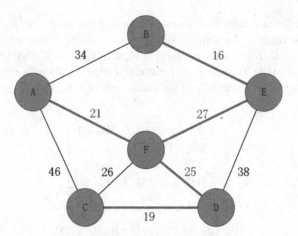

Fig. 4. The minimum spanning tree of the anonymity graph based on Scheme I.

It can be found that the minimum spanning tree of the anonymity graph is the same as the minimum spanning tree of the original weighted graph. This shows that the linear model based on Kruskal algorithm is feasible.

3.2   An Anonymity Model of Edge Weight Based on Prim Algorithm

A. Abstract model based on Prim algorithm

Assume that TE is the set of edges in the minimum spanning tree on G. The algorithm starts from $U = \{u_0\}(u_0 \in V)$, $TE = \{\}$ and repeats the following operations: Find an edge with the least cost among all the edges $(u, v) \in E$ with $u \in U, v \in V - U$. (u_0, v_0) is merged into the set TE, and v_0 is merged into the set U at the same time, until $U = V$. At this time, there must be $n - 1$ edges in TE, then $T = (V, TE)$ is the minimum spanning tree of G.

Constraint **I**: In the Prim algorithm, (u, v) becomes the edge selected for the ith generation, (u', v') is the edge that can be selected but not selected for the ith generation, and the inequality is in the selection $x_{(u,v)} \leq x_{(u',v')}$ will be added to this model when the given weight satisfies $w[u, v] \leq w[u', v']$.

Constraint **II**: The difference between Kruskal algorithm and Prim algorithm is that Prim algorithm is based on all edge weights. The publisher can model based on constraint I and set the anonymity range of the side rights by himself.

Objective function: Prim algorithm and Kruskal algorithm are both MST algorithms, so the objective function is the same.

Based on the Prim algorithm, we establish a concrete anonymity model as follows: First, select (A, F) and add vertex F, then

$$x_3 \leq x_1, x_3 \leq x_5,$$

$$U = \{A, F\}, \ TE = \{(A, F)\}.$$

Second, select (C, F) and add vertex C, then

$$x_6 \leq x_1, x_6 \leq x_4, x_6 \leq x_5, x_6 \leq x_7,$$

$$U = \{A, F, C\}, \; TE = \{(A, F), (C, F)\}$$

Third, select (C, D) and add vertex D, then

$$x_9 \leq x_1, x_9 \leq x_4, x_9 \leq x_7,$$

$$U = \{A, F, C, D\}, \; TE = \{(A, F), (C, F), (C, D)\}$$

Fourth, select (F, E) and add vertex E, then

$$x_4 \leq x_1, x_4 \leq x_8,$$

$$U = \{A, F, C, D, E\}, \; TE = \{(A, F), (C, F), (C, D), (F, E)\}$$

Fifth, select (B, E) and add vertex B, then

$$x_2 \leq x_1,$$

$$U = \{A, F, C, D, E, B\}, \; TE = \{(A, F), (C, F), (C, D), (F, E), (B, E)\}$$

Based on constraint II, assume that the publisher further restricts the edge weight to $1 \leq x_i \leq 10$. The linear model is solved by the exhaustive method, and there are 12,855,337 anonymity solutions for the publisher to choose. The time required to solve the linear model is 16594.8 s.

B. Validation based on Prim specific model.
In this subsection, we choose one solution for verifying the anonymity as follows.

Scheme II: $x_1 = 7, x_2 = 1, x_3 = 7, x_4 = 5, x_5 = 10, x_6 = 1, x_7 = 7, x_8 = 10, x_9 = 2$.
The anonymity graph is listed as follows (Fig. 5):

Through the Prim algorithm, a minimum spanning tree of the anonymity graph of Scheme II is obtained as follows, where the red edges represent the edges of the anonymity graph spanning tree (Fig. 6).

It can be found that the minimum spanning tree of the anonymity graph is the same as the minimum spanning tree of the original weighted graph. This shows that the linear model based on Prim algorithm is feasible.

4 Experiments

Both Kruskal algorithm and Prim algorithm are used for finding the minimum spanning tree. Based on the linear anonymity of MST, the range of anonymous edge weights changes with respect to the time (in seconds), number of anonymity solutions (No. of solutions), and degree of anonymity α (the quotient of number of anonymous edges and number of edges of the original edge weight graph). The experimental results are shown in Tables 1, 2, and Figs. 7, 8, 9, 10.

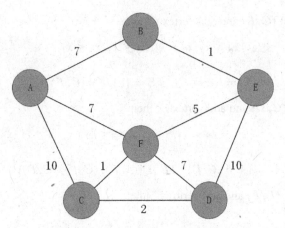

Fig. 5. Anonymity graph based on Scheme II.

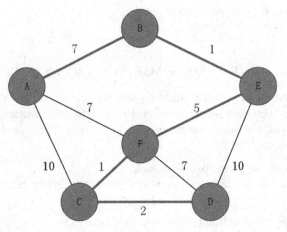

Fig. 6. The minimum spanning tree of the anonymity graph based on scheme II.

Table 1. Anonymity results based on Kruskal algorithm.

Edge weight	No. of solutions	Time	α
1–5	126	0.409	0.56
2–6	126	0.417	0.56
3–7	126	0.579	0.56
4–8	126	0.6	0.56
5–9	126	0.501	0.56
6–10	126	0.707	0.56

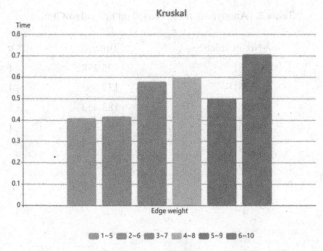

Fig. 7. Anonymity time with different edge weights based on Kruskal algorithm.

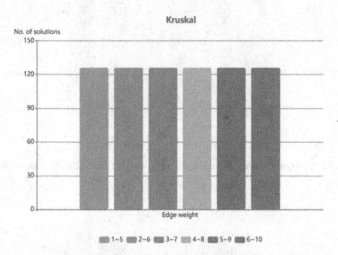

Fig. 8. Number of anonymity solutions based on Kruskal algorithm with different edge weights.

In Table 1, Fig. 7 and Fig. 8, we can get that the number of anonymity solutions based on Kruskal algorithm is 126 for all choices of the edge weights. However, the anonymity time with different edge weights are different. When the edge weights are in 1–5, the anonymity time is 0.409 s. When the edge weights are in 2–6, the anonymity time is 0.417 s. When the edge weights are in 3–7, the anonymity time is 0.579 s. When the edge weights are in 4–8, the anonymity time is 0.6 s. When the edge weights are in 5–9, the anonymity time is 0.501 s. When the edge weights are in 6–10, the anonymity time is 0.707 s.

Table 2. Anonymity results based on Prim algorithm.

Edge weight	No. of solutions	Time	α
1–5	45261	195.288	1
2–6	45261	137.863	1
3–7	45261	183.463	1
4–8	45261	181.371	1
5–9	45261	172.721	1
6–10	45261	154.81	1

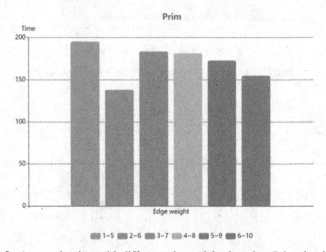

Fig. 9. Anonymity time with different edge weights based on Prim algorithm.

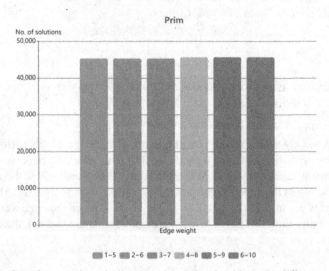

Fig. 10. Number of anonymity solutions based on Prim algorithm with different edge weights.

In Table 2, Fig. 9 and Fig. 10, we can get that the number of anonymity solutions based on Prim algorithm is 45261 for all choices of the edge weights. However, the anonymity time with different edge weights are different. When the edge weights are in 1–5, the anonymity time is 195.288 s. When the edge weights are in 2–6, the anonymity time is 137.863 s. When the edge weights are in 3–7, the anonymity time is 183.463 s. When the edge weights are in 4–8, the anonymity time is 181.371 s. When the edge weights are in 5–9, the anonymity time is 172.721 s. When the edge weights are in 6 ~ 10, the anonymity time is 154.81 s.

It can be seen that the Prim algorithm has significant advantages in the number of anonymity solutions. This gives web publishers a better choice. Although Kruskal algorithm has more advantages in the anonymity time, the Prim algorithm does not cost much more time than that of Kruskal algorithm. To a certain extent, anonymity based on Prim algorithm is better.

5 Conclusion

In this paper, we provided an effective solution to the anonymization of global edge weighted social network graphs. We first proposed a linear programming model to effectively preserve properties of the graph. At the same time, we considered the minimum spanning tree and the shortest path between multiple sources, and showed how to use the Kruskal algorithm and Prim algorithm to anonymize the original edge weighted graph. Finally, we executed the experiments on the number of anonymity solutions and time with different edge weights to analyze the Kruskal algorithm and Prim algorithm to verify their anonymity feasibility.

Acknowledgment. The authors declare that there is no conflict of interest regarding the publication of this paper. This work was supported in part by the National Natural Science Foundation of China (No. 62171132, No. 62102088, No. U1905211, No. 61771140), Fok Ying Tung Education Foundation (No. 171061), Natural Science Foundation of Fujian Province (No. 2021J05228), and Fujian University of Technology (No. GJ-YB-20-06).

References

1. Siddula, M., Li, Y., Cheng, X., Tian, Z., Cai, Z.: Anonymization in online social networks based on enhanced equi-cardinal clustering. IEEE Trans. Comput. Soc. Syst. **6**(4), 809–820 (2019)
2. Huang, H., Zhang, D.J., Xiao, F., Wang K., Wang, R.: Privacy-preserving approach PBCN in social network with differential privacy. IEEE Trans. Netw. Serv. Manage. **17**(2), 931–945 (2020)
3. Safi, S.M., Movaghar, A., Mahmoodzadeh, K.S.: A framework for protecting privacy on mobile social networks. Mobile Netw. Appl. **26**, 1281–1299 (2021)
4. Das, S., Eğecioğlu, Ö., Abbadi, A.E.: Anonimos: an LP based approach for anonymizing weighted social network graphs. IEEE Trans. Knowl. Data Eng. **24**(4), 590–604 (2010)
5. Das, S., Eğecioğlu, Ö., Abbadi, A.E.: Anonymizing weighted social network graphs. In: IEEE International Conference on Data Engineering, pp. 904–907. IEEE, Long Beach (2010)

6. Zhang, X., Zhu, J.: Skeleton of weighted social network. Phys. A Stat. Mech. Appl. **392**(6), 1547–1556 (2013)
7. Wang, S.-L., Tsai, Y.-C., Kao, H.-Y., Ting, I.-H., Hong, T.-P.: Shortest paths anonymization on weighted graphs. Int. J. Softw. Eng. Know. Eng. **23**(01), 65–79 (2013)
8. Tsai, Y.-C., Wang, S.-L., Kao, H.-Y., Hong, T.-P.: Edge types vs privacy in k-anonymization of shortest paths. Appl. Soft Comput. **31**, 348–359 (2015)
9. Liu, Q., Li, F., Yang, S., Wu, J.: Preserving privacy with probabilistic indistinguishability in weighted social networks. IEEE Trans. Parallel Distrib. Syst. **28**(5), 1417–1429 (2017)
10. Dou, K., Gou, B., Kuang, L.: A privacy-preserving multimedia recommendation in the context of social network based on weighted noise injection. Multimedia Tools Appl. **78**(6), 26907–26926 (2019)
11. Wang, D., Long, S.: Boosting the accuracy of differentially private in weighted social networks. Multimedia Tools Appl. **78**(24), 34801–34817 (2019)
12. Walia, G.S., Jain, G., Bansal, N., Singh, K.: Adaptive weighted graph approach to generate multimodal cancelable biometric templates. IEEE Trans. Inf. Forensics Secur. 15, 1945–1958 (2020)
13. Zhao, P., Yu, J., Zhang, H., Qin, Z., Wang, C.: How to securely outsource finding the min-cut of undirected edge-weighted graphs. IEEE Trans. Inf. Forensics and Secur. **15**, 315–328 (2020)
14. Yin, L., Feng, J., Xun, H., Sun, Z., Cheng, X.: A privacy-preserving federated learning for multiparty data sharing in social IoTs. IEEE Trans. Netw. Sci. Eng. **8**(3), 2706–2718 (2021)

Security and Privacy in Big Database

Trajectory Privacy Protection Scheme for Different Travel Modes

Yanzi Li[1,2], Jing Zhang[1,2]([✉]), Peng Gao[3], and Sitong Shi[1,2]

[1] School of Computer Science and Mathematics, Fujian University of Technology, Fuzhou 350118, Fujian, China
[2] Fujian Provincial Key Laboratory of Big Data Mining and Applications, Fujian University of Technology, Fuzhou 350118, Fujian, China
[3] Southest University, Nanjing 210096, Jiangsu, China

Abstract. The problem of trajectory privacy is getting more attention in recent years. It is unreasonable to adopt the same privacy protection scheme in diversified travel modes, since the trajectories have different constraints under different travel modes. Aiming at this problem, a mobile trajectory privacy protection scheme for different travel modes is proposed in this paper. At first, the overall privacy protection scheme is designed according to the classification of privacy level of road sections and different travel modes of users. And then, by considering both service and privacy, two false trajectory generation algorithms are designed, which can protect the real trajectory. The simulation experiments show that, the proposed scheme can process trajectory anonymity effectively. Compared with the algorithm in non-road network environment, the road network based algorithm can improve the average service accuracy by 36%, and decrease the privacy leak by 78%, which can provide users with more efficient and secure location services.

Keywords: Privacy protection · Trajectory · Road network · Anonymity

1 Introduction

Due to the rapid development of intelligent terminals with location function and mobile Internet, more and more LBS (Location Based Service) have been integrated into people's daily life [1]. For example, querying the hotel, hospital, gas station within one kilometer, the least time-consuming path to a place. However, in the case of obtaining the convenience of LBS intelligent service, privacy will certainly confront the danger of being maliciously used. The location information is provided by people to obtain accurate services. And this information will also be obtained by malicious users. The malicious users can even obtain users' trajectory information through continuous query, so as to analyze their sensitive information, such as personal preferences, behavior patterns, financial status, etc. How can people enjoy het convenience of intelligent services while avoiding information leakage? This has become an urgent problem to be solved in today's society, and also the focus of scholars in recent years [2].

At present, the main method of location privacy protection is to confuse the attackers by mixing real and false location [3]. Location K-anonymity is a location confusion

© Springer Nature Singapore Pte Ltd. 2021
L. Lin et al. (Eds.): SocialSec 2021, CCIS 1495, pp. 133–144, 2021.
https://doi.org/10.1007/978-981-16-7913-1_10

privacy protection model first proposed by Marco Gruteser [4]. Later, scholars have studied a variety of protection schemes around this idea, mainly including schemes based on false location [5, 6], spatio-temporal correlation combined anonymity scheme [7], K-anonymity based on Hilbert curve value [8], etc. They focus on single point query in European space. For example, when shopping mall, it is possible to initiate the query service in any location of the mall. However, if people initiate the query on the vehicle, the situation will be different. At this time, the privacy scheme in the traditional European space cannot meet the privacy requirements of the road network [9]. Literatures [9–15] are all aimed at the privacy protection of vehicle information and consider the problem of trajectory leakage from the perspective of prediction, etc., but seldom consider the environmental information of road network. Throughout the existing studies, there is still a lack of trajectory privacy protection scheme for different travel modes. It is not feasible to use the same scheme for free European space and road network environment. It is also not feasible to use the same method for the protection of trajectory position as for the protection of single point position.

Based on the above information, trajectory privacy protection schemes under different environments are designed:

1) Formulate non-road network or road network protection methods according to travel forms and demands;
2) According to the privacy level of road network map, the trajectories on the road with high risk are protected;
3) Avoid trajectory matching and associating with user to prevent potential information leakage.

2 Model Description

2.1 System Model Description

K-anonymous trajectory set: an anonymous trajectory set composed of the user's real trajectory and $K - 1$ false trajectories generated by the false trajectory generation algorithm, represented by ATS = $\{L_1, L_2, ..., L_K\}$. In this paper, L_1 represents the real trajectory, and others represent false trajectories.

Location privacy protection system consists of three parts: user, privacy protection server and LBS. The privacy protection server includes a module for generating false trajectory set and a module for query feedback. Among them, the generation module of false trajectory set is responsible for generating multiple virtual trajectories, which are published after confusing with the real trajectory; the query feedback module is responsible for filtering the feedback results of LBS. Request query includes travel mode, location, request content and so on. according to the travel modes and privacy requirements, the privacy protection server selects the false trajectory generation algorithm to generate and process the anonymous set of trajectory, and sends the processed anonymous information to LBS. The matching results which calculated by LBS are fed back to the privacy protection server. The filtered real service is fed back to the requesting user by the privacy protection server.

2.2 Trajectory Privacy Protection Scheme

This scheme is composed of three modules: area map matching module; section privacy level determination module; virtual trajectory generation module.

Area map matching: First, the query service is initiated by the user, single point or continuous query. Such as query point A to point B of the best driving path or several continuous queries surrounding food. The trajectory area is preliminarily determined through query, and the road network structure of this region is established.

Determine the privacy level of the road: each road section in the area is divided, and the privacy level of each road section is determined. For example, the urban main road has dense traffic flow and almost 90% of vehicles choose this section, so the privacy level can be set as a low level, and the probability of densely populated areas being located by attackers is low. The privacy level of the road with few people should be set higher. In extreme cases, this section has only one user at the moment, it must be the query user, the risk is very high. In this model, the privacy protection server assumes that information such as road privacy level can be obtained.

The false trajectory generation algorithms are determined according to the privacy level of road section and user demand: A. False Trajectory Algorithm without Road Net (FTA); B. False Trajectory Algorithm Based on Road Network (RNFTA). The algorithms, which are the focus of this article, will be discussed in detail in part 3.

3 False Trajectory Generation Algorithm

3.1 False Trajectory Algorithm Without Road Net (FTA)

FTA algorithm is suitable for walking users, without road network environment. Finding the appropriate distance between true and false trajectory points is the key of this algorithm: if the distance is too close, the generated false trajectory does not meet the anonymity principle; if the distance is too far, the generated false trajectory and the real trajectory feature are too different, and the requested service cannot be obtained. Therefore, both privacy and service requirements need to be taken into account.

K is defined as the degree of anonymity, that is, the number of false trajectories; θ is the threshold value of the included angle between two adjacent sections in the false trajectory. In order to prevent the motion trajectory from being too small, the included angle between two adjacent sections should be greater than this threshold value; d is the maximum distance threshold between the false trajectory point and the corresponding user's real trajectory point. If the threshold is too large, the false position is too far away from the real position, so it is difficult to get the required service. If it is too close, it is difficult to ensure privacy. Therefore, it can be set according to the customer's requirements. (x_i, y_i) and $\left(x_i', y_i'\right)$ respectively represent the coordinates of the i-th sampling position point in the true and false trajectories. The specific algorithm is described as Algorithm 1:

Algorithm 1: False Trajectory Generation Algorithm without Road Net (FTA-r1)

Input: K, θ, d

Output: K false trajectories

begin

1. obtain the starting coordinate (x_i, y_i) of the true trajectory, $i = 1$;

2. $k = 1$, in the d range of starting coordinate, the initial section $[(x_1', y_1')(x_2', y_2')]$ of false trajectory is randomly generated;

\\find the initial position of the k-th $(1 \leq k \leq K)$ false trajectory

3. obtain the true trajectory node coordinate (x_{i+1}, y_{i+1}) at the next moment;

4. randomly generate false trajectory point (x_{i+1}', y_{i+1}');

5. obtain angle θ_k, which is the included angle between line segments $[(x_i', y_i')(x_{i+1}', y_{i+1}')]$ and $[(x_{i-1}', y_{i-1}')(x_i', y_i')]$;

6. if the included angle does not satisfy the condition $(\theta \leq \theta_k \leq 180°)$, return to 4;

7. (x_{i+1}', y_{i+1}') is added to the false trajectory;

8. if the trajectory point is not the endpoint, return to 3;

9. this false trajectory L is added to the false trajectory set ATS, if $k < K$, return to 2;

end

FTA-r1 only takes into account the angle problem of false trajectory when generating position points. The random generation of false coordinates makes the feature difference between the false trajectory and the real trajectory relatively large. Therefore, the FTA-r2 algorithm specifies the following requirements to generate false trajectory points: the included angle between the direction angle of false trajectory segment and that of true trajectory segment must be less than a certain angle; the real trajectory section and the false trajectory section should meet the requirement of distance deviation.

The generation of false trajectory points is shown in Fig. 1, where the black point is the real trajectory point and the gray point is the false trajectory point. It can be seen from Fig. 1 that the false track segment generated in Fig. 1(a) meets the two requirements of the FTA-r2 algorithm and is qualified. The false track segment generated in Fig. 1(b) exceeds the set range and does not meet the requirements of distance offset. The included angle between the direction angle of the false trajectory segment generated in Fig. 1(c) and that of the true trajectory segment exceeds the set angle threshold, which does not meet the angle requirements.

Two parameters φ_i and φ_i' are added in algorithm FTA-r2, which respectively represent the direction angle of the i-th line segment of the real trajectory and the false trajectory. The line segment in the false trajectory has to satisfy $\left|\varphi_i - \varphi_i'\right| \leq \theta$. FTA-r2 false trajectory generation algorithm is to replace the 5th and 6th lines of code in Algorithm 1 (FTA-r1) with:

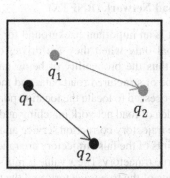 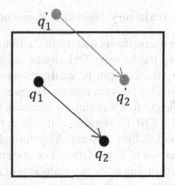

(a) The false trajectory meets the requirements   (b) False trajectory path out of range

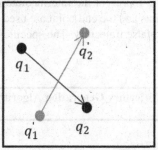

(c) False trajectory direction angle deviation is too large

Fig. 1. Generation of false trajectory points

Algorithm 2: False Trajectory Generation Algorithm without Road Net (FTA-r2)

Input: K, θ, d

Output: K false trajectories

begin

1. obtain the starting coordinate (x_i, y_i) of the true trajectory, $i = 1$;

2. $k = 1$, in the d range of starting coordinate, the initial section $[(x_1', y_1')(x_2', y_2')]$ of false trajectory is randomly generated;

   \\find the initial position of the k-th $(1 \leq k \leq K)$ false trajectory

3. obtain the true trajectory node coordinate (x_{i+1}, y_{i+1}) at the next moment;

4. randomly generate false trajectory point (x_{i+1}', y_{i+1}');

5. obtain the direction angles of true and false trajectories, φ_i is the direction angle of line segment $[(x_i, y_i)(x_{i+1}, y_{i+1})]$, and φ_i' is the direction angle of line segment $[(x_i', y_i')(x_{i+1}', y_{i+1}')]$;

6. if the included angle does not satisfy the condition ($|\varphi_i - \varphi_i'| \leq \theta$), return to 4;

7. (x_{i+1}', y_{i+1}') is added to the false trajectory;

8. if the trajectory point is not the endpoint, return to 3;

9. this false trajectory L is added to the false trajectory set ATS, if $k < K$, return to 2;

end

3.2 False Trajectory Algorithm Based on Road Network (RNFTA)

For vehicle users, the road network environment is an important background for maintaining false trajectories. Trajectories are normal only when they are driven on the road, otherwise they can be easily eliminated, thus the probability of being targeted is increased. Digital maps contain a common type of structured road data, and the map matching function of planning the route can be processed to locate the location points on the real road. RNFTA algorithm introduces the idea of road network matching and route planning, and realizes map matching through the trajectory correction service and route planning service of Baidu server. The two endpoints of the false trajectory are randomly generated according to the two endpoints of the true trajectory. The x value is introduced to represent the number of trajectory feature points of the true trajectory, and the trajectory feature points are used to represent the intermediate points of the trajectory. The starting point, the feature points and the end point are used for route planning and route matching, so as to obtain the false trajectory. The specific RNFTA algorithm is shown in Algorithm 3:

Algorithm 3: False Trajectory Generation Algorithm Based on Road Network (RNFTA)

Input: K, x, d
Output: K false trajectories
begin
  1. obtain the starting coordinate (x_1, y_1) and the ending coordinate (x_{-1}, y_{-1}) of the true trajectory;
  2. divide the true trajectory into x trajectory segments;
  3. calculate the feature points of each trajectory segment;
  \\find the initial position of the k-th false trajectory
  4. obtain the true trajectory node coordinate (x_i, y_i) at the next moment, and determine whether to generate false positions according to the privacy level of the section where each feature point is located;
  5. if it is at a lower level, no change is required and return to 4; if it is at a higher level, run step 6;
  6. generate false trajectory points $(x_i', y_i')(x_{i+1}', y_{i+1}')$ randomly;
  7. plan the route for $(x_i', y_i')(x_{i+1}', y_{i+1}')$;
  8. the obtained planned route fragment is added to the false trajectory;
  9. if the trajectory point is not the endpoint, return to 4;
  10. trajectory correction is performed by the true trajectory timestamp set and false trajectory.
  11. get the false trajectory after repair;
  12. if (the number of false trajectory points after repair is closer to the number of true trajectory points)
    {false trajectory = false trajectory after repair;}
  13. correct the number of false trajectory points;
  14. the false trajectory is added to false trajectory set;
  15. this false trajectory L is added to the false trajectory set ATS, if $k < K$, return to 1;
end

---

4 Simulation Analysis

In this section, the solution is simulated and analyzed. The simulation platform is implemented by using PYTHON language. The computer platform used in the experiment is a Windows 10 64-bit computer with Intel core i5-6300HQ and 8 GB memory. The true trajectory data used in the experimental analysis are ten trajectories randomly labeled in Nanjing. The sum of the total length of the trajectory is about 53 km. The number of sampling points for each trajectory is between 10 and 35, and the sampling distance is about 200 m.

The platform first needs to import the real trajectory. Users can import the real trajectory into the simulation platform in the form of files or load the real trajectory from the database. After importing the trajectory, the simulation system will display the effect of the current trajectory, as shown in Fig. 2.

Fig. 2. Simulation system

4.1 Feasibility Analysis of False Trajectory Generation Algorithm Without Road Net

Firstly, the FTA algorithm and the influence of different generalization scope is analyzed. As shown in Fig. 3, three false trajectories with $K = 3$ are generated. L_1 is the real trajectory, L_2, L_3 and L_4 are false trajectories, and the distance threshold of the trajectory is set to 200 m, 500 m and 1000 m respectively.

As shown in Fig. 3, the larger the distance threshold, the greater the false trajectory deviation, which can well protect the real trajectory. However, the false trajectory has some problems that the route is too false and the service accuracy is insufficient. For example, walking to a few meters away in a second, driving too far off the road, and insufficient feedback when querying the surrounding gas stations.

The comparison of the two FTA algorithms is shown in Fig. 4. It can be seen that the false trajectory generated by FTA-r2 is smoother and closer to the reality, which is suitable for walking users. However, it is not applicable to the vehicle trajectory. The false trajectory deviates seriously from the road, and the attacker can easily locate the real trajectory.

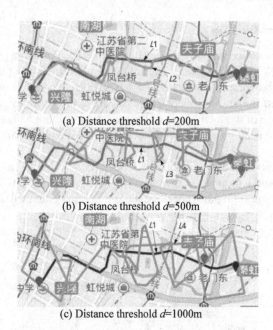

(a) Distance threshold *d*=200m

(b) Distance threshold *d*=500m

(c) Distance threshold *d*=1000m

Fig. 3. One simulation example of FTA algorithm

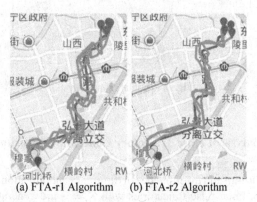

(a) FTA-r1 Algorithm   (b) FTA-r2 Algorithm

Fig. 4. Comparison of two FTA algorithms

4.2 Feasibility Analysis of False Trajectory Generation Algorithm Based on Road Network

One example of RNFTA algorithm is shown in Fig. 5, where L_1 is the real trajectory, L_2 and L_3 are false trajectories generated by setting different privacy levels. In Fig. 5(a), R1 and R2 are set to a low level of privacy; in Fig. 5(b), R3 and R4 are set to a low level of privacy. These sections are main roads with dense vehicles and do not require trajectory anonymity. In both cases, the two false trajectories are both on the road, so the trajectories produced do not deviate from the road, and both are feasible. Another

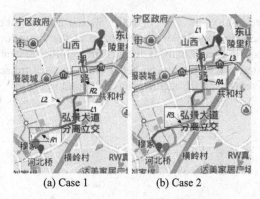

(a) Case 1   (b) Case 2

Fig. 5. Example 1 of RNFTA algorithm

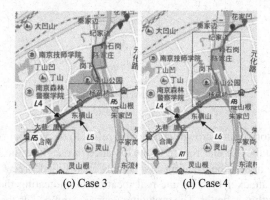

(c) Case 3   (d) Case 4

Fig. 6. Example 2 of RNFTA algorithm

example of the RNFTA algorithm is shown in Fig. 6. By comparing Fig. 5 and Fig. 6, it can be seen that RNFTA algorithm can adapt to different simulation environments.

4.3 Performance Analysis

Next, the algorithm performance will be analyzed from the perspective of trajectory coverage and crowding degree. These two indicators can well measure the ability of the constructed false trajectory to obtain accurate service and resist aggression. Trajectory coverage means that for a point in the real trajectory, the circular region of the distance threshold always contains false trajectory points, indicating that the real trajectory can be covered by the false trajectory. Trajectory coverage refers to the proportion of the covered true trajectory points T' in the total number of true trajectory points T, that is,

$$\text{Trajectory coverage} = \frac{T'}{T} \times 100\% \tag{1}$$

A higher coverage indicates that accurate services can still be obtained under the condition of anonymity.

The distance threshold value $d = 50$, 100, 150 and 200 are taken respectively to compare their impacts, and the trajectory coverage of the algorithm is calculated as shown in Fig. 7. According to the analysis, the false trajectories generated by the RNFTA algorithm for road network matching can better cover the real trajectories and obtain accurate services. Average service accuracy has increased by 36%.

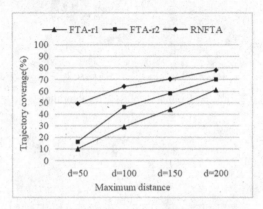

Fig. 7. Trajectory coverage analysis chart

The true trajectory points crowding degree F refers to the number of false trajectory points contained in the circular region of the distance threshold value for a point in the real trajectory. The higher the true trajectory points crowding degree F is, the lower the probability of the attacker locating the real location is, indicating that the anti-attack ability of the algorithm is better. The crowding degree is defined as the ratio of the sum of true trajectory points crowding degree F to the total number of true trajectory points T, which is

$$\text{crowding degree} = \frac{\sum_{i=1}^{T} F_i}{T} \tag{2}$$

The distance threshold value $d = 50$, 100, 150 and 200 are taken respectively to compare their influences, and the trajectory crowding degree is calculated, as shown in Fig. 8. According to the analysis, the false trajectory and true trajectory set generated by the RNFTA algorithm for road network matching have higher crowding degree of trajectory points, which reduces the degree of privacy leakage by 78%. In conclusion, the scheme in this paper can be applied to users of different travel modes. Meanwhile, RNFTA based on road network has better ability to obtain accurate services and resist attacks.

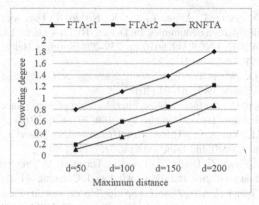

Fig. 8. Crowding degree analysis chart

5 Conclusion

In view of the problem that privacy protection cannot be mixed when people travel in different ways, this paper proposes a mobile trajectory privacy protection scheme facing different travel modes. Firstly, the overall privacy protection scheme is designed according to the classification of route section privacy level and different modes of user travel; then, a false trajectory generation algorithm for non-road environment (FTA) is designed, taking into account the requirements of service and privacy; finally, the false trajectory generation algorithm under road network environment (RNFTA) is designed, thus the real trajectory can be hidden and protected. The simulation experiment shows that the scheme can handle the anonymous trajectory quickly for the users of different travel modes, and can provide the users with more efficient and safe location services.

Funding. This work is funded by the National Natural Science Foundation of China (No.61902069 and U1905211), the Science Foundation of Fujian University of Technology (GY-Z21048, GY-Z18181, GY-Z21024), the Natural Science Foundation of Fujian Province of China (2021J011068).

References

1. Feng, D., Zhang, M., Ye, Y.: Research on location trajectory publishing technology based on differential privacy model. J. Electron. Inf. Technol. **42**(1), 74–88 (2020)
2. Wu, Z., Wang, R., Li, Q.: A location privacy-preserving system based on query range cover-up or location-based services. IEEE Trans. Veh. Technol. **69**(5), 5244–5254 (2020)
3. Xu, C., Luo, L., Ding, Y.: Personalized location privacy protection for location-based services in vehicular networks. IEEE Wirel. Commun. **9**(10), 1633–1637 (2020)
4. Zeng, H., Zuo, K., Wang, Y.: Semantic diversity location privacy protection in road network environment. Comput. Eng. Appl. **56**(7), 102–108 (2020)
5. Gruteser, M., Grunwald, D.: Anonymous usage of location-based services through spatial and temporal cloaking. In: Conference: Proceedings of the First International Conference on Mobile Systems, Applications and Services, San Francisco, CA, USA, pp. 31–42 (2003)

6. Kato, R., Iwata, M., Hara, T., Arase, Y., Xie, X., Nishio, S.: User location anonymization method for wide distribution of dummies. In: Decker, H., Lhotská, L., Link, S., Basl, J., Tjoa, A.M. (eds.) DEXA 2013. LNCS, vol. 8056, pp. 259–273. Springer, Heidelberg (2013). https://doi.org/10.1007/978-3-642-40173-2_22

7. Zhang, S., Liu, Q., Wang, G.: Trajectory privacy protection method based on location obfuscation. J. Commun. **39**(7), 81–91 (2018)

8. Li, Z., Li, W., Wen, Q.: A efficient blind filter: location privacy protection and the access control in FinTech. Futur. Gener. Comput. Syst. **100**, 797–810 (2019)

9. To, Q.C., Dang, T.K., Kueng, J.: A Hilbert-based framework for preserving privacy in location-based services. Int. J. Intell. Inf. Database Syst. **7**(2), 113 (2013)

10. Ye, A., Meng, L., Zhao, Z., Diao, Y., Zhang, J.: Trajectory differential privacy protection mechanism based on prediction and sliding window. J. Commun. **41**(4), 123–133 (2020)

11. Xu, Z., Zhang, J., Tsai, P., Lin, L., Zhuo, C.: Spatiotemporal mobility based trajectory privacy-preserving algorithm in location-based services. Sensors **21**(6), 113–134 (2021)

12. Squicciarini, A.C., Qiu, C.: Location privacy protection in vehicle-based spatial crowdsourcing via geo-indistinguishability. In: 2019 IEEE 39th International Conference on Distributed Computing Systems (ICDCS). IEEE (2019)

13. Arain, Q.A., Memon, I., Deng, Z., Memon, M.H., Mangi, F.A., Zubedi, A.: Location monitoring approach: multiple mix-zones with location privacy protection based on traffic flow over road networks. Multimedia Tools Appl. **77**(5), 5563–5607 (2017). https://doi.org/10.1007/s11042-017-4469-4

14. Ji, Y., Gui, X., Dai, H., Peng, Z.: A two-stage user interest zone construction method to support trajectory privacy protection. Chin. J. Comput. **40**(12), 2734–2747 (2017)

15. Kuang, L., Wang, Y., Zheng, X., Huang, L., Sheng, Y.: Using location semantics to realize personalized road network location privacy protection. EURASIP J. Wirel. Commun. Netw. **2020**(1), 1–16 (2019). https://doi.org/10.1186/s13638-019-1618-7

Migration Privacy Protection Based on Scheduling Algorithm for Online Car-Hailing

Qian Ding[1,2], Jing Zhang[1,2(✉)], Liwei Lin[1,2], Zhiping Xu[1,2], and Yichun Wang[3]

[1] School of Computer Science and Mathematics, Fujian University of Technology, Fuzhou 350118, Fujian, China
[2] Fujian Provincial Key Laboratory of Big Data Mining and Applications, Fujian University of Technology, Fuzhou 350118, Fujian, China
[3] Shanghai Oriental Pearl Digital TV Company Limited, 1 Century Avenue, Pudong District, Shanghai 200120, China

Abstract. In the era of rapid development of mobile Internet technology and big data technology, people enjoy more convenient travel because of Online Car-hailing. At the same time, the location privacy of drivers and passengers has also been leaked due to the use of Online Car-hailing. The traditional privacy preserving encryption technology for Online Car-hailing has a large amount of computation and low efficiency. In order to solve these problems, the Migration Privacy Protection based on Scheduling Algorithm (MPSA) for Online car-hailing is proposed in this paper. Firstly, the road network model is established through the road network matching technology. Secondly, the shortest path between the passenger and the car is calculated through A* algorithm and Dijkstra algorithm. Finally, the location privacy protection between the driver and the passenger is realized through the offset technology. In this paper, a scientific experiment is carried out on real data to verify the superiority of MPSA in privacy protection effect and operation efficiency.

Keywords: Online Car-hailing · Location privacy protection · Road network matching · Migration technology

1 Introduction

In the era of rapid development of Internet technology, Online Car-Hailing services are closely integrated with the lives of people. According to the 47th statistical report on Internet development in China released by China Internet Network Information Center, the number of Online car-hailing users in China has reached 365 million by December 2020 [1]. In the Online car-hailing system, the passenger sends their current location and riding demand through mobile intelligent devices, and the nearest car will be assigned to the passenger. Although the fast Online car-hailing platform improves people's travel efficiency greatly. It also triggers a series of vicious social events, which resulting leakages of the passenger's privacy and threatening the passenger's safety. For example, in order to facilitate the monitoring of online cars, the Online car-hailing platform requires

L. Lin et al. (Eds.): SocialSec 2021, CCIS 1495, pp. 145–158, 2021.
https://doi.org/10.1007/978-981-16-7913-1_11

all drivers and passengers to register their real names and save a large amount of user information [2]. Once the location information in the process of driving is obtained by the criminals, the passenger's safety is vulnerable. Therefore, the Online car-hailing platform should not only provide convenience for people, but also protect the location privacy and security of users.

At present, there are three main technologies for location privacy protection: K-anonymity [3, 4], Encryption [5], and Differential privacy [6]. The privacy protection degree can be defined by K-anonymity according to the user's needs, but the K-anonymity does not consider the attacker's background knowledge and will be attacked by replay. The Differential privacy doesn't need to consider the attacker's background knowledge, so it has good privacy protection effect and can make up for the disadvantage of K-anonymity. However, it is difficult to allocate the privacy budget ε, and unreasonable privacy budget will make the location data distorted. Encryption technology has better privacy protection effect, but the use of cryptography related algorithms leads to too much calculation, resulting in the low efficiency of the overall algorithm.

Another technique is migration, which protects the location privacy of users by changing the location coordinates [7, 8]. Ms. Apurva K. Kini *et al.* [7] proposed the K-dummy Position Generation Algorithm (KDPA), which make the true location and dummy location hard to be distinguished. Although migration technology can protect users' location privacy, it has not been applied in the field of Online car-hailing location privacy protection at present. Therefore, the Migration Privacy Protection based on Scheduling Algorithm (MPSA) is proposed in this paper. It not only realizes the Online car-hailing scheduling function, but also protects the location privacy information of drivers and passengers.

2 Related Works

This paper mainly solves the problems of effective scheduling and privacy protection of Online car-hailing. The following is the research status of these two aspects.

2.1 Shortest Path Calculation

Dijkstra [9] algorithm is a typical single source shortest path algorithm, which is used to calculate the shortest path from a node to all other nodes. Its basic principle is as follows: given a road network graph $G = (V, E)$, the vertex set V in the graph is divided into two groups: S and U, where S is the vertex set for which the shortest path has been solved, U is the vertex set for which the distance from the initial point to it has not been solved, and the distance of the non-directly connected vertices is ∞. The shortest path of each vertex to the initial point is computed circularly. In the process of calculating the shortest path, continuously add the vertices of the shortest path length (set to P) in U to S, and take the shortest path length as the shortest distance from U to each vertex. At the same time, if the distance from P to each vertex in U + distance from initial point to P < initial point to the distance of each vertex, the distance will be updated to the smaller number. The algorithm ends when all the vertices in U are added to S.

A* [10] algorithm is similar to Dijkstra algorithm in principle. Its efficiency is higher than Dijkstra algorithm. The specific reasons are: Dijkstra algorithm only calculates the minimum cost a from the initial node to each node, and finally finds the target node through traversal. The A* algorithm judges the cost between nodes by the sum of the shortest cost a from the initial node to a node and the precomputing cost b from the node to the target node. That is, the cost $f = a + b$. This precomputation including heuristics improves the efficiency of the whole algorithm.

2.2 Implementation of Location Privacy Protection

Privateride [11] is the first system to protect the location privacy of passengers and prevent the driver's information from being captured. It can complete the journey matching service without exposing the location privacy. However, the Privateride can not protect the privacy of driver's information. Then, Yu et al. proposes the pRMatch scheme [12]. In pRMatch, the shortest road distance over encrypted data is computed by using road network embedding and partially homomorphic encryption and further efficiently compare encrypted distances by using ciphertext packing and shuffling. Although the pRMatch protects the location information of both drivers and passenger, it still has a large computational cost.

Li et al. proposes an efficient trajectory privacy protection scheme based on false trajectory. In this scheme, the real trajectories are offset by the method of trajectory rotation, so as to construct $K - 1$ false trajectories that are difficult to be distinguished by the enemy with background information, thus achieving the privacy protection of user trajectories at K-anonymity level [13]. Xu et al. proposes a distributed location privacy protection method based on offset grid [14]. In this method, the location area is divided into grids, the user calculates the offset grid area according to the regularly updated grid information, and sends the offset grid area to the anonymous server. Although the offset technology in references [13] and [14] can be used to protect location privacy, the generated false location may be easily recognized by attackers because it does not conform to the reality.

The main contribution of this paper is to propose MPSA algorithm, which can not only effectively complete the Online car-hailing scheduling function, but also protect the location privacy of users. Specifically, in this paper, the real road network data is offset according to a certain offset by the offset technology, so as to get the pseudo road network data different from the real road network. Under this technology, the offset pseudo positioning data will be uploaded to the server by passengers and drivers, and the offset road network data is used by the server for function calculation. In this way, only pseudo data different from the real location data is saved in the server platform, which can not be directly applied to the actual map. Thus, the encryption effect of privacy protection is achieved.

3   Algorithm Design

The goal of this paper is to realize the Online car-hailing scheduling and privacy protection. Based on this goal, the Euclidean Distance based Scheduling Algorithm for Online car-hailing (EDSA) is proposed, but it can not be combined with the actual road network, resulting in large matching error. Therefore, the Road Network Embedding based Scheduling Algorithm for Online car-hailing (RNSA) is proposed. Although this algorithm realizes the matching of online car hailing and passengers on the real road network, it can not protect the location privacy information of passengers and drivers. Therefore, this paper proposes the Migration Privacy protection technology based Scheduling Algorithm for Online car-hailing (MPSA), which can not only realize the intelligent service of the Online car-hailing system, but also effectively protect the location information of both drivers and passengers.

Table 1 shows the relevant variables and meanings that will be used in this paper.

Table 1. The variable meaning table

Variable	Meaning
user	Passenger's longitude, latitude, and number
clist	Information collection of longitude, latitude and number of taxi
car	Location information of a car
rlist	The set of distances between vehicles and passengers
clist'	The shortest distance and shortest path set between each vehicle and passenger
U	Passenger boarding road node
C	Next road node for a single taxi
r	The calculated Euclidean distance
blat	Latitude value of the original position point
blng	The longitude value of the original position point
z	Excess value
zlng	Longitude value after offset
zlat	Latitude value after offset
$n1$	Offset used for longitude
$n2$	Offset used for latitude
i	Calculate dimension variables

3.1 Euclidean Distance Based Scheduling Algorithm for Online Car-Hailing (EDSA)

In this section, the detailed design of EDSA algorithm will be introduced. Firstly, the algorithm obtains the longitude and latitude of passengers and Online car-hailing. Secondly, the Euclidean distance between the passenger and the randomly generated online car is calculated according to the longitude and latitude. Finally, the calculation results are sorted, and the vehicle with the smallest euclidean distance of passengers is the optimal vehicle to match.

EDSA algorithm is shown in algorithm 1.

Algorithm 1: EDSA algorithm

Input: user, clist.
Output : The vehicle information with the smallest r in the **clist** set.
  begin
  1. enter the generated **user**, **clist**; Create **rlist** set;
  2.   for **car** (the Euclidean distance between the passenger and the last car is calculated){
  3.   the euclidean distance r between **car** and **user** is calculated;
  4.   the calculation results r, user's information and car corresponding vehicle information are stored in **rlist** together;
  }
  5. sort **rlist** according to the size of r in **rlist**;
  6. Returns the vehicle information with the smallest r in **rlist**;
  end

Running the EDSA algorithm through the operating platform, the results are shown in Fig. 1.

Fig. 1. An example of the EDSA algorithm

As shown in Fig. 1, the number of the vehicle closest to passenger **U** calculated by EDSA algorithm is 13. However, there is no road between passenger **U** and vehicle 13 in the actual road network, so this algorithm is not applicable in the real road environment. Therefore, the second algorithm is proposed in this paper: Road Network Embedding based Scheduling Algorithm for Online car-hailing (RNSA).

3.2 Road Network Embedding Based Scheduling Algorithm for Online Car-Hailing (RNSA)

The Road Network Embedding based Scheduling Algorithm for Online car-hailing (RNSA) is proposed in this section. Firstly, the road network map is preprocessed to obtain the real road network vector data. Secondly, Dijkstra algorithm and A * algorithm are used to calculate the shortest path to realize the online car scheduling function in the real road network.

Firstly, the algorithm obtains the shortest path between nodes in the road network through Dijkstra routing algorithm and A* algorithm. Then, an intersection node near passenger **U** is defined as **S**, and the distance between **U** and **S** is dist (**U, S**), the node of an intersection near vehicle **C** is **T**, the distance between **C** and **T** is dist (**C, T**), and the distance between node **T** and node **S** is dist (**T, S**), so the distance between passenger **U** and vehicle **C** is: dist(**U, C**) = dist(**U, S**) + dist(**C, T**) + dist(**T, S**). As shown in Fig. 2.

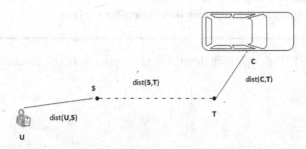

Fig. 2. Schematic diagram of route distance between passengers and taxis

Where dist(**U, S**) and dist(**S, T**) are calculated by euclidean distance respectively. Then, the shortest distance dist (**S, T**) and the shortest driving path between road node **T** and **S** are obtained by combining Dijkstra algorithm and A* algorithm of road network.

To sum up, the set of (**P, E**) is defined as a road network in this algorithm. **P** is the intersection node in the road network, **E** is the edge connecting two intersection nodes, and n is the number of intersection nodes. According to the passenger's position **U**, the target road point **U'** is defined and calculated at the same time. According to the car location set in the vicinity $R = \{P_1, P_2, P_3...P_i\}$, the starting road node set corresponding to the taxi set $R' = \{P_1', P_2', P_3' ... P_i'\}$ $(i < n)$ is obtained. The path distance between the passenger and the car is shown in Formula (1):

$$dist(U, P_1) = dist(U, U') + min(dist(U', P_1')) + dist(P_1, P_1') \qquad (1)$$

Based on the above definition, the possible path distances between the target point **U** and the set **R** are combined into a set **HD(UR)**, The minimum value in **HD(UR)** is the shortest path distance.

$$HD(UR) = (dist(U, P_1), dist(U, P_2), dist(U, P_3), ... dist(U, P_i)) \qquad (2)$$

RNSA algorithm is shown in algorithm 2.

Algorithm 2: RNSA algorithm

Input: user, clist.

Output: The shortest distance and shortest path set between each vehicle and passenger.
  begin

    1. enter the generated **user, clist'**; Create **rlist** set;

    2. According to the user's regional information, read the corresponding road
       intersection and road vector data from the database;

    3. for (the road network distance between the passenger and the last car is
       calculated) {

    4. The distance between **user** and each road intersection is calculated and
         compared to get the nearest road node **u**, and the distance is recorded as uu;

    5. Traverse the road data, calculate the vector road closest to **car**, obtain the
         end point **c** of vector road, and calculate the distance between **car** and **c** as cc;

    6. Call the routing algorithm to calculate the shortest path between road node
         u and road node **c**, and the shortest distance is uc;

    7. Compute the value of $uu + cc + uc$, and the shortest path information is stored
       together in **rlist**;

  }

    8. The **rlist** is sorted according to the path distance in the **rlist**;

    9. return **rlist**;

  end

Running the RNSA algorithm through the operating platform, the results are shown in Fig. 3

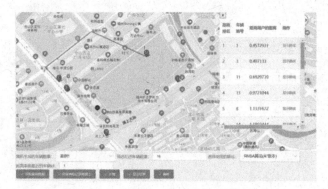

Fig. 3. An example of the RNSA algorithm.

It can be seen from the above Fig. 3 that the matching results obtained by RNSA algorithm are obviously consistent with the actual road network scenarios. Therefore, RNSA algorithm is more accurate than EDSA algorithm.

3.3 Migration Privacy Protection Technology Based Scheduling Algorithm for Online Car-Hailing (MPSA)

Although the RNSA algorithm realizes the matching of Online car-hailing and passengers on the real road network, it can not protect the location privacy information of passengers and drivers. Therefore, the Migration Privacy protection technology based Scheduling Algorithm for Online car-hailing (MPSA) is proposed in this section. Firstly, the road network map is offset to obtain pseudo road network data different from the real road network. Secondly, passengers and drivers upload pseudo-location data with the same offset to the server. Finally, these offset data are used by the server for business function calculation, thus protecting the location privacy of both the drivers and passengers.

The offset calculation in this paper refers to the positioning offset of Badu Map API[1], and the specific calculation is shown in Eq. (3) and (4).

$$\begin{cases} zlng = z * cos(t) + n1 \\ zlat = z * sin(t) + n2 \end{cases} \tag{3}$$

$$\begin{cases} z = \sqrt{blng^2 + blat^2} + \alpha * sin(blat * \pi) \\ t = atan2(blat, blng) + \beta * cos(blng * \pi) \end{cases} \tag{4}$$

The longitude and latitude after offset can be calculated by Eq. (3), in which the values of z and t are calculated by Eq. (4), and the offset $n1$ and $n1$ are adaptive and can be set according to specific application scenarios.

MPSA algorithm is shown in algorithm 3.

---

[1] https://www.cnblogs.com/arxive/p/7511468.html.

Algorithm 3: MPSA algorithm

Input: user, clist.

Output: The nearest **car** to the **user**.

    begin

        1. Randomly generates **user**, **clist**;

        2. The **user** and **clist** location information is offset by the offset algorithm and uploaded to the server;

        3. The server reads the corresponding road intersection and road vector data from the database according to the user's area, and offsets them at the same time;

        4. Create **rlist** set;

        5.   for (the road network distance between the passenger and the last car is calculated) {

        6.   The distance between **user** and each road intersection is calculated and compared to get the nearest road node **u**, and the distance is recorded as uu;

        7.   Traverse the road data, calculate the vector road closest to the **car**, obtain the vector road end point **c**, and calculate and save the distance between the **car** and **c** as cc;

        8.   Call the road network routing algorithm to calculate the shortest path between road node **u** and road node **c**, and the shortest distance is recorded as uc;

        9.   The **car** information is calculated to calculate the path distance $uu+cc+uc$, and the shortest path information is stored in **rlist** together;

        }

        10. The **rlist** is sorted according to the size of the path distance in the **rlist**;

        11. return **rlist**;

    end

Similarly, Running the MPSA algorithm through the operating platform, the results are shown in Fig. 4.

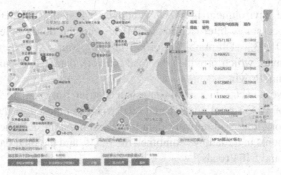

Fig. 4. An example of the MPSA algorithm

It can be seen from Fig. 4 that the MPSA algorithm can obtain the same number of the vehicle closest to the passenger position under the same conditions as RNSA algorithm, which proves its feasibility. When the data obtained from the server is also put on Baidu Map, the result is shown in Fig. 5.

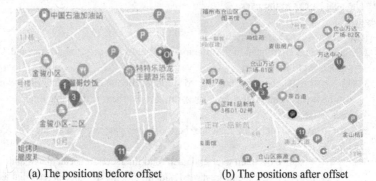

(a) The positions before offset   (b) The positions after offset

Fig. 5. An example of position comparison before and after migration algorithm

It can be seen intuitively that the location of driver and passenger in reality is different from the original after the offset algorithm is calculated, which can ensure that the location privacy of drivers and passengers will not be leaked by the server. Moreover, because all the offset positions are calculated by the same offset algorithm, the relative distance of each point does not change after the position offset, which indicates that the calculation result of RNSA algorithm after the offset is not different from that before the offset, which proves the feasibility of MPSA algorithm.

4 Experimental Simulation

4.1 Experimental Environment and Data Set

The experimental environment is 64 bit windows10 system, the memory (RAM) is 8.00 GB, the processor is Intel (R) core (TM) i7, and the development environment is IntelliJ idea 2019.3.3 (Ultimate Edition). The main source of experimental data is OpenStreetMap map, which provides the road network data set of Cangshan District, Fuzhou City, Fujian Province.

The road network vector data set of Cangshan District, Fuzhou City, Fujian Province contains a total of 16453 road nodes and 17801 roads composed of these road nodes. We simplify the original road network data to a certain extent. For the case that there are multiple segments in a road, we combined the roads, and the final data set contained 4116 road nodes and 5464 roads.

4.2 Road Network Area Division

In order to improve the matching efficiency of the algorithm, the road network map is divided into several rectangular areas according to the preset longitude and latitude interval. In the specific division process, the fineness of 10*10 is adopted in this experiment to segment the road network map of Cangshan District. In this way, taxis and passengers will be calculated in their assigned regions before sending their offset coordinates to the server, and then send the calculated region ID to the server along with the encrypted coordinates, so as to reduce the computing amount of the server and improve the efficiency of the algorithm.The specific division effect is shown in Fig. 6.

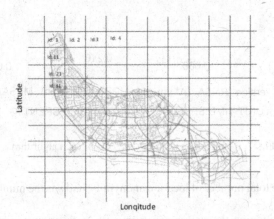

Fig. 6. Diagram of road network division in Cangshan District, Fuzhou City

4.3 Analysis of Algorithm Time Accessibility

The current network car software single time calculation reaction time is about 2S. The time calculation methods of the three algorithms in this paper are as follows: first of all, the time stamp sets at the beginning and end of the algorithm are recorded. And then the average speed of each vehicle for passengers under different algorithms is calculated in turn. The time effect diagram of the specific algorithm is shown in Fig. 7. The letter "D" in the Fig. 7 is the abbreviation of Dijkstra.

It is easy to find out form Fig. 7 that MPSA algorithm has a slightly larger time cost than RNSA algorithm, but the difference is only a few milliseconds, which can be ignored. Moreover, the total time calculated by MPSA algorithm, which is in line with the market expectation.

4.4 Location Privacy Anonymity Rate Analysis

In this paper, the privacy anonymity rate is used to measure the degree of protection of location privacy. Anonymous privacy rate η is the probability of successful location protection. Its calculation method is as follows:

$$\eta = \frac{n}{m} \times 100\% \tag{5}$$

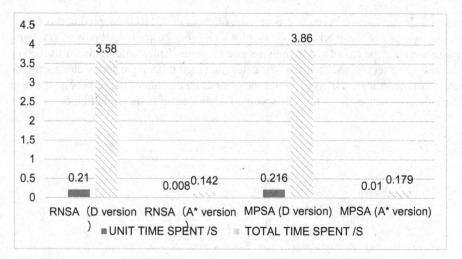

Fig. 7. Comparison chart of time cost of each algorithm.

Where m is the total number of location anonymity, and n is the number of successful location anonymity.

The basis for judging the success of anonymity in this paper is as follows: given a threshold R. The Euclidean distance between the post offset position and the preoffset position is represented as d. If $d > R$, the anonymity is successful, otherwise the anonymity is failed. Where d is calculated as follows:

$$n = \sum_i^m \chi(d_i - R) \tag{6}$$

Where $\chi(x)$ is the logical judgement function, $\chi(x) = 1$ if $x > 0$. Otherwise, $\chi(x) = 0$.

In this experiment, the KDPA algorithm in literature [7] and the Coordinate Transformation Algorithm (CTA) in literature [8] are used to compare with MPSA algorithm. Finally, the anonymous success rate comparison results of the three algorithms are shown in Fig. 8:

As shown in Fig. 8, the anonymous success rate of MPSA algorithm is increasing with the number of passengers, and the anonymous success rate is higher than KDPA algorithm and CTA algorithm. When the number of passengers is 25, the anonymous privacy rates of MPSA, CTA and KDPA are 0.88, 0.78 and 0.71 respectively. Therefore, the security degree of MPSA algorithm is higher than the other two algorithms, and the privacy protection effect is the best.

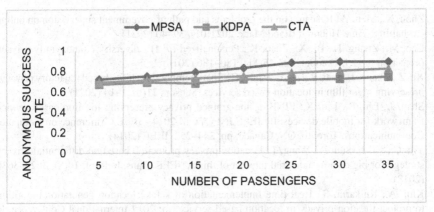

Fig. 8. Comparison of anonymous success rate of algorithms

5 Conclusion

In order to solve the problem of effective scheduling and privacy protection of Online car-hailing, the MPSA algorithm is proposed in this paper. The design of this algorithm is divided into three steps. Firstly, this paper proposes EDSA algorithm, which calculates the nearest Online car-hailing from passengers through Euclidean distance, so as to realize the effective scheduling of Online car-hailing in Euclidean space. Secondly, aiming at the problem of large matching error caused by Euclidean distance calculation in EDSA algorithm, the road network matching model is established in this paper, and the RNSA algorithm is proposed to realize the driver passenger matching on the real road network. Finally, because RNSA algorithm can only realize scheduling and can not protect the location privacy of Online car-hailing drivers and passengers, the MPSA algorithm is proposed, which is based on RNSA algorithm and hides the real location of Online car-hailing drivers and passengers through offset technology, so as to effectively protect the location information of both drivers and passengers.

Meanwhile, the scheme proposed in this paper has some shortcomings. The actual vector road network data used in this paper are not completely accurate. In the future, we will continue to improve the road network matching model to achieve more accurate scheduling matching.

Funding. This work is funded by the National Natural Science Foundation of China (No. 61902069 and U1905211), the Science Foundation of FuJian University of Technology (GY-Z21048, GY-Z18181 and GY-Z21024), the Natural Science Foundation of Fujian Province of China (2021J011068), and the Key Project of Shanghai Science and Technology Innovation Action Plan under Grant (19DZ1100400).

References

1. 21st Century Business Herald. https://m.21jingji.com/article/20210715/020f3c860939158 be3eb50add203838a.html. Accessed 15 July 2021

2. Zhou, X., Men, Z.: Research on the problems and path of government supervision on online car-hailing. Time-Honored Brand Mark. **2021**(01), 39–40 (2021)
3. Cao, M., Zhang, L., Bi, X., Zhao, K.: Personalized (α, I) - diversity K-anonymity privacy protection model. Comput. Sci. **45**(11), 180–186 (2018)
4. Xu, Z., Zhang, J., Tsai, P., Lin, L., Zhuo, C.: Spatiotemporal mobility based trajectory privacy-preserving algorithm in location-based services. Sensors **21**(6), 1–14 (2021)
5. Shao, J., Liu, R., Lin, X.: FINE: a fine-grained privacy-preserving location-based service framework for mobile devices. In: IEEE INFOCOM 2014 - IEEE Conference on Computer Communications, Toronto, ON, Canada, pp. 244–252. IEEE (2014)
6. Yin, C., Xi, J., Sun, R., Wang, J.: Location privacy protection based on differential privacy strategy for big data in industrial internet of things. IEEE Trans. Ind. Inf. **14**(8), 3628–3636 (2018)
7. Kini, A., Kulkarni, S.: Real time implementation of k fake location generation algorithm to protect location privacy in location based service. In: 2017 International Conference on Advances in Computing, Communications and Informatics (ICACCI), Udupi, India, pp.142–148. IEEE (2017)
8. Lin, S., Ye, A., Xu, L.: K-anonymity location privacy protection method based on coordinate transformation. Mini-Micro Syst. **37**(1), 119–123 (2016)
9. Yue, Y., Gong, J.: An efficient implementation of shortest path algorithm based on Dijkstra algorithm. J. Wuhan Tech. Univ. Surv. Mapp. **24**(3), 209–212 (1999)
10. Ju, C., Luo, Q., Yan, X.: Path planning using an improved a-star algorithm. In: 2020 11th International Conference on Prognostics and System Health Management (PHM-2020 Jinan), Jinan, China, pp. 23–26. IEEE (2020)
11. Pham, A., et al.: PrivateRide: a privacy-enhanced ride-hailing Service. In: Proceedings on Privacy Enhancing Technologies, pp. 38–56. PETS, American Samoa (2017)
12. Yu, H., Zhang, X., Yu, X.: Hail the Closest Driver on Roads: privacy-preserving ride matching in online ride hailing services. Secur. Commun. Netw. **2020**(2), 1–13 (2020)
13. Li, F., Zhang, C., Niu, B., Li, H., Hua, J.: Efficient trajectory privacy protection scheme. J. Commun. **36**(12), 114–123 (2015)
14. Xu, J.: Decentralized location privacy protection method of offset grid. In: Modern Computer, pp. 113–120 (2019)

Security of AI

A Survey of Adversarial Examples and Deep Learning Based Data Hiding

Zijing Feng⑩, Chengyu Liu⑩, Xiangmin Ji⑩, and Xiaolong Liu$^{(\boxtimes)}$ ⑩

Fujian Agriculture and Forestry University, Fuzhou 350002, China
xlliu@fafu.edu.cn

Abstract. Nowadays, the emergence of deep learning technology has brought breakthroughs to many fields and has been widely used in many practical scenarios. At the same time, the concept of adversarial examples are gradually known. By adding tiny disturbances to the original samples, the accuracy of the original classification depth model is successfully reduced, and the purpose of confronting deep learning is achieved. In this paper, the survey of adversarial examples and deep learning based data hiding are presented, and then the idea and possibility of combining them well are then puts forward, for providing a novel concept of data hiding based adversarial examples. In addition, this paper introduces the generation of adversarial examples and defense against them. The future research is prospected by using watermark to generate adversarial examples. Making use of the imperceptibility of data hiding, we present a novel concept of adversarial examples adding meaningful watermarks to the original image and attacking the deep neural network model.

Keywords: Adversarial examples · Deep learning · Data hiding

1 Introduction

Adversarial examples [1] refer to examples formed by manually adding subtle disturbances invisible to the naked eye or visible to the naked eye that do not affect the whole after processing in the original data set. Such examples will cause the trained model to give different classification outputs with high confidence.

Seeing is not always believing, i.e. a natural-looking image can contain secret information that is invisible to the general public. Data hiding [18] enables concealing a secret message within a transport medium, such as a digital image, and its essential property lies in imperceptibility for achieving the fundamental goal of being hidden. With easy access to the Internet and gaining popularity of the social media platform, digital media, such as image or video, has become the most commonly used host for secure data transfer in applications ranging from secret communication, copy-right protection to content authentication. Data hiding schemes are characterized by three requirements: capacity regarding the embedded payload, security in terms of being undetectable by steganalysis, robustness against distortions in the transmission channel.

© Springer Nature Singapore Pte Ltd. 2021
L. Lin et al. (Eds.): SocialSec 2021, CCIS 1495, pp. 161–171, 2021.
https://doi.org/10.1007/978-981-16-7913-1_12

In this article, in the part of adversarial examples, firstly, the specific introduction of adversarial examples and the generation of adversarial example are given. There are many ways to generate adversarial examples. This paper mainly introduces FGSM [1], C&W [2] and DeepFool [3], and then introduces defense against adversarial examples. . Including Modified Training/input (brute force training, image compression …), modified network and additional network. Then, we discuss the deep learning based data hiding. Firstly, the formula of deep hiding is proposed [2], and then several basic meta-architectures are discussed, focusing on hiding secret messages in image carriers. We describe its three applications, namely secure steganography, light field messaging and robust watermarking. Finally, we discuss the combined application of anti-samples and information hiding based on deep learning.

2 Adversarial Example

2.1 Basic Principle of Adversarial Example

Adversarial example is an interesting phenomenon of machine learning model, which can be accepted by attackers by adding machine learning model to the original data, but it is difficult for human beings to make wrong classification decisions through subtle changes in sensory recognition. A typical scene is the adversarial example of the image classification model. By adding slight disturbance to the image, it makes the classification model misjudge when it is hard to be detected by naked eyes. As shown in the figure, the original image is identified as a panda by the image classification model, with a confidence of 57.7%. By adding a disturbance to the original image, the image classification model is identified as a gibbon with a confidence of 99.3% (Fig. 1).

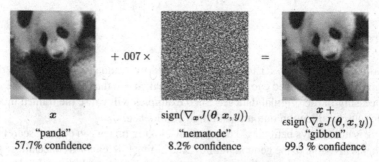

$+ .007 \times$
$\operatorname{sign}(\nabla_x J(\theta, x, y))$
$=$

x
"panda"
57.7% confidence

$\operatorname{sign}(\nabla_x J(\theta, x, y))$
"nematode"
8.2% confidence

$x + \epsilon\operatorname{sign}(\nabla_x J(\theta, x, y))$
"gibbon"
99.3 % confidence

Fig. 1. Examples of adversarial example [1]

2.2 Generation of Adversarial Example

Fast Gradient Sign Methods (FGSM). FGSM was first proposed by Goodfellow in his paper Explaining and Harnessing Advanced Examples [1]. Taking the most common image recognition as an example, it is difficult to identify the original image with naked eyes, but it can make the image recognition model misjudge [4]. Assuming that the original data of the picture is x, and the result of picture recognition is y, it is difficult to recognize the subtle changes η in the original image, which is expressed by the following mathematical formula [5].

$$\tilde{x} = x + \eta \tag{1}$$

The modified image is input into the classification model, and x is multiplied by the parameter matrix.

$$\omega^t \tilde{x} = \omega^t x + \omega^t \eta \tag{2}$$

The impact on the classification results is also affected by the activation function, and the generation process of attack examples is to make maximum changes to the classification results through the activation function. Goodfellow pointed out that if our change is completely consistent with the gradient change direction, it will maximize the change of classification results.

$$\eta = \text{sign}(w) \tag{3}$$

FGSM is an algorithm for generating adversarial examples based on gradient, which belongs to the target-free attack in adversarial attack. (that is, it is not required that the adversarial examples go through the categories specified by the model prediction, as long as they are different from those predicted by the original samples).

After understanding the formula, FGSM is not difficult. Its idea is similar to deep neural network, but it is more like an inverse process. In our machine learning algorithm, we hope that the loss function can be as small as possible; The counter sample is different. It is a destructive thing in itself. Of course, it is hoped that the greater the loss value, the better, so that the algorithm cannot predict it and will fail.

Carlini and Wagner Attacks (C&W). C&W algorithm is an attack algorithm based on optimization [6]. The innovation lies in setting a special loss function to measure the difference between input and output. This loss function contains adjustable hyperparameters and parameters that can control the confidence of the generated counter samples. By selecting the appropriate values of these two parameters, excellent countermeasures samples can be generated. According to different norms, C&W algorithm is divided into L_0, L_2 and L_∞ [7].

L_2: Strike a balance between the degree and quantity of modification.

L_0: Step by step, find those pixels that have little influence on the classification results, and then fix these pixels (because changing them has no effect), until no such pixels can be found. The remaining pixels are the points to be changed.

L_∞: Limit the degree of change.

DeepFool. DeepFool is a gradient-based white-box attack algorithm, which was proposed by Seyed-Mohsen Moosavi-Dezfooli et al. in the paper "Deep Fool: A Simple and Accurate Method to Fool Deep Neural Networks" [3]. DeepFool is usually used as an undirected attack algorithm. Compared with FGM, the learning rate ε is not specified, and the algorithm itself can calculate smaller disturbance than FGM to achieve the attack purpose. Taking the simplest binary classification problem as an example, as shown in the figure, it is assumed that the segmentation plane is a straight line, and the two sides of the straight line correspond to different classification results.

2.3 Defense Against Adversarial Example

At present, there are three main directions in the defense against attack [8]:

- Modify the training process or modify the input samples in the learning process
- Modify the network, such as adding more layers, changing loss/activation functions, etc.
- When classifying unseen samples, external models are used as additional networks

The first method does not directly deal with the learning model. On the other hand, the other two classifications are more concerned about the neural network itself. These methods can be further subdivided into two types: (a) complete defense; (b) detection only. The goal of the "complete defense" method is to let the network identify the adversarial example as the correct class. On the other hand, the "probe only" method means that an alarm is sent on the adversarial example to reject any further processing (Fig. 2).

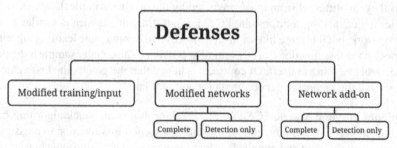

Fig. 2. Three main directions in the defense against attack [8].

Modify Training Process/Input Data. In this paper, four examples are given in modifying the training process/input data. They are brute force adversarial training, data compression, defense based on concave mechanism, and data randomization method.

Brute Force Adversarial Training. By continuously inputting new types of adversarial examples and performing confrontation training, the robustness of the network is continuously improved. In order to ensure its effectiveness, this method needs to use high-strength adversarial examples, and the network architecture should have sufficient expression ability. This method needs a lot of training data, so it is called brute force training. Many literatures mentioned that this kind of brute force training can regularize the network to reduce over-fitting [1, 9]. However, Moosavi-Dezfooli [10] pointed out that no matter how many anti-attack samples are added, there are new anti-attack samples that can deceive the network again.

Image Compression. Since most training images are in JPG format, Dziugaite et al. [11] use JPG image compression method to reduce the impact of adversarial disturbance on accuracy. Experiments show that this method is effective for some adversarial attack algorithms, but usually it is far from enough to use compression method, and the accuracy of normal classification will be reduced when compressing images. This is a disadvantage of this method.

Foveation Based Defense. Luo et al. [12] put forward that foveation mechanism can defend against disturbance generated by L-BFGS and FGSM. the assumption is that image distribution is robust to conversion variation, but disturbance does not have this characteristic. But the universality of this method has not been proved.

Data Randomization. Xie et al. [13] found that introducing random rescaling to training images can weaken the strength of anti-attack, and other methods include random padding, image enhancement during training and so on.

Modified Network

Deep Compression Network. It has been observed that simply stacking Denoising Auto Encoders on the original network will only make them more vulnerable. Therefore, Gu and Rigazio [14] introduced Deep Contractive Networks, which used a smoothness penalty similar to that of Contractive Auto Encoders.

Gradient Regularization. Input gradient regularization [15] is used to improve the robustness against attack [14]. This method combined with brute force training has a good effect, but the computational complexity is too high.

Defensive Distillation. Distillation refers to the transfer of knowledge from complex networks to simple networks, which was proposed by Hinton [16]. Papernot [17] proposed Defensive distillation by using this technology, and proved that it can resist the counter attack with small amplitude disturbance.

Additional Network

Defend Against General Disturbance. A separately trained network is added to the original model, so as to achieve the method of immunity adversarial examples without adjusting coefficients [8].

GAN Based Defense. GAN-based networks can resist confrontation attacks, and the author proposes that all models can resist adversarial examples by using the same method [8].

3 Deep Learning Based Data Hiding

3.1 Problem Formulation

Basic data hiding takes into account the scenario of secret communication between two agents: Alice and Bob, in which Alice is the sender and Bob is the receiver. Alice is responsible for hiding the secret information in the transmission medium, and then the result becomes a container, which contains the coded medium of the secret information. Bob got the secret message from C', that is, the secret that was solved. These operations are shown in Formula 4, where H and R are hidden and displayed neural networks respectively. θ_H and θ_R are their parameters.

$$C' = H(S, C; \theta_H); \quad S' = R(C'; \theta_R) \tag{4}$$

For secure steganography and robust watermarking, there is a new player named Eve, who plays Alice and Bob's opponent, trying to distinguish containers from covers by steganography analyzer A in secure steganography, or interfering containers with distortion represented as noise attack N to destroy the secret information in watermark.

Imperceptibility is the basic requirement of successful deep hiding. In other words, it is to minimize the difference between C and C' and between S and S'

$$\theta_H^* = \arg \oint \min dist_c\left(C, C'\right) = \arg \min dist_c(C, H(S, C; \theta_H)) \tag{5}$$

$$\theta_R^* = \arg \oint \min dist_S\left(S, S'\right) = \arg \min dist_S(S, R(C'; \theta_R)) \tag{6}$$

where $dist_c$ $(\cdot)$ and $dist_s$ $(\cdot)$ are the metrics of distances between two distributions. They are crucial in deep hiding as they guide the direction of neural networks' training convergence. L2 distance is the most widely used one. One commonly used optimization loss is defined as $L = ||C' - C|| + \beta||S' - S||$, where β is a weight factor for balancing the parts. A higher β often results in a higher quality of the retrieved secret at the cost of lower quality for the container. Alternatively, L1 distance, SSIM and LPIPS are also adopted commonly associated with L2 distance to evaluate perceptual quality [18]. For secret messages in the form of binary bits, the cross-entropy loss is widely used.

A steganography algorithm with high security is expected to confuse A such that it cannot perform better than random guess, i.e. the confidence score of an image being C or C' is approximately equal to each other:

$$|A(H(S, C; \theta_H)) - A(C)| < \varepsilon \tag{7}$$

where ε is a sufficiently small positive number. A robust scheme applied for robust watermarking should maintain secret information even after container C' is attacked by N:

$$\min dist_s(S, R(N(H(S, C; \theta_H)); \theta_R)) \tag{8}$$

3.2 Deep Hiding Meta-architectures

In an article in 2017 [19], deep steganography introduced by Baluja defined a new task of hiding a complete image in another image. This task is different from the traditional steganography, which needs to decode the secret information perfectly. On the contrary, the goal is to improve the image quality of the retrieved secret images. In other words, the secret image does not need perfect decoding, but the gap between the retrieved secret image and the original secret image needs to be minimized. In addition, the hiding capacity of traditional steganography is generally low. Because of the trade-off between capacity and confidentiality, some steganalysis algorithms can easily detect deep steganography. It can be seen that this task is roughly called "data hiding", rather than "steganography", and a distinction should be made.

At present, three simple meta-architectures are summarized from the existing researches, which can be directly applied to data hiding tasks. At the same time, through some targeted strategies, these meta-architectures can be extended to other applications, including steganography, light field messaging and watermarking.

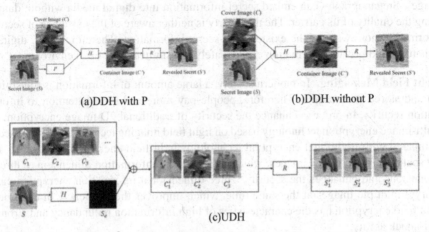

Fig. 3. Schematic diagram for three meta-architectures in the form of hiding images within images, where P, H and R represent preparation, hiding and reveal network respectively.

DDH with P. Specifically, it includes three networks: prepare network, hide network and reveal network [19, 20]. As shown in figure (a). A preparation network (P) is used to transform the secret image S into features that are usually useful for compressed images, such as marginal and orthogonal components. The hidden network adopts the overlay image C and the prepared secret image in series. S′ from the container image C′. In Fig. 3(a), how secret image is encoded in container image is dependent on the cover image. Thus, following the terminology, we call it cover-dependent deep hiding, or DDH in short, meta-architecture. Specifically, it also has an additional P network, this kind of architecture is called DDH with P in this survey.

DDH without P. After continuous research, P is not absolutely necessary [18, 21, 22]. Without p network, DDH is simpler. As shown in Fig. 3.

UDH. The framework [18] is mainly composed of H and R, and the goal is that H only encodes the secret information S, which has nothing to do with the carrier image

C. Back propagation only affects how S is encoded and does not modify C. When embedding information, the framework directly adds the secret information features Se and C generated by H. When the same S needs to be embedded in multiple carrier images Ci, using this framework only needs to generate Se once by H, which reduces a lot of work load compared with DDH. When decoding, the secret information S' can be recovered directly from R.

3.3 Applications

Secure Steganography. In recent years, steganography has become the focus of information security. Because every Web site depends on multimedia, such as audio, video and images. Steganography can embed secret information into digital media without damaging the quality of its carrier. The third party is neither aware of the existence of secret information nor aware of the existence of secret information. Therefore, keys, digital signatures and private information can be safely transmitted in an open environment.

Light Field Messaging. In modern society, a large amount of information is transmitted and stored all the time. Therefore, people pay more and more attention to information security. In order to enhance the security of traditional 2D image encryption, a multi-image encryption technology based on light field imaging technology is proposed. Compared with traditional encryption technology, light field encryption makes use of the spatial information of images, which improves the information dimension to three dimensions and enhances the security. Three-dimensional information encryption can encrypt multiple images at the same time, which improves the efficiency. In addition, light field encryption has the characteristics of high information redundancy and strong anti-attack ability.

At present, some redundant information still remains in the final decryption process of the image decrypted by light field, which affects the quality of the decrypted image. Removing these defects manually will consume a lot of manpower and material resources. Because these defects have certain regularity and the repair logic is simple, the deep learning method is proposed to let the artificial neural network learn how to distinguish and remove the defects in the light field decrypted image, so as to achieve the purpose of automatically repairing the image.

Robust Watermarking. The framework of robust watermarking network is mainly composed of four parts: encoder, decoder, discriminator and distortion. encoder is used to embed watermark, decoder is used to extract watermark, discriminator usually uses a confrontation network to ensure the visual quality of image, and distortion layer is introduced by distortion to make watermark robust.

According to the different forms of hidden watermark, it can be divided into two cases, one is binary string, the other is image. When embedding binary strings into images as information, different researchers have done different preprocessing on the strings. In references, researchers use channel coding strategy to encode character strings, and the redundancy generated is used to correct errors caused by character strings in channel transmission. In addition, reference proposes a different strategy, which uses a special information coding network to extract character string features and embed a short feature into the carrier.

How to deal with the attack distortion in the network can make the watermarking algorithm more robust in practice, which is a research hotspot in recent years. Attacks are mainly divided into two types, known attacks and unknown attacks. At present, there are two main solutions to known attacks, one is to generate distorted data of real attacks, but the disadvantage is that the cost is too high. The other is simulated attack data. Many researchers do research, but the biggest difficulty is to solve the problem of non-micro-compression, such as JPEG compression.

4 Deep Learning Based Data Hiding with Adversarial Attack

There are many methods to generate adversarial example, but they all add adversarial disturbances to the original image. However, the author is studying how to use watermark to generate adversarial example. Making use of the imperceptibility of the watermark, we make a fuss about the watermark, so as to generate adversarial example. That is, adding meaningful watermarks to the original image to attack the deep neural network model. The watermark mentioned here has watermark characteristics, which can be used for security authentication, copyright protection, etc. At the same time, it also has the function of resisting examples, which can lead to the wrong classification of trained models. Here, we need to grasp that there is nothing against disturbance except watermark area. At present, there are few researches on this aspect, and the embedded adversarial watermark is visible in the adversarial watermark image, which needs to be improved. Recently, Zhang's research in 2021 [23] has performed a joint investigation of such misalignment phenomenon in both tasks, and providing a unified Fourier perspective on why such small perturbation can dominate the images in the context of universal attack and hiding. The reason for the misalignment has been attributed to the fact that the DNNs being sensitive to high-frequency content Zhang's research in 2021 [23] with the observation that frequency is a key factor that influences the performance for both tasks. The joint investigation of deep watermarking and adversarial attack has also been previously explored in Quiring' research in 2018 [24] with a unified notion of black-box attacks against both tasks, the efficacy of which is demonstrated by applying the concepts from adversarial attack to watermarking and vice versa. For example, counter-measures in watermarking can be utilized to defend against some model-extraction adversarial attacks and the techniques for improving the model adversarial robustness can also help mitigate the attacks against the watermarking in Quiring' research in 2018 [24]. Moreover, the lesson in multimedia forensics has also be found useful for facilitating the detection of adversarial examples [25]. On the other hand, adversarial machine learning against watermarking has also been explored in Quiring and Rieck's research in 2018 [26] thorough adopting a neural network to detect and remove the watermark. Therefore, in the future research, it is suggested to continue working on the study of adversarial examples in the hope of realizing the concealment of anti-watermarking in the image.

5 Conclusion

In this article, we introduce the concepts of adversarial example and deep learning based data hiding, and finally present a novel concept of data hiding based adversarial examples by combining them. At first, this paper introduces the generation of adversarial example and the defense against adversarial example. The characteristics of adversarial example are the same input plus some slight disturbance, which may make the neural network give different outputs. At the same time, data hiding based on deep learning has become a new technology and attracted more and more attention. This paper briefly introduces three basic meta-architectures, and further discusses the application of deep hiding in steganography, light field information, robust watermarking and so on. Finally, the combination of adversarial attack and data hiding is introduced, which is a new insight and an interesting direction for future research on the filed of information security.

References

1. Goodfellow, I.J., Shlens, J., Szegedy, C: Explaining and harnessing adversarial examples. In: 3rd International Conference on Learning Representations, ICLR, San Diego, CA, USA (2015)
2. Carlini, N., Wagner, D.: Towards evaluating the robustness of neural networks. In: IEEE Symposium on Security and Privacy 2017, pp. 39–57. IEEE, San Jose (2017)
3. Moosavi-Dezfooli, S.M., Fawzi, A., Frossard, P.: DeepFool: a simple and accurate method to fool deep neural networks. In: 2016 IEEE Conference on Computer Vision and Pattern Recognition, pp. 2574–2582. IEEE, Las Vegas (2016)
4. Szegedy, C., et al.: Intriguing properties of neural networks. In: 2nd International Conference on Learning Representations, ICLR, Banff, AB, Canada (2014)
5. Goodfellow, I.J., Shlens, J., Szegedy, C.: Explaining and harnessing adversarial examples. In: 3rd International Conference on Learning Representations, ICLR, San Diego, CA, USA (2015)
6. Papernot, N., McDaniel, P., Wu, X., Jha, S., Swami, A.: Distillation as a defense to adversarial perturbations against deep neural networks. In: IEEE Symposium on Security and Privacy 2016, pp. 582–597. IEEE, San Diego (2016)
7. Carlini, N., Wagner, D.: Towards evaluating the robustness of neural networks. In: IEEE Symposium on Security and Privacy 2017, pp. 39–57. IEEE, San Diego (2017)
8. Akhtar, N., Mian, A.: Threat of adversarial attacks on deep learning in computer vision: a survey. IEEE Access 6(6), 14410–14430 (2018)
9. Sankaranarayanan, S., Jain, A., Chellappa, R., Lim, S. N.: Regularizing deep networks using efficient layer wise adversarial train. In: Thirty-Second AAAI Conference on Artificial Intelligence, AAAI, New Orleans, Louisiana, USA (2018)
10. Moosavi-Dezfooli, S. M., Fawzi, A., Fawzi, O., Frossard, P.: Universal adversarial perturbations. In: 2017 IEEE Conference on Computer Vision and Pattern Recognition, pp. 86–94. IEEE, Honolulu (2017)
11. Dziugaite, G.K., Ghahramani, Z., Roy, D.M.: A study of the effect of JPG compression on adversarial images. CoRR, abs/1608.00853 (2016)
12. Luo, Y., Boix, X., Roig, G., Poggio, T., Zhao, Q.: Foveation-based mechanisms alleviate adversarial examples. CoRR, abs/1511.06292 (2015)
13. Xie, C., Wang, J., Zhang, Z., Zhou, Y., Xie, L., Yuille, A.: Adversarial examples for semantic segmentation and object detection. In: IEEE International Conference on Computer Vision, pp. 1378–1387. IEEE, Venice (2017)

14. Gu, S., Rigazio, L.: Towards deep neural network architectures robust to adversarial examples. In: 3rd International Conference on Learning Representations, ICLR, San Diego, CA, USA (2015)

15. Ross, A.S., Doshi-Velez, F.: Improving the adversarial robustness and interpretability of deep neural networks by regularizing their input gradients. In: Proceedings of the Thirty-Second AAAI Conference on Artificial Intelligence, pp. 1660–1669. AAAI, New Orleans (2018)

16. Hinton, G., Vinyals, O., Dean, J.: Distilling the knowledge in a neural network. CoRR abs/1503.02531 (2015)

17. Zhang, J., Xu, Q.: Attention-aware heterogeneous graph neural network. Big Data Min. Anal. **4**(4), 233–241 (2021)

18. Bie, Y., Yang, Y.: A multitask multiview neural network for end-to-end aspect-based sentiment analysis. Big Data Min. Anal. **4**(3), 195–207 (2021)

19. Baluja, S.: Hiding images in plain sight: deep steganography. In: Annual Conference on Neural Information Processing Systems 2017, Long Beach, CA, USA, pp. 2069–2079 (2017)

20. Baluja, S.: Hiding images within images. IEEE Trans. Pattern Anal. Mach. Intell. **42**(7), 1685–1697 (2020)

21. Weng, X., Li, Y., Chi, L., Mu, Y.: High-capacity convolutional video steganography with temporal residual modeling. In: Proceedings of the 2019 on International Conference on Multimedia Retrieval, pp. 87–95. ACM, Ottawa (2019)

22. Niu, K., Yang, X., Zhang, Y.: A novel video reversible data hiding algorithm using motion vector for H.264/AVC. Tsinghua Sci. Technol. **22**(5), 489–498 (2017)

23. Wang, W., et al.: Anomaly detection of industrial control systems based on transfer learning. Tsinghua Sci. Technol. **26**(6), 821–832 (2021)

24. Quiring, E., Arp, D., Rieck, K.: Forgotten siblings: unifying attacks on machine learning and digital watermarking. In: 2018 IEEE European Symposium on Security and Privacy, pp. 488–502. IEEE, London (2019)

25. Schöttle, P., Schlögl, A., Pasquini, C., Böhme, R.: Detecting adversarial examples-a lesson from multimedia forensics. CoRR, abs/1803.03613 (2018)

26. Quiring, E., Rieck, K.: Adversarial machine learning against digital watermarking. In: 26th European Signal Processing Conference, pp. 519–523. IEEE, Roma (2018)

Trust and Reputations in Social Networks

A New Measure of Network Robustness: Network Cluster Entropy

Jiafei Liu[1,2] and Shuming Zhou[1,2(✉)]

[1] College of Computer and Cyber Security, Fujian Normal University,
Fuzhou 350117, Fujian, People's Republic of China
qbx20190070@yjs.fjnu.edu.cn, zhoushuming@fjnu.edu.cn
[2] School of Mathematics and Statistics, Fujian Normal University,
Fuzhou 350117, Fujian, People's Republic of China

Abstract. Online social networks have gained tremendous popularity and have dramatically changed the way we communicate in recent years. It is a challenging problem, however, due to the difficulties of handling complex social network topologies and conducting accurate assessment in these topologies. Therefore, the robustness analysis of network topologies has been a hot research topic in recent years. To characterize the structure feature of complex social network quantificationally, we propose a new measure for network robustness, namely, network cluster entropy, which takes the impact of cluster density on the network structure into consideration. Besides, the relationship between the network cluster entropy and network connectivity reliability is established. To show the effectiveness of the proposed method, we compute the network cluster entropy of the Zachary's Karate Club network with two existing indices under disparate divisions, and we also compare the results by measuring the ability of each index to characterize network heterogeneity. Both of experimental results and empirical analysis show that our proposed method has the more excellent performance compared with two existing methods. Therefore, it is indicated that the cluster entropy and network connectivity reliability will be an important tool to study the online social network.

Keywords: Online social network · Network cluster entropy · Network connectivity reliability · Zachary's Karate Club network

1 Introduction

In recent decades, with the rapid growth of computer science, graph theory has developed fast as an interdisciplinary subject between mathematics and computer science. An online social network is usually modeled by a connected

Supported by the National Natural Science Foundation of China (Nos. 61977016 and 61572010), Natural Science Foundation of Fujian Province (Nos. 2020J01164, 2017J01738).

graph G, where nodes represent users, and edges represent communication links between processors. Study of network robustness has laid a solid foundation for development of network security [1]. The network structure entropy is an important indicator to assess the resilience of online social networks, which has served as one of indices of measuring the social network heterogeneity. Furthermore, network structure entropy has applications in other disciplines including operations research, chemistry, biomedicine, telecommunications, computer science, and network security. It is of great theoretical and practical significance to conduct in-depth research on the network cluster entropy, and use it to further reveal the structural properties of networks.

Entropy was first introduced by the German physicist Clausius in 1865, which is a concept in chemistry and thermodynamics. Later, Shannon [2] proposed the concept of Shannon entropy, which is applied to information theory. If X is a set of possible events $x_1, \ldots, x_n$, and p_i is the probability that event x_i occurs such that the entropy of X is calculated by $E = -\sum_{i=1}^{n} p_i ln p_i$, where $\sum_{i=1}^{n} p_i = 1$. The entropy referred to in chemistry and thermodynamics is a measure of the total amount of energy that cannot be done in terms of kinetics, which is widely used to quantify the heterogeneity of a complex network.

The research on network structure entropy has achieved great advance in recent years. Until now, there are many researches on network structure entropy. Wen and Jiang [3] proposed the structure entropy depending on Tsallis entropy, which combines the fractal dimension and local dimension, and if the fractal dimension equals to one, it would degenerate to the Shannon entropy based on the local dimension. Duan, Wen and Jiang [4] proposed the Rényi dimension, combined with Rényi entropy and information dimension, and introduced a modified box-covering algorithm to calculate the minimum number and the length of the boxes needed covering the whole network. Feng et al. [5] established von Neumann entropy based on its first and second neighbors, and investigated the differences of nodes features in the view of spectrum eigenvalues distribution. Chen et al. [6] introduced the information entropy as a measurement of the relationship between nodes including direct and indirect neighbors, and proposed a new belonging coefficient to describe the weight of the label. Almog and Shmueli [7] took into consideration both the number of subnetworks and their sizes, which generated a single representative value. Cai et al. [8] characterized network heterogeneity by proposing an evolving caveman network that reveals the differences among four existing structure entropy indices by comparing the sensitivities during the network evolutionary process. Garcia et al. [9] opened a new standpoint in the detection of emotional distress by entropy-based measures, which may gain new insights about the brain's behavior under this negative emotion. Aziz et al. [10] extracted the set of all graphlets of a specific sizes and compute the network entropy, and embed a network in a feature space using entropies estimated from graphlets of different sizes. Mishra et al. [11] proposed entropy based defensive mechanism against DDoS attack in SDN-Cloud enabled online social networks. Zhang et al. [12] measured nodes structure similarity based on relative entropy. Tan et al. [13] has defined *the degree entropy* as an index of network heterogeneity expressed by $E = -\sum_{i=1}^{n} p_i ln p_i$, where $p_i = \frac{d_i}{\sum_{i=1}^{n} d_i}$, and d_i denotes the degree of the i-th node. If the i-th node is isolated node, then $p_i = 0$. Hence, E becomes meaningless. Observing that the degree entropy gives no consideration to the impact of isolated nodes on the network structure, Wu et al. [14] established a new index, *the partition entropy*, expressed by $E = -\sum_{i=1}^{n} \frac{n_i}{n} ln \frac{n_i}{n}$, where n_i denote the size of the i-th subgraph, which takes the impact of isolated nodes on the network structure into consideration.

The network reliability may be defined as an ability or probability that a network system has to completely fulfill customer-tailored communications tasks during the stipulated successive operation procedure. The literature concerning network reliability has prospered, ranging from the network connectivity reliability [15], network capacity reliability [16], to network performance reliability [17], and so on. Network connectivity reliability was first proposed by Mine and Kawai [18] in 1982, and it merely considers network topology or introduces the probability of connectivity achieved by network as a reliability measurement criterion. In fact, our proposed index, network cluster entropy, which is an amelioration of the network structure entropy, is able to reflect the characteristics of network connectivity effectively.

The main contributions of this paper are summarized as follows:

- The first attempt to associate the cluster density to network entropy, and introduce a new index for network reliability, network cluster entropy, which takes the impact of cluster density on the network structure into consideration.
- We propose the network connectivity reliability based on cluster entropy. And the relationship between the network cluster entropy and connectivity reliability is explored.
- To show the effectiveness of the proposed method, we compute the network cluster entropy of the Zachary's Karate Club network under different divisions. Meanwhile, we empirically verify that our proposed index is more superior compared with previous existing indices.

The remainder of this work proceeds as follows. In the next section, we present the definition of network cluster entropy and its properties; Sect. 3 establishes the definition of network connection reliability and its properties; Experimental results and empirical analysis are presented in Sect. 4. Finally, the paper concludes with some discussions and future directions of research in Sect. 5.

2   Preliminaries

For convenience of discussion, we remind that, for a graph $G(V, E)$, the notation $V = V(G)$ and $E = E(G)$ will denote the vertex and edge sets, respectively. Also, the order of G is defined by $n = |V(G)|$, and the size of G is defined by $m = |E(G)|$. For any $v \in V(G)$, we denote $N_G(v) = \{w \in V(G) \mid (v, w) \in E(G)\}$ as the neighbourhood of v in G. Moreover, the degree of a vertex v is represented as $d_v = |N_G(v)|$. For a vertex set S of a graph G, we use $N_G(S)$ to denote the neighbour set of S. That is, $N_G(S) = \{w \in V(G) \backslash S \mid v \in S, \ (v, w) \in E(G)\}$. S and T are two disjoint nonempty subsets of G, and we use $E_G[S, T]$ to represent the crossing edges between subgraph S and subgraph T. For further details on graph theory , we refer the reader to [19].

So far, a great number of works on network structure entropy have been proposed. A more specific description of network reliability is to compare its values according to network structure entropy in complex network. Some well-known metrics for structure entropy are listed as follows:

– Spectrum Entropy

The spectrum entropy [20], denoted by E_S, of a network G relates to a tuple $(\lambda_1, \lambda_2, \ldots, \lambda_2)$ derived from G is constructed by

$$E_S = -\sum_{i=1}^{k} \frac{\lambda_i}{\sum_{i=1}^{k} \lambda_i} log \frac{\lambda_i}{\sum_{i=1}^{k} \lambda_i},$$

where every element of the tuple $(\lambda_1, \lambda_2, \ldots, \lambda_2)$ refers to the eigenvalue of network G.

– Degree Distribution Entropy

Under the condition that indeterminacy of the distribution probability of node number with a prescribed edge number reflects network heterogeneity, degree distribution entropy [21], denoted by E_{DD}, is defined by

$$E_{DD} = -\sum_{d=0}^{n-1} p(d) log p(d),$$

where $p(d)$ is the distribution function in which the node degree is d and network size is n. The maximum value of E_{DD} corresponds to a network in which any two nodes have differing degree values.

– Degree Entropy

The degree entropy [13] as an index of network heterogeneity is expressed as

$$E_D = -\sum_{i=1}^{n} p_i ln p_i,$$

where $p_i = \frac{d_i}{\sum_{i=1}^{n} d_i}$, and d_i denotes the degree of the i-th node.

– Partition Entropy

The partition entropy [14] can be phrased as

$$E_P = -\sum_{i=1}^{n} \frac{n_i}{n} ln \frac{n_i}{n},$$

where n_i denote the size of the i-th subgraph, which takes the impact of isolated nodes on the network structure into consideration. More specifically, in the social network with k communities, $\frac{n_i}{n}$ represents the probability of randomly drawing a node from each community. Partition entropy [7] is calculated based on the number of communities and their sizes. The calculation does not take into account the internal structure of the communities. Consider a network of n nodes. The minimal value for the structural entropy of a network is 0, and this value is obtained when all nodes in the network are assigned to the same community.

3   Network Cluster Entropy and Its Properties

To reconcile the antagonistic organizing principles of communities and hierarchy, Ahn et al. [22] proposed a measure of clustering density in 2010. Later, Lee et al. [23] applied the clustering density to the partition of community structure. In the following, we further improve the index, which take the generalized case that views an isolated node as a cluster into consideration (Fig. 1).

Definition 1. *(Local clustering density) To measure the quality of a network, the local clustering density, denoted as LCD, can be elaborated as follows,*

$$LCD = \begin{cases} \dfrac{1}{n}, & m = 0 \text{ and } n = 1 \\[2mm] \dfrac{m - (n-1)}{C_n^2 - (n-1)}, & \text{otherwise} \end{cases} \tag{1}$$

where m and n are the numbers of edges and nodes in network G, respectively. Here, $C_n^2 = \frac{n(n-1)}{2}$ is the number of links of the fully connected graph. If the connected graph is an isolated node, we denote LCD as $\frac{1}{n}$. Clearly, $0 \le m \le C_n^2$, then we show $0 \le LCD \le 1$.

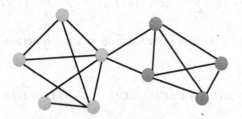

Fig. 1. Local clustering coefficient (LCD) of the yellow subgraph is 4/5, local clustering coefficient (LCD) of the blue subgraph is 1. (Color figure online)

Definition 2. *(Network cluster entropy) Let G be a graph, which contains n nodes and k connected subgraphs such that the i-th connected subgraph contains n_i nodes as well as m_i edges. Then the network cluster entropy, denoted by E_C, is defined as*

$$E_C = -\sum_{i=1}^{k} LCD_i ln LCD_i \tag{2}$$

where

$$LCD_i = \begin{cases} \dfrac{1}{n}, & m_i = 0 \text{ and } n_i = 1 \\[2mm] \dfrac{m_i - (n_i - 1)}{C_{n_i}^2 - (n_i - 1)}, & \text{otherwise} \end{cases}$$

and $C_{n_i}^2 = \frac{n_i(n_i-1)}{2}$ is the number of links of the fully connected graph.

Regarding the property of network cluster entropy, we start with the following observation.

Theorem 1. *If the size of network diminishes, then the network cluster entropy will grow larger.*

Proof. Let G be a network with k connected subnetworks, denoted by $G_1, G_2, \ldots, G_k$. Without loss of generality, we suppose that the network G reduces some edges to obtain the network G'. Next we distinguish between two cases as follows.

Case 1. The number of components is unchanged.
Assume that G'_j is generated by reducing x edges from the j-th subnetwork G_j. Then the size of G'_j is equal to $m_j - x$, where m_j represents the size of G_j. Hence, the clustering density of the j-th subnetwork $LCD'_j = \frac{m_j - x - (n_j - 1)}{C_{n_j}^2}$, where n_j represents the order of G_j. Therefore,

$$E'_C = -\left(\sum_{i=1,\ i\neq j}^{k} LCD_i ln LCD_i + LCD'_j ln LCD'_j \right).$$

Since $f(x) = x ln x$ $(x \geq 1)$ is a monotonic increasing function,

$$E'_C - E_C$$

$$= -\left(\sum_{i=1,\ i\neq j}^{k} LCD_i ln LCD_i + LCD'_j ln LCD'_j \right) - \left(-\sum_{i=1}^{k} LCD_i ln LCD_i \right)$$

$$= -\frac{m_j - x - (n_j - 1)}{c_{n_j - (n_j - 1)}^2} ln \frac{m_j - x - (n_j - 1)}{c_{n_j}^2 - (n_j - 1)} - \left(-\frac{m_j - (n_j - 1)}{c_{n_j}^2 - (n_j - 1)} ln \frac{m_j - (n_j - 1)}{c_{n_j}^2 - (n_j - 1)} \right)$$

$$= \frac{m_j - (n_j - 1)}{c_{n_j}^2 - (n_j - 1)} ln \frac{m_j - (n_j - 1)}{c_{n_j}^2 - (n_j - 1)} - \frac{m_j - x - (n_j - 1)}{c_{n_j}^2 - (n_j - 1)} ln \frac{m_j - x - (n_j - 1)}{c_{n_j}^2 - (n_j - 1)}$$

$$> 0,$$

which implies the assertion.

Case 2. The number of components increases.

Assume that the k-th subnetwork gets rid of one edge such that the k-th subnetwork is divided to two disconnected subnetworks, whose orders are n_{k_1} and n_{k_2}, whose sizes are m_{k_1} and m_{k_2}, respectively. Clearly, it follows that $n_{k_1} + n_{k_2} = n_k$ and $m_{k_1} + m_{k_2} + 1 = m_k$. Then,

$$E'_C = -(\sum_{i=1}^{k-1} LCD_i lnLCD_i + LCD'_k lnLCD'_k + LCD'_{k+1} lnLCD'_{k+1})$$

Hence,

$$E'_C - E_C$$

$$= -(\sum_{i=1}^{k-1} LCD_i lnLCD_i + LCD'_k lnLCD'_k + LCD'_{k+1} lnLCD'_{k+1})$$

$$- (-\sum_{i=1}^{k} LCD_i lnLCD_i)$$

$$= LCD'_k lnLCD'_k + LCD'_{k+1} lnLCD'_{k+1} - LCD_k lnLCD_k$$

$$= \frac{m_{k_1} - (n_{k_1} - 1)}{c^2_{n_{k_1}} - (n_{k_1} - 1)} ln \frac{m_{k_1} - (n_{k_1} - 1)}{c^2_{n_{k_1}} - (n_{k_1} - 1)} + \frac{m_{k_2} - (n_{k_2} - 1)}{c^2_{n_{k_2}} - (n_{k_2} - 1)} ln \frac{m_{k_2} - (n_{k_2} - 1)}{c^2_{n_{k_2}} - (n_{k_2} - 1)}$$

$$- \frac{m_k - (n_k - 1)}{c^2_{n_k} - (n_k - 1)} ln \frac{m_k - (n_k - 1)}{c^2_{n_k} - (n_k - 1)}$$

$$> 0,$$

which yields the desired result.

When the network G gets rid of at least two edges such that the number of the network's component become larger, and the analogous results occurs.

To summarize, when the size of network diminishes, the network cluster entropy will grow larger.

Corollary 1. *If the size of network diminishes continuously, the network cluster entropy will reach the maximum value, $E_{Cmax} = lnn$.*

Proof. Clearly, when the number of edges diminishes continuously, all vertices of the network become isolated nodes. It follows from Definition 2 that the local clustering density of every isolated vertex is $\frac{1}{n}$. Here, the network cluster entropy reaches the maximum value

$$E_{Cmax} = -\sum_{1}^{n} \frac{1}{n} ln \frac{1}{n} = lnn,$$

the corollary follows.

Theorem 2. *If the size of network increases, the network cluster entropy will decrease.*

See **Appendix** for this proof of Theorem 2.

Corollary 2. *If the size of network increases continuously, the network cluster entropy will reach the minimum value, $E_{Cmin} = 0$.*

4   Network Connectivity Reliability Based on Cluster Entropy

In this section, we firstly give the definition of network connectivity reliability, and determine its properties. Then we establish the relationship between network cluster entropy and network connectivity reliability.

Definition 3. *(Network connectivity reliability) To measure the robustness and reliability of network, the concept of the network connectivity reliability in a network, denoted by NCR, can be elaborated as follows,*

$$NCR = \frac{E_{Cmax} - E_C}{E_{Cmax} - E_{Cmin}} \tag{3}$$

where E_{Cmax} is the maximum value of network structure entropy, and E_{Cmin} is the minimum value of network structure entropy.

Clearly, we observe that $NCR \in [0, 1]$. When the network G is connected, $E_C = 0$ and $NCR = 1$.

In the following, we will establish the relationship between network cluster entropy and connectivity reliability.

Theorem 3. *If the size of network reduces, connectivity reliability of the network will become weaker. Conversely, if the size of network increases, connectivity reliability of the network will grow stronger.*

Proof. By Theorem 1, the network cluster entropy becomes larger when the number of edge of the network decreases. By Eq. (3), network cluster entropy and network connectivity reliability are inversely proportional. Hence, network connectivity reliability becomes weaker when the network cluster entropy enlarges. On the contrary, using analogous arguments as above, there will yield the desired results accordingly.

Now, we establish the relationship between network cluster entropy and network connectivity reliability.

Theorem 4. *The larger value of network cluster entropy becomes, the network connectivity reliability will weaken. Conversely, the smaller value of network cluster entropy becomes, the stronger network connectivity reliability will grow.*

Therefore, the network cluster entropy and network connectivity reliability are very meaningful to research structural characteristics and connection properties of the complex network.

5 Empirical Analysis of the Zachary's Karate Club Network

In recent years, there have been a lot of measuring methods for network structure entropy in complex networks. For comparisons, we draw into two classical models: degree entropy [13] and partition entropy [14] in the network system. In the following, we introduce the Zachary's Karate Club network.

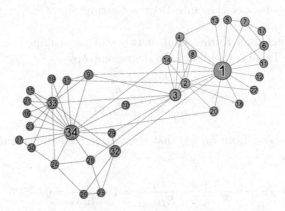

Fig. 2. Zachary's Karate Club network of friendships ($k = 2$). (Color figure online)

Table 1. Distribution of vertex degree of Zachary's Karate Club network ($k = 1$)

node	degree	node	degree	node	degree
1	16	13	2	25	3
2	9	14	5	26	3
3	10	15	2	27	2
4	6	16	2	28	4
5	3	17	2	29	3
6	4	18	2	30	4
7	4	19	2	31	4
8	4	20	3	32	6
9	5	21	2	33	12
10	2	22	2	34	17
11	3	23	2		
12	1	24	5		

Zachary's Karate Club network is a well-known and widely-used data set for social network, which is the network of friendships among the 34 members of a karate club at a US university and described by Wayne Zachary [24] in

1977. Zachary spent more than two years observing 34 members in a karate club and found that the division of opinion of instructor and administrator of the club leaded to the split of club into two factions. A simple unweighted version of Zachary's network is shown in Fig. 2, where nodes 1 and 34 represent the instructor and the administrator respectively and two factions caused due to the disagreement are demonstrated in two different color (red and blue). Moreover, The network consists of 34 nodes and 78 edges, in which each node in the network refers to a member of the club, and each edge in the network stands for a tie between two members of the club. Degree distribution of Zachary's network is shown in Table 1.

When the Zachary's Karate Club network of friendships is connected, i.e., $k = 1$. Through Table 1, we obtain the degree entropy

$$E_D = - \sum_{i=1}^{34} \frac{d_i}{\sum_{i=1}^{n} d_i} ln \frac{d_i}{\sum_{i=1}^{n} d_i} = 3.26095;$$

accordingly, it follows from Eq. (3) that connectivity reliability under the degree entropy is

$$NCR_D = \frac{E_{Dmax} - E_D}{E_{Dmax} - E_{Dmin}} = 1 - \frac{E_D}{ln34} = 0.07526.$$

When the Zachary's Karate Club network is connected, the partition entropy is

$$E_P = - \sum_{i=1}^{1} \frac{n}{n} ln \frac{n}{n} = - \frac{34}{34} ln \frac{34}{34} = 0;$$

accordingly, it follows from Eq. (3) that connectivity reliability under the partition entropy is

$$NCR_P = \frac{E_{Pmax} - E_P}{E_{Pmax} - E_{Pmin}} = 1 - \frac{E_P}{ln34} = 1.$$

But, by our proposed method, the network cluster entropy is

$$E_C = - \frac{m - (n-1)}{C_n^2 - (n-1)} ln \frac{m - (n-1)}{C_n^2 - (n-1)} = \frac{78 - 33}{\frac{34*33}{2} - 33} ln \frac{78 - 33}{\frac{34*33}{2} - 33} = 0.2071;$$

accordingly, it follows from Eq. (3) that connectivity reliability under the cluster entropy is

$$NCR_C = \frac{E_{Cmax} - E_C}{E_{Cmax} - E_{Cmin}} = 1 - \frac{E_C}{ln34} = 0.94127.$$

Table 2. Distribution of vertex degree of Zachary's Karate Club network ($k = 2$)

node	degree	node	degree	node	degree
1	14	13	2	25	3
2	8	14	4	26	3
3	5	15	2	27	2
4	6	16	2	28	3
5	3	17	2	29	2
6	4	18	2	30	4
7	4	19	2	31	3
8	4	20	2	32	4
9	3	21	2	33	11
10	1	22	2	34	15
11	3	23	2		
12	1	24	5		

When we remove 10 crossing edges so that $k = 2$, Zachary's Karate Club network of friendships is split into two subnetworks, which are represented by red and blue (see Fig. 2). Red subnetwork has 18 nodes as well as 33 edges, while blue subnetwork has 16 nodes as well as 35 edges. There exist 10 crossing edges between red subnetwork and blue one. The degree distribution of Zachary's network is shown in Table 2. Then the degree entropy is

$$E_D = -\sum_{i=1}^{34} \frac{d_i}{\sum_{i=1}^{n} d_i} ln \frac{d_i}{\sum_{i=1}^{n} d_i} = 3.27362;$$

under the condition, accordingly, connectivity reliability is

$$NCR_D = \frac{E_{Dmax} - E_D}{E_{Dmax} - E_{Dmin}} = 1 - \frac{E_D}{ln34} = 0.07167.$$

While the partition entropy is

$$E_P = -\sum_{i=1}^{2} \frac{n_i}{n} ln \frac{n_i}{n} = -(\frac{18}{34} ln \frac{18}{34} + \frac{16}{34} ln \frac{16}{34}) \doteq 0.6914;$$

accordingly, it follows from Eq. (3) that connectivity reliability under the partition entropy is

$$NCR_P = \frac{E_{Pmax} - E_P}{E_{Pmax} - E_{Pmin}} = 1 - \frac{E_P}{ln34} = 0.80393.$$

But, by our proposed method, the network cluster entropy is

$$
\begin{aligned}
E_C' &= -\sum_{i=1}^{2} \frac{m_i - (n_i - 1)}{C_{n_i}^2 - (n_i - 1)} ln \frac{m_i - (n_i - 1)}{C_{n_i}^2 - (n_i - 1)} \\
&= -\left(\frac{m_1 - (n_1 - 1)}{C_{n_1}^2 - (n_1 - 1)} ln \frac{m_1 - (n_1 - 1)}{C_{n_1}^2 - (n_1 - 1)} + \frac{m_2 - (n_2 - 1)}{C_{n_2}^2 - (n_2 - 1)} ln \frac{m_2 - (n_2 - 1)}{C_{n_2}^2 - (n_2 - 1)} \right) \\
&= -\left(\frac{33 - 17}{\frac{18*17}{2} - 17} ln \frac{33 - 17}{\frac{18*17}{2} - 17} + \frac{36 - 15}{\frac{16*15}{2} - 15} ln \frac{36 - 15}{\frac{16*15}{2} - 15} \right) \\
&= 0.6097;
\end{aligned}
$$

accordingly, it follows from Eq. (3) that connectivity reliability under the cluster entropy is

$$
NCR_C = \frac{E_{Cmax} - E_C}{E_{Cmax} - E_{Cmin}} = 1 - \frac{E_C}{ln34} = 0.82710.
$$

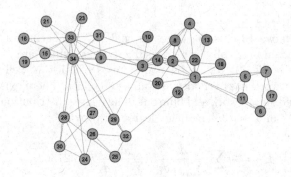

Fig. 3. Zachary's Karate Club network of friendships ($k = 4$). (Color figure online)

When removing 21 crossing edges subject to $k = 4$ [25], Zachary's Karate Club network of friendships is split into four subnetworks, which are represented by purple, green, blue and orange (see Fig. 3). Purple subnetwork has 9 nodes as well as 16 edges, green subnetwork has 12 nodes as well as 26 edges, blue subnetwork has 8 nodes as well as 9 edges, while orange subnetwork has 5 nodes as well as 6 edges. There exist 21 crossing edges among 4 subnetworks. So $k = 4$, the degree distribution of Zachary's network is shown in Table 3. Then the degree entropy is computed as

$$
E_D = -\sum_{i=1}^{34} \frac{d_i}{\sum_{i=1}^{n} d_i} ln \frac{d_i}{\sum_{i=1}^{n} d_i} = 4.0116;
$$

accordingly, it follows from Eq. (3) that connectivity reliability under the degree entropy is

$$
NCR_D = \frac{E_{Dmax} - E_D}{E_{Dmax} - E_{Dmin}} = 1 - \frac{E_D}{ln34} = 0.
$$

Table 3. Distribution of vertex degree of Zachary's Karate Club network ($k = 4$)

node	degree	node	degree	node	degree
1	10	13	2	25	3
2	8	14	5	26	3
3	6	15	2	27	1
4	6	16	2	28	2
5	2	17	2	29	1
6	3	18	2	30	2
7	3	19	2	31	3
8	4	20	2	32	3
9	3	21	2	33	8
10	1	22	2	34	8
11	2	23	2		
12	1	24	3		

While the partition entropy is computed as

$$E_P = -\sum_{i=1}^{4} \frac{n_i}{n} ln \frac{n_i}{n} = -(\frac{9}{34} ln \frac{9}{34} + \frac{12}{34} ln \frac{12}{34} + \frac{8}{34} ln \frac{8}{34} + \frac{5}{34} ln \frac{5}{34}) = 1.34175;$$

accordingly, it follows from Eq. (3) that connectivity reliability under the partition entropy is

$$NCR_P = \frac{E_{Pmax} - E_P}{E_{Pmax} - E_{Pmin}} = 1 - \frac{E_P}{ln34} = 0.61951.$$

But, by our proposed method, the network cluster entropy is

$$E'_C = -\sum_{i=1}^{4} \frac{m_i - (n_i - 1)}{C^2_{n_i} - (n_i - 1)} ln \frac{m_i - (n_i - 1)}{C^2_{n_i} - (n_i - 1)}$$
$$= -(\frac{2}{7} ln \frac{2}{7} + \frac{3}{11} ln \frac{3}{11} + \frac{2}{21} ln \frac{2}{21} + \frac{1}{3} ln \frac{1}{3})$$
$$= 1.30242;$$

accordingly, it follows from Eq. (3) that connectivity reliability under the cluster entropy is

$$NCR_C = \frac{E_{Cmax} - E_C}{E_{Cmax} - E_{Cmin}} = 1 - \frac{E_C}{ln34} = 0.63066.$$

For the ease of understanding, in Table 4, we present the entropy compared results among the methods by Tan and Wu [13], Wu, Tan and Zhang [14] and our proposed one in the Zachary's Karate Club network in detail. When $k = 1$, the value of network cluster entropy(E_C) is approximately equal to 0.2071. Our method is prior to the method of degree entropy [13]. When the Zachary's Karate Club network is divided into two subnetworks, the degree entropy $E_D \approx 3.2736$, the partition entropy $E_P \approx 0.6914$ and the cluster entropy $E_C \approx 0.6097$. Clearly,

Table 4. Entropy comparison under 3 different methods in the Zachary's Karate Club network

Methods k	Degree Entropy	Partition Entropy	Cluster Entropy
K=1	3.2610	0	0.2071
K=2	3.2736	0.6914	0.6097
K=4	4.0116	1.3418	1.3024

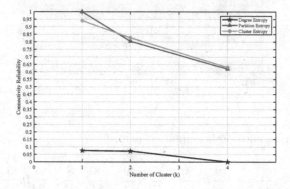

Fig. 4. Connectivity reliability under different partitions.

the cluster entropy our proposed is better than other two methods when $k = 2$. Next, we analyse the case that the Zachary's Karate Club network is divided into four subnetworks by the divided method [25]. When $k = 4$, our method is superior to other two methods in terms of Table 4. Therefore, it is observed that our proposed method shows better performance compared to two methods on degree entropy and partition entropy under the Zachary's Karate Club network's different divisions.

We next analyzed the performance of connectivity reliability based on network cluster entropy with degree entropy as well as partition entropy, respectively. From Fig. 4, we observe that degree entropy performs the poor connectivity reliability as the number of components increases. Nevertheless, cluster entropy and partition entropy show desirable connectivity reliability. In particular, when $k = 2$ or 4, it is clearly observed that connectivity reliability of Zachary's Karate Club network by our proposed method performs better than other two methods.

6   Conclusions

With the development of the network technology, network robustness analysis has witnessed a great progress in recent years. But the traditional robustness evaluation methods are hard to be applied to network evaluation due to the complexity, dynamic and multi-state characteristics of a network. To characterize the structure feature of complex network quantificationally, we propose a new measure index for network robustness, named network cluster entropy, which takes the impact of cluster density on the network structure into consideration. Besides, the relationship between the network cluster entropy and network connectivity reliability is expounded. To show the effectiveness of the proposed method, we compute the network cluster entropy of the Zachary's Karate Club network with existing indices under disparate divisions, and compare the results by measuring the ability of each index to characterize network heterogeneity. Both of mathematical analysis and computational simulation show that our proposed method has the more excellent performance compared with existing methods.

Appendix: The proof of Theorem 2.

Proof. Let G be a network with k connected subnetworks, denoted as G_1, $G_2, \ldots, G_k$. Without loss of generality, we suppose that G' is obtained by adding some edges to G. Next we distinguish between two cases as follows.

Case 1. The number of components is unchanged.
Assume that G'_j is generated by adding x edges from the j-th subnetwork G_j. Then the size of G'_j is equal to $m_j + x$. Hence, the clustering density of the j-th subnetwork is $LCD'_j = \frac{m_j + x - (n_j - 1)}{C^2_{n_j}}$. Therefore,

$$E'_C = -(\sum_{i=1,\ i \neq j}^{k} LCD_i lnLCD_i + LCD'_j lnLCD'_j).$$

Since $f(x) = xlnx$ $(x \geq 1)$ is a monotonic increasing function,

$$E'_C - E_C$$
$$= -(\sum_{i=1,\ i \neq j}^{k} LCD_i lnLCD_i + LCD'_j lnLCD'_j) - (-\sum_{i=1}^{k} LCD_i lnLCD_i)$$
$$= -\frac{m_j + x - (n_j - 1)}{c^2_{n_j}} ln \frac{m_j + x - (n_j - 1)}{c^2_{n_j}} - (-\frac{m_j - (n_j - 1)}{c^2_{n_j}} ln \frac{m_j - (n_j - 1)}{c^2_{n_j}})$$
$$= \frac{m_j - (n_j - 1)}{c^2_{n_j}} ln \frac{m_j - (n_j - 1)}{c^2_{n_j}} - \frac{m_j + x - (n_j - 1)}{c^2_{n_j}} ln \frac{m_j + x - (n_j - 1)}{c^2_{n_j}}$$
$$< 0.$$

So $E'_C < E_C$, which implies the assertion.

Case 2. The number of components diminishes.
Assume that we add one or more edges to G such that the number of subnetwork reduces. Without loss of generality, we suppose that the $(k-1)$-th subnetwork

and k-th subnetwork is connected by some edge, which generates a new subnetwork G'. One can easily check that G' is of $(n_{k-1}+n_k)$ vertices as well as $(m_{k-1} + m_k + 1)$ edges. Then,

$$E'_C = -(\sum_{i=1}^{k-2} LCD_i lnLCD_i + LCD'_{k-1} lnLCD'_{k-1}).$$

Hence,

$$E'_C - E_C$$
$$= -(\sum_{i=1}^{k-2} LCD_i lnLCD_i + LCD'_{k-1} lnLCD'_{k-1}) - (-\sum_{i=1}^{k} LCD_i lnLCD_i)$$
$$= LCD_{k-1} lnLCD_{k-1} + LCD_k lnLCD_k - LCD'_k lnLCD'_k$$
$$= \frac{m_{k-1}-(n_{k-1}-1)}{c_{n_{k-1}}^2 - (n_{k-1}-1)} ln \frac{m_{k-1}-(n_{k-1}-1)}{c_{n_{k-1}}^2 - (n_{k-1}-1)} + \frac{m_k-(n_k-1)}{c_{n_k}^2-(n_k-1)} ln \frac{m_k-(n_k-1)}{c_{n_k}^2-(n_k-1)}$$
$$- \frac{m'_k-(n'_k-1)}{c_{n'_k}^2-(n'_k-1)} ln \frac{m'_k-(n'_k-1)}{c_{n'_k}^2-(n'_k-1)}$$
$$< 0,$$

which yields the desired results.

References

1. Li, A., Hu, Q., Liu, J., Pan, Y.: Resistance and security index of networks: structural information perspective of network security. Sci. Rep. **6**(1), 26810 (2016)
2. Shannon, C.-E.: Mathematical theory of communication. Bell Syst. Tech. J. **27**(4), 623–656 (1948)
3. Wen, T., Jiang, W.: Measuring the complexity of complex network by Tsallis entropy. Phys. A **526**, 121054 (2019)
4. Duan, S., Wen, T., Jiang, W.: A new information dimension of complex network based on Rényi entropy. Phys. A **516**, 529–542 (2018)
5. Feng, X., Wei, W., Zhang, R., Wang, J., Shi, Y., Zheng, Z.: Exploring the heterogeneity for node importance by von Neumann entropy. Phys. A **517**, 53–65 (2018)
6. Chen, N., Liu, Y., Chen, H., Cheng, J.: Detecting communities in social networks using label propagation with information entropy. Phys. A **471**, 788–798 (2017)
7. Almog, A., Shmueli, E.: Structural entropy: monitoring correlation-based networks over time with application to financial markets. Sci. Rep. **9**(1), 10832 (2019)
8. Cai, M., Cui, Y., Stanley, H.: Analysis and evaluation of the entropy indices of a static network structure. Sci. Rep. **7**, 9340 (2017)
9. Garcia, M.-B., Martinez, R.-A., Cantabrana, R., Pastor, J., Alcaraz, R.: Application of entropy-based metrics to identify emotional distress from electroencephalographic recordings. Entropy **18**(6), 221 (2016)

10. Aziz, F., Akbar, M., Jawad, M., Malik, A., Uddin, I., Gkoutos, G.: Graph char-
    acterisation using graphlet-based entropies. Pattern Recogn. Lett. **147**, 100–107
    (2021)
11. Mishra, A., Gupta, B., Perakovic, D., Yamaguchi, S., Hsu, C.: Entropy based defen-
    sive mechanism against DDoS attack in SDN-Cloud enabled online social networks.
    In: 2021 IEEE International Conference on Consumer Electronics, pp. 1–6. IEEE,
    Las Vegas (2021)
12. Zhang, Q., Li, M., Deng, Y.: Measure the structure similarity of nodes in complex
    networks based on relative entropy. Phys. A **491**, 749–763 (2018)
13. Tan, Y., Wu, J.: Network structure entropy and its application to scale-free net-
    works. Syst. Eng. Theory Pract. **6**, 1–3 (2004)
14. Wu, L., Tan, Q., Zhang, Y.: Network connectivity entropy and its application on
    network connectivity reliability. Phys. A **392**, 5536–5541 (2013)
15. Zhang, X., Jia, L.-M., Dong, H., Wang, Z., Wang, K., Qin, Y.: Analysis and eval-
    uation of connectivity reliability for dynamic transportation network. In: Fifth
    International Joint Conference on INC, IMS and IDC IEEE, Seoul, South Korea,
    pp. 353–356 (2009)
16. Sumalee, A., Kurauchi, F.: Network capacity reliability analysis considering traf-
    fic regulation after a major disaster. Netw. Spat. Econ. **6**(3–4), 205–219 (2006).
    https://doi.org/10.1007/s11067-006-9280-0
17. Zhang, H., Huang, N., Liu, H.: Network performance reliability evaluation based
    on network reduction. In: 2014 Annual Reliability and Maintainability Symposium.
    IEEE (2014)
18. Main, H., Kawai, H.: Mathematics for Reliability Analysis. Asakura-shoten,
    Japanese (1982)
19. Xu, J.-M.: Combinatorial Theory in Networks. Science Press, Beijing (2013)
20. Wan, P., Tu, J., Dehmer, M., Zhang, S., Emmert-Streib, F.: Graph entropy based
    on the number of spanning forests of c-cyclic graphs. Appl. Math. Comput. **363**,
    124616 (2019)
21. Solé, R., Valverde, S.: Information theory of complex networks: on evolution and
    architectural constraints. In: Ben-Naim, E., Frauenfelder, H., Toroczkai, Z. (eds.)
    Complex Networks. Lecture Notes in Physics, vol. 650, pp. 189–207. Springer,
    Heidelberg (2004). https://doi.org/10.1007/978-3-540-44485-5_9
22. Ahn, Y.-Y., Bagrow, J., Lehmann, S.: Link communities reveal multiscale com-
    plexity in networks. Nature **466**(7307), 761–764 (2010)
23. Lee, J., Zhang, Z.-Y., Brooks, B.R., Ahn, Y.-Y.: Inverse resolution limit of partition
    density and detecting overlapping communities by link-surprise. Sci. Rep. **7**(1),
    12399 (2017)
24. Zachary, W.: An information flow model for conflict and fission in small groups. J.
    Anthropol. Res. **33**(4), 452–473 (1977)
25. Li, X., Zhou, S., Liu, J., Lian, G., Chen, G., Lin, C.-W.: Communities detection
    in social network based on local edge centrality. Phys. A **531**, 121552 (2019)

Correction to: Anonymizing Global Edge Weighted Social Network Graphs

Jiaru Wang, Ziyi Wan, Jiankang Song, Yanze Huang (iD), Yuhang Lin,
and Limei Lin (iD)

Correction to:
Chapter "Anonymizing Global Edge Weighted Social Network
Graphs" in: L. Lin et al. (Eds.): *Security and Privacy in Social*
Networks and Big Data, **CCIS 1495,**
https://doi.org/10.1007/978-981-16-7913-1_9

In the originally published chapter 9 some of the paragraphs were presented in their unfinished version, which affected the readability of the paper. The sections Introduction, Preliminary and References have been revised and updated.

The updated version of this chapter can be found at
https://doi.org/10.1007/978-981-16-7913-1_9

© Springer Nature Singapore Pte Ltd. 2022
L. Lin et al. (Eds.): SocialSec 2021, CCIS 1495, p. C1, 2022.
https://doi.org/10.1007/978-981-16-7913-1_14

Author Index

Printed in the United States
by Baker & Taylor Publisher Services